The Psalms

introduced and newly translated for today's readers by Harry Mowvley

❧ The Psalms

*introduced and newly translated
for today's readers*

by Harry Mowvley

Collins

Collins Liturgical Publications
8 Grafton Street, London W1X 3LA

Collins Dove
PO Box 316
Blackburn, Victoria 3130

Collins New Zealand
PO Box 1
Auckland

distributed in Canada by
Novalis
375 Rideau Street
CP 9700 Terminal, Ottawa
Ontario

First published 1989
© *1989 Harry Mowvley*
ISBN 0 00 599172 2

Typographical design
by Malcolm Harvey Young

Typesetting by Swains (Glasgow) Limited

Made and printed by
William Collins Sons & Co Ltd,
Glasgow

✦ Contents

Preface   vii

Introduction   1

The Psalms   9

❧ Preface

This translation of the Psalms began its life as an attempt to see how far it was possible to capture their flavour and to represent in clear modern English the poetic and religious vitality of the original Hebrew. Working through many of them with generations of students made me aware how difficult this is. Indeed, perhaps in the end it is impossible to be wholly satisfied with any translation. Having made a start, however, I then tried out some of my efforts both in the College Chapel and in worship in various churches. The reception they received there encouraged me to persevere with the task and bring it to completion.

My thanks are due to those students who shared with me the study of many of the Psalms, who sometimes challenged my translations and interpretations and who often contributed new insights. I am especially grateful to Mrs Pearl Woolnough whose willingness to provide the first typescript from a manuscript which only she and I could read and whose enthusiastic encouragement have contributed much to this volume.

Lastly I must thank the Senior Editor of Collins Liturgical Publications, Sally Ferard, for her careful work on the manuscript and for her helpful comments and suggestions throughout.

❧ Introduction

The Psalms of the Old Testament have long been and still remain vehicles to convey to God the many moods, thoughts and feelings which all religious people feel. In them worshippers can find words with which to express their thanks and praise, their anxieties and fears, their confidence and hopes. The Authorised Version and the Prayer Book made them familiar to many people and several psalms have continued to be well-loved and well-used by Jews and Christians alike. The 16th century language retains its hold on us and its familiarity makes us loth to let it go. Yet it ought to be possible to allow the Psalms to speak to us in 20th century language as well. To many, however, the modern versions leave something to be desired in terms of either clarity of meaning or poetic quality, especially when they are used in public worship. It may seem rather foolhardy, therefore, to make another attempt at translation but this has to be done again and again so as to make the Psalms available to each new generation.

Traditionally the Psalms have been associated with David, the great Israelite king who lived and reigned in the 10th century BC. As early as the 5th century BC in the Book of Chronicles David was credited with the beginnings of Israelite worship (1 Chron. 16) while even earlier in the Book of Samuel he is portrayed as a musician (1 Sam. 16.14). The result of this was that the Psalms became known as the Psalms of David and David came to be regarded as their author. It is not impossible that he composed some of the psalms but there are many others like those which refer to the Solomonic Temple or the Babylonian Exile which cannot have been written by David but which were linked with his name because they belonged to the same literary category. Similar processes gave rise to the idea of the Law of Moses and the Wisdom of Solomon. The tradition of Davidic authorship was strengthened by the fact that many of the psalms were at some point

1

provided with a heading associating them with him. The phrase which does so does not necessarily imply authorship. It could be translated 'A Psalm for David', perhaps meaning 'belonging to a Davidic collection', just as others seem to belong to collections compiled by the 'sons of Korah' (Psalm 84 etc.) among whom were Heman (Psalm 88) and probably Ethan (Psalm 89) and by Asaph (Psalm 73 etc.) all of whom are mentioned as Temple singers in 1 Chronicles 15.19. Later still, however, some of these headings were expanded to associate the psalm with a particular episode in David's life. Psalm 51, for instance, had a heading which links it with David's repentance following his affair with Bathsheba. Such headings are not part of the psalms themselves but are later attempts to provide a historical setting for them. The headings have therefore been omitted from the present translation as they have from many modern ones. Often in the Hebrew Bible the heading becomes verse 1 and the actual psalm begins at verse 2. This explains why in this translation some psalms have no verse 1.

If the Psalms were not composed by David then the question arises as to who did compose them and why. Some of them are highly personal poems and yet they are anonymous giving no clue as to the author's identity; others seem intended for public worship offered in the Temple in Jerusalem. Certainly we can say that the collection as we have it at present is an anthology of hymns and songs which were used in the Temple after it had been rebuilt in the 6th century BC by those Jews who had returned from exile in Babylon. Having said that, however, the origin of individual psalms goes back much further than this. The view which has become common among scholars this century is that virtually all the psalms were composed for use in Israel's worship but, as is the case with most worship material, it is usually impossible to say exactly when. Some bear all the marks of having been used at a king's coronation (Psalm 2) or his wedding (Psalm 45). Many are thought to have been used at the great autumn Feast of Tabernacles. This celebrated the grape harvest but there were possibly other elements involved including a symbolic humiliation, death and rising of the king representing the death and rising of the rain-giving god or, more likely, of the people whose life was threatened by the heat and drought of the summer months. There may have been a procession into the Temple and a reaffirmation of the LORD's Kingship. Even though there is little evidence for all this outside the Psalms such a view does give many of the psalms a sharper focus. If all this is correct perhaps we can attribute some psalms to Temple poets and musicians whose names are no longer known to us, but who were the forerunners of people like Isaac Watts and Charles Wesley who wrote hymns specifically for use in public worship. On the other hand it may well be that some individual Israelites expressed in poetry the deep feelings which they and their contemporaries experienced in the varied circumstances of life, and that their compositions found their way into the stock of worship material in the way that poems by J.G. Whittier and William Cowper have done in more recent times. Again, though, these poets remain anonymous. Questions about the authorship of the Psalms cannot be answered any more specifically than this at the present time. In the long run, of course, what matters is not who wrote a particular psalm but rather what personal or national circumstances underlie it and how the psalm may address us and be used by us in our present day situations.

If the origins of the Psalms must be left in comparative obscurity, we are better placed to say something about the way they were used. As we have seen, they came to be used in Jewish worship after the Exile and have continued to be used by Jews and Christians alike ever since. Many of them could not be so used, however, unless they were reinterpreted and used in a different way. To take a specific example, Psalm 2 was first used as part of a coronation ceremony for one of the kings of Israel. Which king we cannot say, but it doubtless continued to be used in this way for the crowning of subsequent kings. It appears that at each coronation there was a renewed hope that the king being crowned would be the one to make Israel great and powerful in the Ancient Near East. During the Babylonian exile, however, King Jehoiakin died and no king succeeded him throughout the next five centuries. The psalm already had this forward look and so when no coronations were possible the whole of it was used as an anticipation of a future king and his universal reign. So it became a 'Messianic' psalm. The early Christians who saw Jesus fulfilling that Messianic hope therefore applied the psalm to him and used it in the description of his baptism (Luke 3.22) and his transfiguration (Luke 9.35). Since then Christians (Hebrews 1.5) have seen the psalm as looking forward not only to Jesus' incarnation but beyond that to the consummation of his universal kingship. In this way the Psalms have been kept alive and have continued to provide Jews and Christians with songs which are relevant to the present as well as to the distant past.

It is not clear just how the Psalms were collected into their present order. As the individual introductions will show, some small groups seem to have been put together because they have something in common (e.g. Psalms 46-48) but in most cases no such principle can be detected. After they had all been collected together the Psalter was divided into five books, separated by a doxology, perhaps on the analogy of the five books of the Law.

The process of reinterpretation outlined above poses severe problems for the translator. It is sometimes said that translation should be independent of interpretation but in practice this proves to be impossible. Psalm 93, for example, begins with a statement about the kingship of the LORD. It is quite likely that it was used in a ceremony at the autumn Feast of Tabernacles when, each year, the LORD was symbolically enthroned again and recognised as King by his people. If we see this as the background then we should translate the opening phrase as 'The LORD has become king'. During the Exile when such ceremonies were no longer possible the psalm was probably reinterpreted to affirm that the LORD and no other god was king and his reign was universal. If this is seen as the background then we should translate the opening phrase as 'It is the LORD who is king'. The Hebrew will tolerate either of these translations and so I ought to indicate my own approach. As a general rule I have tried to translate the psalms as I think they were originally intended by their original poets. At the same time I have sought as far as possible to ensure that my translation does not rule out the later interpretations but rather encourages them. The introductions are meant to help the reader with this problem.

There are other problems too. The Psalms are, of course, poems and poetry always says much more than the sum of its words. It uses sounds, rhythms and images to conjure up deeper layers of meaning. Indeed it does not address the mind so much as the emotion and the will. Any translation has to seek as far as possible to reproduce this. One of the ways in which poetry seeks to achieve its aims is often by using metaphors, the point of which would have been obvious to those who first spoke or heard the Psalms but which now may be less apparent to us. It is possible simply to translate the metaphor literally and leave it at that, but I have tried to elucidate the significance not so much by paraphrase as by the careful choice and ordering of words. Hebrew parallelism can not only help us to solve this problem, it is an essential component of the poetry. Through it a thought or idea expressed in one line is repeated in different words in the next. This is much more than repetition. The second line, by looking at the same idea from a slightly different point of view expands, enhances, enlarges and deepens the meaning. It is therefore important to carry this style over into the English translation not only to assist in the clarification of metaphor but also to produce the same emotional and volitional impact as the original.

It may be thought that the use of a good dictionary would ensure an accurate translation of words from one language to another but again it is not as simple as that. No word in one language can exactly reproduce the significance of a word in another language for every word we use has a range of ideas, thoughts and meanings attached to it. For instance the word 'tent' in English probably conjures up pictures of a group of Boy Scouts on an adventure holiday or of a family relaxing in the freedom of a camp site with coloured tents and awnings. The Hebrew word 'ohel which may be translated 'tent' would have conjured up for the Israelite the goat-skin home in which many people actually lived and brought up their families as they moved about the land seeking new pastures for their flocks. Like the English word 'home' it can signify the people who live in it. Moreover words take their meaning from the context in which they are used. The word 'time' may mean the 'hour' ('it's four o'clock') or the occasion ('the time we went to London') or the experience ('we had a good time'). It is essential therefore for the translator to reproduce not only the meaning of the word but also to catch its more precise flavour and to convey this in the translation.

Because we have scarcely any Hebrew literature from the Old Testament period apart from the Old Testament itself the meaning of words and phrases is sometimes uncertain. Indeed on occasions it is hard if not impossible to be sure what the Hebrew means. In these cases the translator has to use any clues he can find and may, in the end,

5

have to make an educated guess at the meaning. Fortunately this does not happen all that frequently. At one time it was customary, where the meaning was unclear, to read slightly different Hebrew words on the assumption that errors were made in the copying of manuscripts. Our knowledge about the ways in which the text was copied and transmitted has made scholars today much more cautious in this regard. In this translation I have endeavoured, where possible, to make sense of the Hebrew text found in the 3rd edition of *Biblia Hebraica*. Sometimes it is helpful to look at variant manuscripts and the early translations into Greek or Syriac for help. Just occasionally it has been thought necessary to change a Hebrew consonant or to assume a different set of vowels but those occasions are rare. I have not drawn attention to them in the English text because footnotes of this kind tend to divert attention from the reading of the psalm.

Finally, since the Psalms are meant to be used in public reading as well as privately I have avoided using the personal name of Israel's God, YHWH, sometimes pronounced Yahweh, because it seems to my ears to jar when used in public and to be an intrusion of the original language into the English. Moreover, we ought, I believe, to respect those who find the use of the name difficult or even offensive. For these reasons I have followed the Jewish and Christian tradition of using the word LORD, putting it in capital letters to represent this proper name. The form 'Lord' represents a more general Hebrew noun.

I do not pretend that other scholars will necessarily approve wholeheartedly of either the translation or the introductions, but I hope what I have done may bring to the reading of the Psalms, both in private devotion and in public worship, a freshness and vitality which will ensure their usefulness to those who wish to use them to express and to nourish their devotion to God.

🎋 The Psalms

🎕 Psalm 1

This psalm was deliberately chosen to open the whole collection of psalms because it sets out clearly the familiar doctrine of the Two Ways, the way of righteousness which leads to prosperity and the way of wickedness which leads to disaster. This finds its clearest expression in the so-called Wisdom Literature (e.g. Proverbs 2.21-22), but it may be found frequently elsewhere too. It is common in the Book of Deuteronomy (e.g. Deut. 11.13-17) and in the historical books of Samuel and Kings which were probably composed by the successors of those responsible for Deuteronomy (e.g. 2 Kings 17.19-20). It may be found too in the preaching of the prophets (e.g. Isaiah 1.19-20). Originally statements about these two ways and their destinations were meant as guidelines, as general advice by which people could live their lives. There may be exceptions to their teaching but this did not invalidate it as a means of persuading people to live life according to God's will. The fact that the advice was given in such black and white terms made it all the more effective. It also left room, however, for a dangerous development, namely, the belief that this was a fixed system from which there could be no exceptions. The Book of Jeremiah clearly sees the value of the general statements in a passage which closely resembles this psalm (Jeremiah 17.5-8) but also recognises with some pain that there are exceptions. The prophet himself has had to bear much verbal and physical abuse although he has been obedient to God (Jeremiah 20.7-12). The most conspicuous example of an exception in the Old Testament is in the Book of Job where the wholly righteous man has to bear the most extreme sufferings. His friends, drawing on the fixed dogma of the Two Ways, conclude that he must have sinned, but Job resists this conclusion and maintains that he is an exception to what had now become a rule. His view is vindicated by God.

We must beware, therefore, of seeing this and subsequent psalms as theological statements of absolute validity. This particular psalm may have had its origin in the context of Temple worship where priests pronounced blessings on the innocent and curses on the guilty. It remains, however, a call to all believers to be obedient to God.

1   Happy is the man who has spurned the advice of the wicked,
        who has not stood alongside sinners in their sin,
        who has not sat among scoffers in their mockery of God,

2   But who rather finds enjoyment in the LORD's instruction
                and muses upon it day and night.

3   He is like a tree which grows near flowing streams,
                which bears fruit at the right time
                and its foliage does not wither;
        so in whatever he undertakes he prospers.

4   Not so the wicked!
                He is like husks of grain scattered by the wind.

5   Wicked men cannot stand where justice is found,
                nor sinners where the righteous assemble.

6   For the LORD cares for him who does what is right,
                while he who does what is wrong will perish.

✥ Psalm 2

There is every reason to believe that this psalm was used at the time of the coronation of the Judaean king. It is best understood if different parts of the psalm are regarded as being sung by different persons. Verses 1-6 may have been sung by a prophet. Disturbances in the balance of power were common enough on the death of a king and generally his successor needed time to establish himself securely on the throne. The prophet, however, makes light of such confusion since it is the LORD who has placed the king on the throne. According to the tradition in 2 Samuel 7 God, through Nathan the prophet, had promised that David's descendants would succeed him as king. This prophet now confirms this but makes the important point that God is the true king and his successor rules only on his behalf. In vv. 7-9 the king himself recites the decree of God by whose authority he rules. He is now, 'today', at his accession, brought into a relationship with God which is most fittingly expressed by the metaphor of father and son in which the son must always obey the father and the father will protect the son. It follows that since God's rule was universal so ideally should be the rule of Judah's king.

Of course, historically it never was; it remained an unfulfilled ideal. Finally in vv.10-12 the prophet probably takes up the psalm again, calling on the nations to acknowledge the LORD and worship him. The Hebrew of v.11 is difficult to understand, especially the last line which you will find variously translated. Some think there is a reference to the Judaean king, in which case people are called upon to submit to him.

The psalm was probably used on more than one occasion but the ideal of a king who would rule the world remained an ideal. During and after the exile in Babylon, when Israel had no king, the psalm must have been reinterpreted and used to anticipate the coming of the ideal king, the new David, the coming Messiah.

It was natural, then, for Christians to use the psalm in respect of Jesus whom they came to see as the Messiah. Parts of it are therefore used in the account of Jesus' baptism (Matt. 3.17, and especially in some manuscripts of Luke 3.22), his transfiguration (Matt. 17.4) and his resurrection (Acts 13.33), all of which emphasised his special relationship with God.

1   Why are foreign nations in turmoil?
        Why do people make empty threats?

2   Kings everywhere take up their positions,
        rulers sit together in counsel
        against the LORD and his anointed king,

3   Saying, 'Let us burst their bonds,
        let us discard their cords.'

4   The one who reigns in heaven will laugh;
        the LORD will deride them.

5   Then he will address them in his anger,
        in his fury he will terrify them.

6   'I myself have installed my king
        on Zion, my holy hill.'

7   I will recite the LORD's decree;
        he said to me, 'You are my son,
        I, today, have fathered you.

8   At your request I will make over to you the nations;
        you will inherit the wide world.

9   You shall break them with an iron sceptre,
        you shall shatter them like a pot of clay.'

10   Now, you kings, pay attention!
        Rulers everywhere, learn your lesson!

11   Serve the LORD — with due reverence!
        Rejoice — but tremble!
        Pay homage — sincerely!

12   Lest he be angry and bring life's journey to a quick end,
        for his anger blazes in a flash.
        Happy are those who seek his protection.

❧ Psalm 3

The psalmist expresses his confidence in God even when he is faced by unfortunate circumstances and by wicked people. Many of the psalms are concerned with 'enemies' but we are not given any precise information as to who they are. The descriptions are rather stereotyped, probably because the psalms are meant to be used in public worship where language is often sufficiently unspecific to allow a variety of worshippers in slightly different situations to make use of it. It seems this psalmist was in great difficulty — 'beyond help'. He was therefore regarded as one with whom God was greatly displeased and as a result he was despised and even attacked by some of his fellows.

*   In vv. 2-4 he addresses God directly, first to describe his difficulty and second to affirm his trust. In vv. 5-7 God is not addressed but is spoken of in the third person and so we should assume that the psalmist turns to make his affirmation of trust to his fellow-worshippers. In v.8 he turns back to speak directly to God, calling on him to 'arise'. This is the same as the cry of the Israelites in the wilderness when they lifted up the Ark of the Covenant, God's throne, to lead them on their journey (Numbers 10.9). It may be there-*

fore that the psalmist stood before the Ark in the Temple to make his plea to God. The second half of the verse seems to indicate that he believes his prayer to have been heard and answered by God. This allows him to turn again towards his fellows to proclaim God's power to save (v.9a) before seeking God's blessing on them as well (v.9b).

It is not a psalm which can be linked to any particular occasion. Rather it expresses the mixture of lament and confidence which many religious people feel. In the end it is the confidence which predominates because in worship some event, here perhaps connected with the Ark, stimulates it. This is one of the functions of true worship.

2   LORD, how many are my enemies!
      How many rise up to attack me!

3   They all say about me,
      'He is beyond help, even from God.'

4   But you, LORD, will always shield me;
      through you I can hold up my head in pride.

    5   Whenever I have cried aloud to the LORD
        he has answered me from his holy hill.

    6   I have lain down to sleep and woken again
        because the LORD supports me.

    7   I am not afraid of ten thousand people
        who have laid hands on me from all sides.

8   Arise, LORD!
      Save me, my God!

Now you have struck all my enemies in the face
      and smashed the teeth of those who wronged me.

    9   The power to save belongs to the LORD.

        May your blessing be upon your people.

✿ Psalm 4

Like the previous psalm this is a mixture of lament and confidence and it alternates between addressing God and addressing fellow-worshippers.It differs in the fact that this psalmist sees himself as set apart for God and as a devotee. Many scholars think this latter term may be used to describe any loyal Israelite but there are good grounds for thinking that the Hebrew word translated here as 'devoted servant' (v.4) refers to a particular member of the Temple staff, possibly a Levite. The term is used almost exclusively within the Book of Psalms and we shall meet it again several times later on. One crucial occurrence outside the Psalms is in Deuteronomy 33.8-11. Here blessings are being pronounced on the various tribes and in these verses the tribe concerned is Levi. It indicates that they are responsible for the use of the sacred lot by which the will of God may be discerned and for the preparations for sacrifice. In the course of their work they will experience opposition and even enmity from others.

So v.2 addresses God as one who does what is right and who can therefore be trusted to hear and answer the psalmist's prayer for deliverance. This allows him to turn to his fellow officials, possibly priests, who denigrate his office (vv.3-7). He reminds them of his calling, advises them to be silent and get on with their work of offering sacrifice to God. They are people who pronounce the priestly blessing similar to the one found in Numbers 6.24-26.

Turning back to God (vv.8-9) he who, as a Levite, has no property or land of his own, claims to be happier than those who possess such things; for it is not material blessings which give him confidence, but God who allows him to rest in security.

2   When I call answer me,
      my God, who secures my rights.
  Make room for me when I am hemmed in by misfortune;
      graciously listen to my prayer.

3   You men, how long will you offer me insult instead of honour,
      loving what is utterly useless
      and seeking what can only deceive?

4   Recognise that the L ORD has set apart for himself his
                devoted servant
         and so will answer when I call.

5   When you tremble with anger do not sin.
         Go, lie down; keep your thoughts to yourself
         and remain silent.

6   Offer the appointed sacrifices
         and trust in the L ORD.

7   Many of you say, 'May he let us see prosperity!
         Let your face be radiant, L ORD, with kindness
                towards us.'

8   You have made me happier than they
         when their corn and wine were plentiful.

9   Peacefully I lay down to sleep,
         for you alone, L ORD, give me confident rest.

🌿 Psalm 5

*Once more the psalmist seems to be suffering some attack from enemies
(vv. 9-10) though not much is made of it. More particularly the psalm is a
plea to God to hear his prayer and accept his worship.*

*It has been suggested that the psalmist is himself a priest. This is based
upon v. 4 where the Hebrew simply uses two verbs 'prepare' and 'wait' without any objects. Some have assumed that it is a sacrifice which he prepares
and the translation in RSV makes this explicit. This might mean that, like
Psalm 4, this psalm was also offered by a Levite. My translation supplies
'prayer' as the object since the psalmist is clearly waiting for an answer. This
leaves the identity of the psalmist much more open. Moreover the psalm is
often said to be a morning prayer on the basis of v. 4 but this too is by no
means clear.*

It was widely held by the prophets that worship, if it was to be accept-

able to God, should be accompanied by right behaviour (Isaiah 1.10-17, Hosea 6.6, Amos 5.21-24, Micah 6.8, Jeremiah 7.21-26). Unless the worshippers lived the kind of life which God required then God hated their prayers and sacrifices, that is to say, he found them totally unacceptable. The same point is made in the Psalms. The qualities required of those who wish to enter the Temple for worship are set out in Psalms 15 and 24. This psalmist makes a similar point. The worship of the wicked is hated by God. For his part he comes to the Temple with devotion, a word which includes both love and loyalty.

The psalmist goes beyond this, however (vv.10-13). It is not sufficient that God should reject the worship of the wicked. The prayer is that they may be banished altogether from the Temple and there may be a hint that they should actually be destroyed. These views are not uncommon in the Old Testament. They are based on a firm belief in the absolute justice of God and however necessary we may feel it to be to modify this somewhat harsh prayer in the light of the New Testament we ought to recognise the underlying truth that God is just as well as loving and 'will not be mocked'. His people disobey him at their peril.

2   Listen to my words, LORD;
        discern my scarce-spoken needs.

3   Pay attention to my cry for help,
        my King, my God, for to you I pray.

4   LORD, each morning you will hear me,
        each morning when I frame my prayers
        and wait expectantly for an answer.

5   You are not a God who enjoys the company of the wicked;
        an evil man can never be your guest.

6   The arrogant have no place in your sight;
        you hate all who do wrong.

7   You destroy liars
        and detest violent and treacherous men, LORD.

8   For my part, I come to your house surrounded by rich
            devotion,
        I worship in your holy Temple humbly and reverently.

9   LORD, lead me in whatever way is right
>> for there are those who watch for me with hostility;
>> make straight before me the path you have marked out.

10   For none of their words can be trusted,
>> they are full of harmful talk.
> They are ready to swallow men like an open grave,
>> their words are as smooth as butter.

11   Pronounce them guilty, LORD;
>> let them fall down through their own evil schemes.
> Banish them, so many are their sins,
>> for they have rebelled against you.

12   But let all rejoice who seek safety with you,
>> let them shout for joy as long as they live.
> Protect those who love to acknowledge you,
>> make them happy in your presence.

13   For you will bless those who do right, LORD;
>> your goodwill will surround them like a shield.

❧ Psalm 6

This lament is a very passionate prayer for help from one who is in great distress. This distress has two causes. The immediate cause is that he is very ill and feels he is at death's door. It may be argued that the psalmist is exaggerating at this point, but it is clear that his trouble is most serious. The second cause is that he sees his misfortune as due to God's displeasure. It is often assumed that this in turn is due to the psalmist's sin. Certainly the connection between sin and suffering is often made in the Old Testament. It is worth noticing, though, that this psalmist never mentions his sin; he does not confess it and there is no expression of penitence for it. The plea for deliverance is based solely on God's devotion to him (v. 5).

It is clear that this psalmist had a view of death which excluded any idea of a meaningful after-life. In Sheol there was no possibility of any continuing relationship with God. This, in fact, is the usual view in the Old Testament. Only in the latest parts of it does there emerge any belief in resurrection. We shall meet further references to Sheol in, for instance, Psalms 31.18, 49.15, 88.12 and the description of it there corresponds closely with that in Job 7.9-10 and 10.21-22. In all these cases Sheol is seen as a vague shadowy existence which can in no way be regarded as life. All is darkness and the way back is securely barred. So what the psalmist is praying for is healing so that he shall not pass into Sheol.

In vv. 9-11 we meet again the sudden change of mood which we have already noticed in Psalm 3. Once more there is no indication as to how this change from near despair to confidence is brought about. All we can say is that he received some assurance that God had heard and was answering his prayer. In such a confident mood he can dismiss those who have hitherto shown enmity towards him because they too had believed that God was displeased with him. The importance of a true experience of the presence of God in worship cannot be exaggerated.

2   LORD, though you are angry, do not correct me;
     though you are furious do not discipline me.

3   Rather be gracious to me, LORD, for I am weak;
     heal me, for I am about to collapse.

4   I am totally dismayed,
     but you, LORD — Oh how much longer?

5   Come back, LORD, and rescue me;
     save me, since you are devoted to me,

6   For when we die there is nothing to remind us of you,
     in Sheol no one can praise you.

7   I have groaned until I am weary;
     every night my tears flood my bed,
     they saturate my bed-clothes.

8   My sight is blurred with my crying;
     I can no longer see, so great is my distress.

9   Get away from me, all you wrong-doers
        for the LORD has heard the sound of my weeping.

10   The LORD has heard my pleading;
        the LORD has accepted my prayer.

11   All my enemies will suffer shame and terror;
        in a second they will turn away in terror.

৩৬ Psalm 7

This psalm takes the form of a legal argument in court with God as judge. It may be that this is simply a stylistic, metaphorical way of speaking about his circumstances or it may be that his case was actually being tried in the Temple before the priests. In Deuteronomy 17.1-13 the procedure for dealing with breaches of the law is set out: if possible, cases should be dealt with locally and there must be a careful investigation with at least two witnesses. Cases which are too difficult for the local elders of the town or village to decide are to be referred to the central sanctuary for decision by the priests and the judge, and their decision is binding. Similar procedure is perhaps reflected in 1 Kings 8.31-32 where a wrong-doer may be tried in the Temple, making his defence on oath. Whether the psalm was used by an accused person in an actual case or whether the language is metaphorical, the procedure needs to be understood if we are to read this psalm with understanding.

    It begins with a plea to God who alone can deliver him (vv.2-3) and there follows an oath in which the defendant calls down upon himself all the violence his enemies can muster if anything wrong can be proved against him. A similar 'oath of innocence' may be found in Job 31. This is not a claim to perfection but refers to specific charges made against him (vv.4-6). He then calls upon God to take his stand as judge for he alone is just and is judge of all the earth. This coming of God as judge may well have been represented in some way in a Temple trial, perhaps, for instance, in the person of the presiding priest (vv.7-8). The psalmist then places himself under God's justice, contrasting how God will treat the innocent by giving them protection and how he will treat the wicked by punishing them (vv.9-17). God's justice may be expressed in terms of his direct punishment (vv.13-14) or in

terms of natural retribution (vv.16-17). There is no contradiction here for it
is God who stands behind the process of natural retribution and who causes
things to happen in that way.

The psalm ends on a note of thanksgiving which suggests that God
pronounced him innocent (v.18).

2   LORD, my God, I have taken shelter with you;
        save me from all who pursue me.

3   Deliver me, before they tear me to pieces like a lion
        and there is no one present to rescue me,
        no one else to deliver me.

4   LORD, my God, if I have done anything wrong,
        if I have acted at all unjustly,

5   If I have repaid my friend with evil
        or robbed my assailant without cause,

6   Then may an enemy pursue me,
        may he overtake me,
  may he crush the life out of me,
        may he lay my reputation in the dust.

7   Arise, give vent to your anger, LORD;
        rouse yourself in wrath against my assailants.
  Awake, my God!
        You who have ordered that justice should be done.

8   Summon an assembly of nations around you:
        resume your throne high above them.

9   LORD, who administers justice between the nations,
        judge me, taking account of my rectitude
        and the integrity I have shown.

10   Put an end to the villainy of bad men;
        give stability to those who do right.
  You are a God who does right,
        testing both thoughts and feelings.

11   God on high is my protector;
         he saves those who are true of purpose.

12   God is a just judge,
         a god who consistently denounces wickedness.

13   Unless a wicked man repents
         God will sharpen his sword,
         he will make ready his bow;

14   He prepares for him deadly weapons;
         he will set light to his arrows.

15   See the man in labour with wickedness!
         He has conceived trouble,
         he has given birth to falsehood.

16   He has dug a deep pit
         and fallen into it himself.

17   The trouble he has caused will recoil upon him;
         his violence will fall upon his own head.

18   I will thank the LORD that he always does right,
         I will sing psalms to the LORD most high.

🦋 Psalm 8

*This well-known hymn begins and ends on a note of universal praise to God.
It implies, not that all men recognise his presence and power, but that he has
universal significance. The central section is concerned with the place of
man in the scheme of things. On the one hand it describes his relationship
with God and on the other it sets out his relationship with the rest of the
created world. It is unusual in that its theme is the whole human race and
not just Israel.*

    A comparison of the English translations will show that there is some uncertainty about the sentence division in verses 2 and 3. Moreover most of them require the Hebrew words to be understood in a rather unusual sense and sometimes slight changes in the Hebrew text are made. The present translation requires the substitution of one almost silent letter for another.

The main point of the psalm is, however, clear. It makes a firm distinction between God as Creator and man as created, though this does not imply that God is in any way distant or remote. To forget this distinction or to blur it is to fall into the sin of pride which is the root of all sin, as is clear from Genesis 3 and Ezekiel 28. At the same time man is given authority over the whole animal kingdom where he rules, but always as man and not as God (cf. Genesis 1.26-28). The word 'god' in verse 6 may refer to the one God or to any god or even to the divine beings who surround God. Hebrews 2.6-8, following the Greek translations of the Hebrew, translates it as 'angels'. The teaching of the psalm is not greatly affected by this uncertainty. However exalted a position man has in creation he owes it to God and he remains human.

As the passage in Hebrews shows, the early Christians understood this in a narrower sense. Since 'a mere mortal' in v. 5 can be translated literally 'son of man' and since this title had now been applied to Jesus, the psalm could be seen as referring to him. Nor were they wrong to do so for Jesus, as perfect man, has authority over both creation and mankind. This narrower interpretation ought not to displace the wider one for the psalm has much to say about human responsibility towards God and for the created world.

2   LORD, our Lord,
  how majestically your name resounds through the
    earth;
  your praise is chanted across the heavens!

3   The very cries of babes and infants
  you use to admonish the mighty,
 refusing to listen to your assailants,
  silencing the enemy out for vengeance.

4   When I see your heavens
  made by your own fingers,
 the moon and the stars
  set in their courses by you,

5   What is man
        that you should remember him?
    What is a mere mortal
        that you should notice him?

6   Yet, compared with a god, you have denied him little,
        you have crowned him with honour and majesty.

7   You have made him ruler over all you have made,
        you have placed everything under his control,

8   Not only flocks and herds,
        but animals in the wild,

9   Birds in the sky and fish in the sea,
        creatures which move along the sea-bed.

10 LORD, our Lord,
        how majestically your name resounds through the
            earth!

&ℰ Psalms 9 and 10

These two psalms were almost certainly originally one. The ancient Greek translation known as the Septuagint *regarded them as one and, even more importantly, taken together they form an acrostic. The first short stanza begins with the first letter of the Hebrew alphabet, the second with the second letter and so on. The acrostic, however, is incomplete. For some reason or other the stanza beginning with the fourth letter of the Hebrew alphabet is missing. Moreover the sequence is more seriously broken in the middle. The acrostic form runs as far as Psalm 10.1 using the first twelve letters and then is picked up again in Psalm 10.12 using the last four. The intervening stanzas beginning with the missing six Hebrew letters have been displaced by a lengthy description of the wicked in Psalm 10.2-11.*

If, for the moment, we ignore these ten verses we are left with a psalm which has an air of confidence in God which allows the psalmist to offer

23

praise although his well-being may be threatened. References to the kingship of the LORD in 9.8 and 10.16 may well suggest that the psalm was originally used in an act of worship celebrating the fact that God reigns and so is responsible for justice throughout the earth (cf. Psalms 96.13 and 98.9). That such a celebration was part of the Feast of Tabernacles (or Booths) is indicated by Zechariah 14.16-19. It is noticeable, too, that while the psalm is sung by an Israelite who recognises that God's just rule provides him with security, there are frequent references also to the nations. This leads us to think that the psalm may well have been sung by the Israelite king when he represented his people at a time of national threat. We shall see later on in connection with other psalms that there is good reason for thinking that the king did so represent his people in worship, not only by singing psalms but also by acting out their distress in some ritual connected with the Feast of Tabernacles.

The substitution of the middle section with a passage about the wicked suggests that at some stage the psalm was reinterpreted in a purely individual way and used as a personal psalm of confidence and lament by an individual who was under attack from personal enemies.

| 2 | *Alep* | I will praise you in all sincerity, LORD, |
| | | I will relate all your wonderful deeds. |

| 3 | | I will worship you in gladness and joy; |
| | | I will sing psalms in your honour, Most High. |

| 4 | *Bet* | When my enemies recoil from your presence |
| | | they will stagger and fall. |

| 5 | | For you have secured a just verdict for me, |
| | | you have presided over a just court. |

6	*Gimel*	You have rebuked the nations;
		you have destroyed the wicked;
		you have erased their memory for ever.

7	*He*	As for the enemy they are finished,
		they are ruined for ever.
		You have demolished their cities,
		the very memory of them has perished.

| 8 | | But the LORD's reign is never-ending, |
| | | his throne is set up to safeguard justice. |

9 *Waw*   He judges all mankind justly
                 he gives all peoples a fair trial.

10   So the LORD is a tower of strength to the oppressed,
                 a tower of strength in difficult times.

11   Those who know you well may trust you, LORD,
                 for you have never abandoned those who seek
                 you in prayer.

12 *Zayin*   Sing praises to the LORD who reigns in Zion,
                 recount all he has done among the nations.

13   For he who demands a life for a life has remembered
                 the oppressed,
       he has not turned a deaf ear to their cry.

14 *Het*   Be gracious to me, LORD!
                 See how I am afflicted by those who hate me,
                 bring me back from the very gates of death

15   So that I may relate in Zion all your praise-worthy
                 acts.
       I will rejoice that you have saved me.

16 *Tet*   The nations have dug a pit
                 and fallen into it themselves.
       They have camouflaged a net
                 but their own feet have been caught in it.

17   The LORD is known as one who metes out justice;
                 the wicked get entangled in their own designs.

18   All the nations who forget God,
                 the wicked ones, will go down to Sheol.

19 *Kap*   But the poor will never be overlooked,
                 nor will the oppressed ever lose hope.

20   Rise up, LORD; stop men from feeling too powerful;
             let nations come before you and be judged.

21   Give them some awe-inspiring experience, LORD,
             that they may know they are only human.

Psalm 10

1 *Lamed*   Why do you stand far off, LORD?
             Why do you hide away when times are
                difficult?

2   Proudly and hotly the wicked pursue the afflicted.
             May they be trapped in their own ingenious
              .   schemes!

3   For the wicked boasts about his appetite for evil,
             greedy himself, he congratulates anyone who
               spurns the LORD.

4   Head high in the air, he will not seek God's help.
             He allows him no place in his schemes.

5   He never sees himself in any danger.
             Proudly he ignores your judgements,
             he scorns all his adversaries.

6   He says to himself, 'Nothing can unsettle me.
             My path will always be smooth and without
               misfortune.'

7   His lips are full of curses, deceit and defamation;
             mischievous and wicked talk comes from his
               tongue.

8   He waits in ambush in the villages;
             in dark corners he murders innocent people;
             he looks with evil intent on hapless folk.

9		He waits in his hiding place like a lion in its lair;

9   He waits in his hiding place like a lion in its lair;
            he waits to catch the innocent;
            he catches him by luring him into his net.

10   The innocent is crushed; he sinks down;
            he falls down; his limbs hang helpless.

11   He says to himself, 'God has forgotten me,
            he has turned his back, never to see me again.'

12   *Qop*   LORD God, rise up and show your power;
            do not forget the afflicted.

13   Why does the wicked turn his back on God?
            Why does he say to himself, 'You will not seek
              me out'?

14   *Resh*   But you do see!
            You see the trouble and the distress of the
              afflicted;
            you have regard for him, taking him in your
              hands.
        The unhappy victim may abandon himself to you;
            and as for the orphan, you are his helper.

15   *Sin*   Smash the power of the wicked, evil man.
            Seek out his wickedness until you can find no
              more.

16   The LORD is King for ever and ever;
            the nations have vanished from his land.

17   *Tav*   You have heard the longings of the humble, LORD;
            you will give them courage,
            you will listen attentively to them,

18   Passing judgement in favour of the orphan and the
              oppressed
            so that no man on earth can make them afraid
              again.

🦑 Psalm 11

This psalm expresses confidence in God at a time when many were in despair at the state of their society. Their advice was to run away from life's responsibilities because there was nothing anyone could do about the situation, however well-meaning they might be. As the chosen people of God their social life ought to have been based on those same qualities which God had shown to them, namely truthfulness, faithfulness, devotion and justice. These qualities were no longer to be found and anyone who sought to re-establish them was in personal danger from those who rejected them.

Some translators regard verses 2 and 3 as the psalmist's own comment on the advice given to him in v.2, but it is probably better to see them as part of that advice, closing the quotation marks at the end of v.3. Then the psalmist's response is to turn attention back to God himself, pointing to his justice. The psalmist's own attitudes are to be determined by this rather than by the circumstances in which he lives. God's justice is expressed in the usual way — his hatred of those who do wrong and his love for those who do right. Moreover, this God who does right and demands right behaviour from his people is not restricted to the Temple but is enthroned in heaven (v.4) and consequently has power and authority over all things. No one can escape his scrutiny.

The 'fire and brimstone' of v.6 may recall the tradition of the punishment of Sodom and Gomorrah from which Lot also was told to flee (Genesis 19).

For those who do right in response to God's righteousness there will be the highest reward. They will look on the face of God. This is better than the NEB translation which speaks of the face of God looking upon his people. It was clearly understood, of course, that God's holiness was such that no man could see him and live (Exodus 33.20). Yet occasionally people, like Isaiah, believed they had done so (Isaiah 6.5) and though they felt threatened by it they survived to serve God. It was therefore a great privilege to be so vividly aware of his presence ('face' and 'presence' represent the same Hebrew word) as to speak of seeing his face.

1   In the LORD I have found security.
         How then can you say to me,
         'Flee away like a bird to the safety of the hills;

2   For already wicked men are bending their bows
         and fitting arrows to the strings,
         ready to shoot blindly on those who intend to do right.

3   The very foundations of society are being destroyed;
         what can a good man do?'

4   The LORD is in his holy Temple;
         the LORD is on the heavenly throne.
    He looks down upon mankind
         and makes a close scrutiny of them.

5   The LORD scrutinises good and bad alike;
         he passionately hates those who love violence.

6   He rains fire and brimstone on the wicked,
         they gulp down the scorching wind.

7   For the LORD does right; he loves men who do right.
    Men of virtue shall look on his face.

ॐ Psalm 12

As in the previous psalm so also in this there is a note of pessimism about the state of society. Again, men who show the basic qualities of devotion and faithfulness to one another are totally lacking. The psalmist sees the lack chiefly in the way that people speak. Flattery, insincerity, false promises are rife (vv. 3-4) and these reveal deeper wrongs. The emphasis on the tongue, that is, speech, was common especially in the Book of Proverbs (Prov. 10.11, 18, 31, 32). Nothing can destroy a society so quickly as malicious speech. In v.5 people are claiming the right to say whatever they want without reference to God. Such pride, as we saw in Psalm 8, is the root of sin. It involved refuting the authority of God and breaking free from the generous constraints which God had placed on man.

God's response in v.6 indicates the effect all this has on the poor, to-wards whom Israelite society was meant to have a special responsibility. The psalmist may have been calling to mind words he had already heard or expressing what he felt God was saying in this situation. More likely, however, the words were spoken by a prophet in the context of worship. There is much to be said for regarding vv.2-3 as the psalmist's own plea addressed directly to God. Then vv.4-7, where God is spoken of in the third person, is the prophetic response promising the punishment of the wicked, containing the divine oracle in favour of the poor and assuring the psalmist of the sureness of God's promise. Finally in vv.8-9, where again the LORD is addressed directly, the psalmist accepts the promise in spite of all that is going on around him. The word translated as 'devoted men' in v.2 is the same word as that found in Psalm 4.4 and it is possible that it has the same meaning here. If this is so then the psalmist laments the lack of people on the Temple staff who speak for God (vv.2-3) only to find that one now responds to him (vv.4-7).

There are times when it seems the world is virtually devoid of good, loyal, trustworthy people who will speak God's word. Elijah had once felt the same — 'I only am left' (1 Kings 19.10) — and had fled to Horeb to encounter God there. This psalmist receives a comparable assurance and, like Elijah, has to return to a world where the wicked still walk about all round him; but he has received the assurance he needed to carry on.

2   Save us, LORD, for there are no devoted men left;
      the faithful have disappeared from mankind.

3   People speak sweet nothings and flatter each other;
      they say one thing and mean another.

  4   The LORD will close all flattering lips
        and cut out the tongues which make great promises

  5   And say, 'We confirm our promises;
        our lips are our own, we are our own master.'

  6   'Because of the havoc played with the poor,
        because of the groans of the needy
      I will now rise up', says the LORD,
        'I will place him in the safety he longs for.'

7   The LORD's promises are always true,
            tried like silver in a furnace,
            like gold refined seven times over.

8   You will watch over us, LORD;
            you will always guard us from such people,

9   Though the wicked walk about all round us
            and villainy is highly regarded among men.

🥀 Psalm 13

The opening phrase of this psalm characterises it as a lament. The phrase 'How long?' is not a question about the date at which the psalmist's fortunes will be reversed. It is a cry from a sufferer seeking an end to his sufferings. Exactly what those sufferings were in this case we are not told, except that as usual they aroused people to enmity against him (vv.3-5). More important than the sufferings themselves is the feeling that they indicated God's desertion of him. The word 'forget' does not imply that God, being busy about other things, had accidentally forgotten him. Just as the word 'remember' carries with it the idea of doing something about it, so the word 'forget' implies a deliberate turning away. So the third line of v.2 clarifies the meaning of the second. In the Old Testament there is no escape from theological difficulty by placing the responsibility for misfortune on fate or chance or even the devil. Good and evil alike come from God as Job recognised (Job 1.21). Misfortune may therefore be due to God's displeasure and this, in turn, may be due to human sin, though this psalm doesn't go into the reason for the misfortune but simply accepts it as from God.

Naturally, this lament leads him on to a prayer for deliverance (vv.4-5) which in turn gives way to an expression of trust and praise (vv.6-7). The change from lament and petition to trust and praise is not as abrupt in this psalm as it is in some others. It is brought about by a realisation of God's devotion, his love and loyalty. No outward stimulus for this realisation is strictly necessary, and it may have come from within him as he prayed. But in the light of other psalms where it is more abrupt, and especially Psalm 46.9-10 where something was seen and heard and God's devotion was 'por-

trayed', it may be that here too we ought to think of some 'portrayal' of God's devotion — possibly some word or act of the priest which evoked the psalmist's trust in it. In any case, we are reminded again of the power of worship to change attitudes and renew resolve.

2 How long must it go on, LORD?
     Will you forget me for ever?
     How long will you turn your back on me?

3 How long will you make trouble for me
     and fill me with grief day by day?
     How long will my enemy rise against me?

4 Look on me; answer me, LORD my God.
     Keep my eyes bright; let me not fall asleep in death.

5 Do not allow my enemy to say, 'I have got the better of him',
     or my opponent to be glad that I am shaken.

6 For my part, I have put my trust in your devotion
     and so I will rejoice in your salvation.

7 I will sing songs to the LORD,
     for he has given me all I could wish for.

🕮 Psalm 14

Like Psalms 11 and 12 this is another reflection on the prevalence of wickedness in the world and an affirmation that God will deal with it. Psalm 14 is found again, in a slightly different form, at Psalm 53. The main difference between the two is that this psalm uses the personal name YHWH, translated here as LORD, while 53 uses the more general word 'God'. Their similarity seems to indicate that the psalms were preserved in what were at one time two separate collections, later brought together. The process by which the psalms came to be collected into their present order was complex and is now largely unknown to us.

The psalm opens with a complaint about the universality of sin (vv. 1-3) though the fact that in v.5 it is recognised that there are some who do right means that we have to understand this as hyperbole, as in Psalm 12. It is certainly how people feel from time to time. In Israel's own tradition the time when the whole world was corrupted by evil was just before the Flood. In the account in Genesis God is said to 'see' the wickedness (6.5 and 12) as he does here (v.2). Now, in this psalm (v.4) God responds to the psalmist. Again we have to ask how this response comes. Does it come from within the psalmist? Or is it perhaps the word of God delivered by his prophet? And if so, are vv.5-6 the prophet's own comments on the oracle he has just delivered? The present translation is set out in such a way as to suggest this. Verse 7 is then the psalmist's own response to this, but this verse does not seem to fit very well and it may be that when the psalm was used at some later stage, perhaps during the exile in Babylon, the wicked were identified with the Babylonians and this verse used to conclude the psalm with a longing for Israel's deliverance.

Two points should be made about the familiar opening verse. First, the 'fool' is neither the court jester nor a half-wit; he is a person who has deliberately turned away from showing respect to God, which is the beginning of wisdom. He is therefore morally blameworthy. Second, the more usual translation 'There is no God' is avoided here because the fool was not an atheist denying the existence of God; he is one who ignores him, who makes his own decisions and regards God as irrelevant.

1 The fool says to himself
        'God is irrelevant'.
   Such men are destructive; they behave abominably;
        no one does anything good.

2 The LORD looks down from heaven
            on men everywhere
   to see if there is a prudent man
        who seeks God in worship.

3 But they are all stubborn and corrupt;
            no one does anything good,
            not a single one of them.

4   'Do they not know what will happen, those wicked men,
           who devour my people as readily as food,
           who never address me by my name, the LORD?'

5   They will become terrified
           for God is with those who do right in our day.

6   The wisdom of him they afflicted will become an
               embarrassment to them
           since he has taken refuge with the LORD.

7   If only Israel's deliverance would come from Zion!
           When the Lord restores his people's fortunes
           Jacob will rejoice, Israel will be glad.

✦ Psalm 15

*Psalms such as this are sometimes known as Entrance Liturgies. People
seeking access to God through worship were required to fulfil certain obligations. As they approached the Temple worshippers would ask what
these qualifications were and a priest would give them an answer. Among
other ancient peoples the requirements would be ritual ones to do with
ceremonial cleanness. But in this Israelite psalm and in Psalm 24 they
are moral requirements concerned with right behaviour.*

*Verses 2-5a set out various conditions: right behaviour in general,
right use of the tongue, right attitudes towards friends and neighbours,
right company, the keeping of solemn promises, a readiness to make interest-
free loans to fellow-Israelites, refusal of bribes in court cases. This does seem
a fairly comprehensive list but it should not be understood as exhaustive.
Nor is it a claim that a man must be perfect before he can enter God's sanctuary. These lists, like the Law itself, were meant to indicate the kind of
behaviour which ought to follow from a right relationship with God. The
intending worshipper must recognise the obligations which he now has
towards the God who chose Israel and set the forefathers free from bondage
in Egypt.*

The final line of the psalm may be either the priest's conclusion to the list or the worshipper's own acknowledgement of his obligations and the consequences of fulfilling them. While 'dislodged' may mean dislodged from worship in the Temple, it may also mean dislodged from the security of living in God's presence. Certainly at some stage the psalm came to be used not only in worship, but also more generally as setting out the qualities needed in those who wished to live in God's presence anywhere. Those who acknowledge God's demands upon them and seek to fulfil them may live securely in his presence.

1   LORD, who may lodge in your sacred tent?
       Who may take up residence on your holy hill?

  2 He who behaves with integrity,
       who does what is right;

  3 He who deliberately speaks the truth,
       who never slanders anyone;
    He who does no harm to his friend,
       who brings no disgrace upon his neighbours;

  4 He who has nothing to do with a despicable man
        but who honours those who revere the LORD;
    He who swears and does not change his mind,
       even though it costs him dear;

  5 He who does not lend money on interest,
       who does not take a bribe to testify against an
         innocent man.

Whoever does these things will never be dislodged.

❧ Psalm 16

The singer of this psalm identifies himself as a 'devoted servant' (v.10), a description we have already met in Psalm 4.4 and 12.1. He begins by confessing his own faith and loyalty to God (vv.2-6). The Levites, to whom this psalmist probably belongs, had proved their loyalty in the desert (Exodus 32.25-29). According to tradition when the Israelites reached the Promised Land each tribe was allocated its share, except for the Levites who were not given a share because they were a priestly tribe (Joshua 13.14). Now the psalmist can claim God as his share and so be very happy and content with what has been allotted to him — his place in worship. The Hebrew of vv.3 and 4 is difficult to translate. The translation offered here involves understanding a word which literally means 'holy ones' in the sense of things which carry with them an air of holiness, that is, heathen idols. The word is used in this sense in some Canaanite texts which were found at Ugarit on the northern part of the Syrian coast.

The psalmist's fellowship with God gives him security and happiness and leads him to be confident that God will be with him throughout his life. We have met the idea of Sheol already, in Psalm 6.6. In vv.10 and 11 he is confident that he will not be allowed to come close to Sheol and death before his time, but that God will show him the way to an even fuller, more joyful life. Life and death must never be understood in purely clinical terms in the Old Testament. When a man is ill or suffering misfortune he is already on his way down to Sheol and may be thought of as as good as dead even before he is clinically dead. When a person is prosperous and is moving up the scale towards the highest form of life which includes all material blessings but, most importantly, the presence of God himself, then that is life. It is the abundant life which, according to John 10.10, Jesus came to make available to his followers. The psalmist did not look beyond death for this. Christians, however, see this new life of fellowship with God through Jesus as unassailable by death and therefore continuing into eternity.

1   Keep me safe, LORD, for I have taken refuge in you.

2   I have said to the LORD,
   'I find my happiness in you, LORD,
   and not in the gods on high.

3   Their idols are all over the land
        and strong nobles delight in them;

4   But those who crave for other gods multiply their own
            sorrows.
        I will not pour out to them libations of blood,
        I will not take their names upon my lips.

5   You, LORD, are my share in the promise,
        you give me what I need,
        you hold my fortunes in your hand.

6   What is allotted to me is very pleasant
        what I have inherited is lovely indeed.'

7   I praise the LORD who gives me guidance,
        who nightly instructs me through my conscience.

8   I have never let the LORD out of my sight;
        because he is by my side I shall not stumble.

9   So I rejoice with heart and soul,
        and live my life in security.

10 For you will never abandon me to Sheol,
        nor allow your devoted servant to look into the Pit;

11 Rather you point out to me the way to life,
        in your presence I am full of joy,
        in your safe-keeping I find untold delight.

❦ Psalm 17

*Like Psalm 7 this was quite likely a psalm sung by a person who had been
falsely accused of wrong-doing and whose case had been brought to the
'appeal court' in the sanctuary. There he protested his innocence and called*

down vengeance on his enemies who, by their false accusations, had also made themselves enemies of God. This setting is indicated by v.2. If this was the original setting there is no doubt that in the course of time it came to be understood and used in a more general sense by anyone who felt threatened by personal antagonists.

It opens with the psalmist's plea to God to listen to him with a reminder that he has already tested his integrity and found it to be sound (vv.1-3). There follows a reaffirmation of this, not in the form of an oath as in Psalm 7, but as simple statements of fact (vv.4-5). The intention, however, is much the same. The wrongs which he denies are quite general and not specific. They have to do with sinful speech and disobedient behaviour. Verse 6 marks a transition; the opening phrase is part of the affirmation of innocence but it leads the psalmist straight into a plea for help and protection (vv.6-8). This, in turn, brings him to a description of those who are accusing and attacking him (vv.9-12) and he pleads for vengeance on them (vv.13-14). The Hebrew of v.14 is difficult to understand, as a comparison of the various translations will show. Judgement seems to be called down in such a way that the accuser's children are involved in it too (cf. Psalm 137.9). In a society where family ties were strong and members depended so much on each other, anything which affected one must also affect the rest. If the accompanying translation is correct the psalmist prays that the land which produces the family's wealth and food may cease to do so and that consequently the whole family will suffer.

The concluding verse (v.15) reiterates the psalmist's righteousness and looks forward with confidence to having a vision of God in his sleep which will satisfy him when he awakes.

1   Hear me, for I do right, LORD;
          pay attention to my cry;
    listen to my prayer
          for I speak without deception.

2   Let judgement in my favour be pronounced in your court,
          watch carefully that justice is done.

3   You have visited me at night and tested my thoughts,
          you have tried me with fire and found nothing wrong.

4   I have not sinned in my speaking, as men often do;
          I have kept the word which you have spoken.

5   I have restrained my feet from paths of violence,
      they have never deviated from your ways.

6   I have called to you, for you answer me, God.
      Open your ears to me; hear what I say.

7   Perform wonderful deeds of devotion,
      saviour of all who seek security in you.
  By your powerful right hand
      deliver them from those who arise to attack them.

8   Protect me, as you would the pupil of your eye;
      in the shadow of your wings hide me

9   From wicked men out to destroy me,
      from enemies who hungrily surround me.

10   They close the door on their sympathy,
      they speak arrogantly, 'We are fine'.

11   Now they keep watch on me from all sides,
      they set out to throw me to the ground.

12   They are like lions greedy for prey,
      like lion cubs waiting for me in their lairs.

13   Rise up, LORD; meet them head on and bring them down;
      with your sword rescue me from the wicked.

14   By your power save me from those who would kill me;
      wipe out all that life has given them,
  the good things with which you have filled them,
      which satisfy their children and leave enough for their
        babies.

15   Because I do right I shall have a vision of you;
      when I awake I shall be content to have seen you.

❧ Psalm 18

*This psalm appears in 2 Samuel 22.2-51 on the lips of King David in grati-
tude for his deliverance from Saul and his victories over the Philistines and
other nations. It is entirely appropriate for this occasion but may also have
been used by other kings after hard-won victories. There is, however,
another setting for which the psalm is appropriate and where it may have
originated. There is reason to believe that when David captured Jerusalem
he took over certain patterns of worship used by the Canaanites who lived
there, investing them with new meanings demanded by his own belief in the
one God, the LORD. In Canaan throughout the hot, rainless summer when
the land became parched it was believed that Baal, the giver of rain and fer-
tility, had died. In the autumn when the rains began again it was thought
that his sister, Anath, had restored him to life. These beliefs were probably
depicted dramatically in the Canaanite sanctuaries such as that in Jerusalem, with the king playing the part of the 'dying' and 'rising' God. It was
quite impossible for an Israelite like David to believe that the LORD had
died and been raised to life since he himself was the source and giver of life
(v.47). So the drama was reinterpreted so that the king represented neither
Baal nor the LORD but his people who were threatened by the lack of rain
and whose life was therefore put at risk. It was the LORD himself who raised
the people to life by sending the rains. This present psalm may be interpreted
against this background, even though it subsequently came to be used as a
victory psalm as in 2 Samuel 22.*

*It begins with a confession of God's saving power (vv.2-4). In vv. 5-7
the psalmist, probably the king, regards himself as ritually 'dead' or in such
deep trouble that he can speak of himself as dead. His cry for help (v.7)
results in the LORD'S appearing to rescue him (8-16) and this is described in
the usual vivid imagery (cf. Exodus 19). The rescue itself is reported in vv.17-
20. This he sees as his reward for living according to God's will (vv.21-25). In
vv.26-30 he turns to address God directly as one who rewards people according to their behaviour and particularly as one who exalts the poor and
humbles the mighty (cf. Luke 1.50-53). At v.31 he turns back to his fellow-
worshippers to confess that it is God who gives him strength to behave
properly and to fight battles. Verses 36-46 are again addressed to God to
confess that it is the LORD who overcomes his enemies and brings them in
submission to him (cf. Psalm 2.10-12). In v.47 he sings triumphantly that
God lives and protects him. The psalm ends (vv.47-51) on a note of thanksgiving and praise for God's help not only to him but to all the succession of
kings of the Davidic line.*

2   I love you, LORD, my strength.

3   The LORD is my cliff fortress; he keeps me safe.
        He is my God, my Rock in whom I find security,
        my shield, my mountain fastness, my stronghold.

4   I call on the LORD who deserves my praise
        and so I shall be saved from my enemies.

5   Death twines its ropes around me,
        its destructive streams overwhelm me.

6   Sheol encircles me with its ropes,
        death's snares threaten me.

7   In my distress I call to the LORD
        and cry to my God for help.

8   Then from his temple he hears me,
        my cry for help falls upon his ears.

9   The earth quaked and trembled,
        the bases of the mountains shook
        and rocked because the LORD was angry.

10   Smoke poured from his nostrils,
        devouring fire was emitted from his mouth,
        scorching coals rained from him.

11   He parted the skies and descended,
        his feet resting on a dark cloud.

12   He flew down riding on a cherub,
        he flashed through the air on the wings of the wind.

13   Heavy, watery clouds surrounded him
        and he hid in their darkness.

14   His clouds rolled away leaving his brightness,
        showering hailstones and blazing coals.

15 The LORD thundered from the sky,
       the Most High's voice pealed out loud.
   He shot his arrows in all directions,
       his flashes of lightning crashing through the air.

16 The contours of the sea-bed were uncovered,
       the very foundations of the earth were revealed
   when you spoke sternly, LORD,
       when you blew with your strong wind.

17 He reaches down from the heights and takes hold of me,
       he lifts me out of the deep waters.

18 He rescues me from my powerful enemies,
       from those who hate me and are too strong for me.

19 They confront me in times of distress
       but the LORD supports me.

20 He brings me through those times into freedom,
       he rescues me because he is pleased with me.

21 The LORD rewards me for doing right,
       he repays my innocence.

22 I have behaved as the LORD has demanded,
       I have not deserted God to do wrong.

23 For I keep in mind all the laws he has laid down,
       I do not push his decrees on one side.

24 So I maintained my integrity in his sight,
       I kept myself free from sin.

25 The LORD repays me for doing right
       because I am innocent in his eyes.

26 You devote yourself to whoever is devoted to you,
       to him who acts with integrity you too act with integrity.

27 You behave sincerely with him who is sincere
      but to him whose behaviour is crooked you are devious
         too.

28 For you are the saviour of humble folk
      but those who are proud you bring down to earth.

29 You are the one who lights my lamp, LORD,
      my God who turns my darkness into light.

30 With your help I can crush a detachment of soldiers,
      with divine aid I can leap over their defensive wall.

31 As for God, then, he behaves with integrity;
      the word of the LORD is tried and true;
      he is a shield for all who seek security in him.

32 For there is no other God than the LORD,
      no safe rock other than our God,

33 God who equips me with strength
      and makes me walk with integrity.

34 He makes me as sure-footed as a deer
      and enables me to stand firm on high ground.

35 He teaches me how to fight battles
      so that my arms can bend a bow, a bronze bow.

36 You have given me protection and safety;
      with your strong right hand you support me,
      gently you make me great.

37 You give me room to walk safely
      and my feet never slip.

38 I pursue my enemies and catch up with them;
      I do not turn around until I have put an end to them.

39 I wound them so badly that they cannot get up,
      they fall beneath my feet.

40   You equip me with strength for battle,
         you enable me to subdue my assailants,

41   You make my enemies turn tail,
         you wipe out those who hate me.

42   They cry out but there is no one to help them;
         they call to the LORD but he does not answer them.

43   I will crush them like wind-blown dust,
         I will trample on them like mud in the streets.

44   When I am in dispute with other peoples
         you will deliver me from them;
   You will establish me as the lord of the nations;
         an unfamiliar people will become my vassals.

45   When they hear me they will do as I say,
         foreigners will come cringing to me.

46   Foreigners will lose their courage
         and come trembling out of their fortresses.

47   The LORD lives! Blessed is my Rock!
         My God and Saviour is exalted high!

48   God, who gives me vengeance,
         who puts people in subjection to me,

49   Who delivers me from my enemies,
         you raise me high over my assailants,
         you rescue me from violent men.

50   Therefore among the nations I will praise you,
         I will address my songs to you.

51   For you give your king great victories,
         you show devotion to him you have anointed,
         to David and his descendants for ever.

ঔৠ Psalm 19

It is sometimes thought that two originally separate psalms have been combined to form this hymn in praise of both Creation and Law. Even if this is so it has to be said that whoever put them together had good reason for doing so and it is important to ask why. The answer is surely because these two, Creation and Law, are the ways in which God reveals himself to men. The material universe reveals the 'glory' of God; that is, it shows to men what the holy God is like. God himself cannot be seen by men, but he reveals, through creation, as much as man is capable of seeing and understanding. The psalmist makes particular mention of the sun and it may be that this part of his poem is influenced by his knowledge of a hymn to the Egyptian sun-god. Be that as it may, the sun, for him, was placed in the sky by God and its movements across the sky were controlled by God.

The Law, on the other hand, reveals not only what God is like, but what he requires of men. It is important to know this so that human behaviour can correspond to what God requires. The Law, then, is not seen as a burden imposed upon men but as a God-given guide to the way fellowship with God may be maintained (Psalm 119).

Once God is revealed, whether through creation or law, people are made aware that they are creatures, and sinful creatures at that. Then neither law nor creation are sufficient. They are thrown back on the grace of God in forgiveness, for which the psalmist prays. It is God who is his Rock, his place of safety (Psalm 18.47) and his Redeemer, his kinsman who acts on his behalf to set him free (cf. Job 19.25).

Christians, of course, will want to go one stage further and see God as revealed supremely in Jesus his Son; but this should not blind us to the value of other ways in which God has shown his glory to us.

2   The heavens tell out the glory of God,
      the sky declares what he has done.

3   Today shouts it loud to tomorrow,
      each night tells what it knows to the next.

4   All this without speech or words,
      without any audible sound.

5   Yet out goes their melody through the earth,
        their words to the far corners of the world.
    In the sky God has pitched a tent for the sun.

6   It comes out like a bridegroom from his wedding bower;
        it is exuberant like an athlete running a race.

7   It rises at one end of the sky
        and completes its circuit at the other.
        There is no way of hiding from its heat.

8   The law of the LORD is perfect; it restores vitality,
        the commandments of the LORD are reliable; they
            provide wisdom for those who need it.

9   The rules of the LORD are just; they make men happy,
        the commands of the LORD are proven; they open men's
            eyes.

10   The law of the LORD inspires reverence and is pure; it stands
        firm, for ever,
        the judgements of the LORD are true; they form a good
            code of justice.

11   They are more desirable than gold,
        than a quantity of finest gold.
    They are sweeter than honey,
        the pure honey straight from the comb.

12   By them your servant is shown how not to live;
        when I keep them the consequences are good.

13   No one can see his own mistakes,
        acquit me of my hidden faults.

14   Hold me back, too, from sins I know about,
        do not let them gain mastery over me.
    Then I shall keep my integrity
        and be innocent of any great sin.

15   May the words on my lips and the thoughts in my mind
         both be pleasing to you,
              LORD, my Rock and my Redeemer.

ꙮ Psalm 20

*It is not easy to pin-point the kind of occasion on which this psalm would
have been used. Whoever the singer is he begins by addressing the king, and
then he invokes God's blessing upon him in a time of trouble. We can only
guess at the nature of the difficulty in which the king stands. There is a word
which recurs several times in the psalm (vv.6, 7 and 10) which may be translated as 'victory', in which case the psalm would probably have been used in
war-time. However, it is equally possible that the word should be translated
'salvation' or 'deliverance', in which case the trouble mentioned in v.2
remains unspecified. The person responsible for invoking such help from
God would have been the priest or a Levite in the Temple.*

*In v.7 the singer turns to the congregation and, with an air of confi-
dence, declares that his wishes for the safety of the king (literally, the
anointed one) have been fulfilled. What inspired such confidence we have
no means of knowing, but we have met similar changes of mood earlier in
other psalms. At any rate the confidence he has is in the power of God himself which is greater than that of all instruments of war (cf. Isaiah 31.1-3).*

*As the Hebrew stands the prayer directly to God is reiterated in the
final verse, 'Deliver, O Lord, the King', but it is tempting to think that one
Hebrew letter has been written twice inadvertently. If one letter is omitted
then it is possible to obtain the translation given here in which the psalmist
states again, as in v.7, that the LORD has saved the king in response to the
prayers of the people.*

2   May the LORD answer you on the day when trouble comes,
         may Jacob's God lift you safely above it.

3   From his Temple may he send you help
         and support you from Zion.

47

4 May he take into account all your offerings
      and regard all your sacrifices as generous.

5 May he give you everything you could wish for
      and bring all your plans to fulfilment.

6 May we shout for joy because you have been delivered
      and declare how great our God is.
   May the LORD fulfil all your requests.

7 Now I know that the LORD has given deliverance to his king;
      from his heavenly sanctuary he responds to him,
      sending his mighty power which always saves.

8 Some draw attention to their chariots, some to their horses,
      but for our part we draw attention to the LORD, our God.

9 They crumple and fall,
      but we will rise and continue on our way.

10 The LORD has delivered the king;
      he answers us when we call.

❧ Psalm 21

Here is another psalm concerning the king and the things God has done for him. Unlike Psalm 20 there is no prayer for God's help but rather a recognition and celebration of his power. It is possible that this psalm was used immediately after Psalm 20. In v.2 there is again that word which may be translated either 'victory' or 'deliverance' and so the psalm may have been used either following victory in war or on some other occasion such as a coronation (v.4) or after a ritual 'rescue' in a ceremony such as that suggested in connection with Psalm 18 when the king's crown and sceptre were given back to him. The details are too imprecise for us to be sure and it is best simply to see it as referring to divine help in some undisclosed difficulty.

Verses 2-7 are addressed to God, presumably by a priest celebrating what has happened to the king. Verse 8 is best seen as a kind of chorus which speaks of God in the third person. Verses 9-13 are words addressed by the priest directly to the king promising him power over his enemies, though the second half of v.10 makes it clear that this power is derived from God. As in Psalm 17 the children are involved with their parents in the destruction which God will bring down on the king's enemies who have plotted against him (cf. Psalm 2.1-5). Finally the congregation joins in another chorus of praise to the LORD.

In all these 'royal' psalms it is important to remember that the fortunes of the whole nation are bound up with those of the king and therefore his deliverance is theirs as well.

2   The king rejoices in your help, LORD.
        How glad he is about the deliverance you have given him!

3   You have given him all he has wanted,
        you have not withheld anything he has asked for.

4   You came to meet him with assurances of prosperity
        and crowned him with a golden crown.

5   You have given him the life he has asked of you,
        long life, lasting for ever.

6   Your deliverance has made him rich and famous,
        you have invested him with honour and majesty.

7   So you give him blessing upon blessing,
        you will fill him with joy by your presence.

    8   For the king trusts in the LORD,
            through the devotion of the Most High his throne is
            secure.

9   You will extend your power over all your enemies,
        searching out those who hate you.

10   You will set fire to them as to an oven
        when the time comes to meet them.

The LORD in his anger will engulf them,
    the fire will burn them up.

11   You will wipe out their children from the earth
    and their descendants from the human race.

12   For they have threatened you with disaster,
    they have worked out a plan against you,
    but cannot carry it out.

13   So you will make them bearers of burdens,
    you will fit arrows to your bow while they look on.

14   Be raised on high in your strength, LORD,
    we will sing psalms in praise of your might.

✆ Psalm 22

It is difficult to detach this psalm from the passion of Jesus since he used its opening words on the Cross and the description of the crucifixion corresponds to some of the verses found here (v.16, 18-19). Yet in the first instance the psalm demands to be understood as the lament of an Israelite who is in desperate trouble from sickness and enemies. As he reflects on his situation his mood fluctuates between despair and hope. The first two verses indicate that what perturbs him most is the sense that he has been deserted by God, but he reminds himself in vv.4-6 of the experience of his forefathers. Verses 7-9 again express his distress while vv.10-11 recall God's help to him in the past. Verses 12-19 are a description of his enemies and their attack on him in highly figurative and poetic language, while vv.20-22 are a prayer to the God who, he felt, had forsaken him.

The change of mood which we have noticed in earlier psalms (e.g. Psalm 6) is most marked here, so much so that some have regarded vv.23-32 as a separate psalm, perhaps sung later when the psalmist had been rescued. It may be, however, that either some priestly word of reassurance or some action within the liturgy produces this confidence which allows him to rejoice and to praise God.

It was therefore a particularly appropriate psalm to be on Jesus' lips on the Cross, and probably he had the whole psalm with its fluctuating moods in mind rather than just the opening verse.

It serves as a reminder of the importance of feeling free to express sorrow and even doubt, whilst keeping in mind also those moments of God's goodness which have been experienced both by others and by ourselves so that our doubts give way to renewed confidence.

2 My God, my God, why have you deserted me?
      Why are you too far away to help me
      when I groan as I do?

3 All day I call, God, but you do not answer;
      all night, too, but there is no rest for me.

4 Yet you are holy,
      Israel praises you as King.

5 Our forefathers trusted in you,
      they trusted in you and you set them free.

6 They cried to you for help and escaped,
      they trusted in you and knew no shame.

7 But I am more of a worm than a man,
      taunted by men, despised by people everywhere.

8 Every time they see me they make fun of me;
      they make free with their tongues, shaking their heads.

9 'Prayers roll off his tongue; let God set him free;
      let him rescue him, seeing he is pleased with him.'

10 But you are the one who delivered me when I was born
      and then kept me safe at my mother's breast.

11 I was thrown on your protection from birth,
      from the moment of delivery you have been my God.

12 Do not stand at a distance when trouble is near
      for I have no one to help me.

51

13 Enemies surround me like bulls,
    like fierce bulls from Bashan.

14 They come to me like lions with mouths wide open
    roaring and ready to tear me apart.

15 I am as weak as water poured on the ground,
    my body is falling apart;
my heart is melting away,
    it has become like soft wax within me.

16 My mouth is as dry as a piece of pot,
    my tongue sticks to my teeth.
    You give me over to the dust in death.

17 A pack of evil men surround me,
    like dogs snapping at my hands and feet.

18 As I count up all my bones
    they look on and stare at me.

19 They share out my clothes among them,
    casting lots for my tunic.

20 So please, LORD, do not stand at a distance;
    hurry up, my helper, and help me!

21 Save my life from their swords,
    my precious life from the power of those dogs.

22 Save me from the mouth of the lion,
    from the horns of the wild bull, afflicted as I am.

23 I will tell my fellow-worshippers how great you are;
    I will praise you in the congregation.

24 Praise him, you worshippers of the LORD!
    Honour him, all you descendants of Jacob!
    Stand in awe of him, all you descendants of Israel!

25 For he has not shown disdain for the afflicted
        nor turned away in loathing from his affliction,
        but has heard when he called to him.

26 He inspires the praise I offer in the great congregation,
        I fulfil my vows in the presence of those who worship him.

27 The poor shall eat until they are full,
        those who seek the LORD's presence will praise him.
        May you live prosperously for ever.

28 People everywhere will remember and turn to the LORD,
        all races will pay homage to him

29 For the LORD is sovereign,
        he rules over the nations.

30 Indeed, all the prosperous will pay him homage;
        those who are dying, too, will bow before him
        and the man who cannot keep himself alive.

31 Future generations will worship him,
        generations to come will tell of the LORD.

32 They will announce to those still to be born
        that the LORD has achieved victory.

ॐ Psalm 23

This is probably the best-known and the best-loved psalm of all. In the first four verses the psalmist recalls God's care using the image of a shepherd looking after his flock, and although shepherding was rather different then from what it is now, the significance of the psalm is clear. It should be remembered, however, that the figure of a shepherd is also used quite often in the Old Testament to represent the king. King David started life as a shepherd boy and when the prophet Micaiah foretold the death in battle of King Ahab he said that he had had a vision of Israel as sheep without a shepherd

(1 Kings 22.17). *Ezekiel spoke about the bad shepherds in Judah before the Exile and went on to promise that God was their true shepherd, making clear that the* LORD *was Israel's King (Ezek. 34). Similarly, the prophet of the Exile spoke of God coming with might and his arm ruling for him (Isaiah 40.10) and then immediately passed on to the figure of the shepherd. If it is true that the* LORD *is the King of all Israel it is equally true that he is the King of each individual Israelite. So Israel's Shepherd-King cares for the psalmist.*

In v.4 there occurs a word which traditionally has been regarded as two separate words meaning 'shadow of death'. Almost certainly it should be read as one word meaning 'pitch darkness'. This scarcely alters the meaning for even the traditional translation indicates an experience which threatens like death rather than death itself.

Once we see the shepherd as king it helps our understanding of the second part of the psalm (vv. 5-6) where the king prepares a banquet, fills the psalmist's cup and anoints him with oil. He will be allowed to live in the LORD'S *family as long as he lives. The word in v.6 which is usually translated 'house' may equally well mean 'household', as it often does. There he will live literally 'for length of days', that is, as long as he lives. Eternal life is not intended here.*

In spite of the fact that the present translation loses some of the traditional meanings it still provides a song of matchless beauty and supreme confidence in God.

1   The LORD is my shepherd,
          I have all I need.

2   He lets me rest where the grass is green,
          he leads me to the side of peaceful pools,

3   Where he restores my vitality.
     He guides me along right paths
          to enhance his reputation.

4   Though my way should lie through a dark valley
          I shall not be afraid of any harm,
     for you are with me,
          your staff to protect and support allays my fears.

5 You prepare a banquet for me
    with my enemies looking on;
I enjoy the luxury of your oil upon my head,
    my wine-cup is full to overflowing.

6 Prosperity and devotion will accompany me
    through all my remaining days
and I shall be part of the LORD's family
    as long as ever I live.

❧ Psalm 24

Like Psalm 15 this is an 'entrance liturgy' which, in its original setting, was used by a procession of worshippers seeking to enter the Temple. It begins with the priest affirming God as Creator and Sustainer of the world (vv. 1-2). The worshippers, or perhaps the leader of the procession, then enquire who may draw near God's Temple on the hill (v. 3). The priest's reply (vv. 4-5) is daunting for it demands nothing less than the highest standard of action, will, desire and speech as the condition for receiving God's blessing, his gifts of prosperity and, above all, his presence. Surprisingly the worshippers appear to claim that they have reached this standard (v. 6) and their response sounds to us almost arrogant. It is difficult to believe that the priest demanded and the people claimed perfection in all these areas of life. Much more likely it was a recognition and confession of what they ought to be and do as God's people. At any rate, on the basis of this they seek entrance for themselves and for their King, the LORD (v. 7). We may ask how the LORD comes to be in the procession seeking entrance. The probable answer is that each year there was a procession carrying the Ark, the moveable throne of God, prior to the celebration of God's kingship in the Temple. This would be a recollection and re-enactment of David's bringing the Ark into Jerusalem in 2 Samuel 6. Like a sentry, the priest seeks identification of the enquirers who reply that it is the LORD (v. 8). This exchange of question and answer is then repeated in vv. 9-10.

As with other psalms this one had to be reinterpreted when processions carrying the Ark to the Temple were no longer possible during and after the Exile in Babylon. Then it became a psalm about entering into worship of God in a more general sense. It has retained this meaning for Christians, particularly in connection with the Ascension of Jesus the King to his Father in heaven.

1   The LORD owns the earth and all it contains,
        the world and all that inhabits it.

2   For he was the one who founded it on the seas
        and set it firmly on the underground streams.

3   Who may ascend the LORD's hill?
        Who may stand on the holy site?

4   The one who is innocent of wrong actions;
        the one who is free from wrong intentions;
    the one who cherishes no wrong desires;
        the one who makes no false promises.

5   He will receive blessing from the LORD,
        his saviour God will do what is right for him.

6   So are we who come to worship him,
        we who seek to enter the presence of Jacob's God.

7   Open up, you gates!
        Open up, you ancient doors!
        Let the glorious King enter.

8   Who is this glorious King?

    The LORD — strong and powerful,
        the LORD — powerful in battle!
9   Open up, you gates!
        Open up, you ancient doors!
        Let the glorious King enter.

10   Who is he, this glorious King?

The LORD — Lord of the battle host,
he is the glorious King.

🐌 Psalm 25

*Here is another 'acrostic' psalm in which each verse begins with a different
letter of the Hebrew alphabet in alphabetical order. The pattern is not quite
complete. The final verse stands outside the acrostic leaving 21 verses in it
whereas there are 22 Hebrew letters. The sixth letter of the alphabet which
should occur between verses 5 and 6 is missing. It then proceeds regularly as
far as v.18 which should have started with the 19th letter. Instead both it
and the following verse begin with the 20th letter and the 19th is left out.*

*The use of the acrostic pattern must have been difficult to maintain
and for this reason the logical order is sometimes sacrificed. It is clear,
though, that the psalmist here was in some trouble (vv.2, 16-20), but he
doesn't go into any detail about its nature apart from mentioning enemies.
The psalm is basically a prayer for deliverance from his trouble and it is a
prayer uttered with some confidence in God. Such confidence is fostered by
his own and his people's experience from which he has gained a deep understanding of God. It is above all through worship in the Temple that this
understanding and consequently his confidence have come to him. So it is
among the congregation gathered for worship that he offers God his
thanks.*

*The final verse which stands outside the acrostic form comes from the
whole congregation and is a prayer for all Israel. At first sight it seems to fit
awkwardly with what has gone before, but we should be aware that it is
unlikely that anyone in a deep experience of trouble would cast his prayer in
the rather complicated form of an acrostic. There is some reason for thinking that the psalm was composed for the use of others in worship, and if this
is so then the congregational conclusion becomes more understandable.*

1   You are all I want, LORD.

2   I have trusted you; never let me down,
        do not let my enemies gloat over me.

3 No one who looks expectantly to you will ever be let down,
    they will be let down who break faith without reason.

4 Show me how I am to behave, LORD,
    teach me the path I am to follow.

5 Keep me faithful to you in all I do and instruct me,
    for you are my God who saves me.
    Each day I look expectantly to you.

6 Remember your acts of love and devotion, LORD,
    for you have been doing them for ages.

7 Do not remember my youthful mistakes and rebelliousness,
    but, in your devotion, do remember me,
    because you are good, LORD.

8 The Lord is good and just,
    therefore he instructs sinners in the way of life.

9 He guides the humble in the paths of justice
    and teaches them what conduct he requires.

10 The LORD always acts with true devotion
    to those who observe the rules of the covenant.

11 For the sake of your standing in the eyes of men,
    LORD, forgive my sinfulness, great as it is.

12 Is there a man who is a worshipper of the LORD?
    The LORD will instruct him as to which way he should
    choose.

13 He will live his life in prosperity
    and his descendants will succeed to the land.

14 The LORD shares his plans with his worshippers,
    telling them about his covenant.

15 I look to the LORD continually
         for he alone can release my feet caught in a net.

16 Turn and look favourably on me
         for I am poor and lonely.

17 Release me from the pressures I am under,
         set me free from all that hems me in.

18 Take away my affliction and trouble
         and forgive all my sins.

19 See how numerous my enemies are
         and how violently they hate me.

20 Defend and deliver me;
         never let me down for I seek safety with you.

21 Let integrity and honesty protect me,
         for I look expectantly to you.

   22 Our God, rescue Israel
            from all its troubles.

✖ Psalm 26

Here is a psalm which could easily give the impression of self-righteousness. The first six verses amount to an expansion of the statement in v.1 that the psalmist has lived his life in integrity. This statement of his innocence has led some to believe that the psalm was sung by one falsely accused whose case is being tried in the Temple, like Psalms 7 and 17. The difference, however, is that this psalmist includes his inner thoughts and is anxious to confess his knowledge of God's devotion. It is this which makes him avoid wicked people.

Verses 6-8 suggest that he has come to the Temple not to appeal against a judicial sentence but to meet God there and to do so in worship, washing his hands in preparation and joining in the procession with thanksgiving for all that God has done not just for him but for the whole people. We needn't take him literally when he speaks of God 'living' in the Temple. The Israelite people knew that God did not live in one particular place on earth, though the Temple was a place where his presence could be experienced.

Because he has not associated with the wicked in wrong-doing he can ask and expect that he would not be associated with them either when they were judged, and so he feels secure (vv. 9-12). This security is based not on his own behaviour so much as upon the devotion and goodness of God.

The closing line suggests that he made his intention clear not just to God but to his fellow-worshippers as well.

1 Judge me, LORD, for I have behaved with integrity,
   I have trusted in you, LORD, without faltering.

2 Examine me, LORD, try me;
   test my feelings and my thoughts.

3 For I am always aware of your devotion,
   I live my life knowing that you are faithful.

4 I do not sit in the company of vacuous people,
   I never enter into relationships with hypocrites.

5 I hate gatherings of criminals,
   I avoid the company of the wicked.

6 I wash my hands to show my innocence
   and then join in the procession round your altar, LORD,

7 Singing a song of thanksgiving
   and reciting your marvellous deeds.

8 I love the Temple where you live, LORD,
   the place where you reside in all your glory.

9 Do not take my life when you take sinners',
   or put me to death along with men out for blood,

10   Who work out evil schemes
          and always have a bribe to hand.

11   For my part, I live my life with integrity;
          set me free, look with favour on me.

12   I stand with my feet on firm ground!

          In the congregation I will thank the LORD for his
          goodness.

❦ Psalm 27

The confidence which this psalmist feels in the first part of the psalm is strongly and beautifully expressed. With God he is absolutely safe (vv.1-3). There is only one thing more he could wish for and that is to remain day and night in God's Temple. If this is understood literally it may suggest keeping vigil throughout the night and waiting expectantly for the morning light. But it may be a vivid way of expressing his desire to remain in the presence of God, a presence of which he was so conscious in the Temple. Doubtless as time went on it came to be understood in this way.

Verse 7 shows a certain change of mood and this and the following two verses are a prayer for God's help. For this reason it has sometimes been regarded as a separate psalm later combined with vv.1-6. It is true of human experience, however, that such 'high' moments of confidence can and do suddenly give way to questions and doubts and there is no reason to think that this was not the case with the psalmist. Verse 8 is not easy to translate, as a glance at the various English versions will show. This present translation requires no change in the Hebrew text at all. It simply recognises 'Come, seek my presence' as a thought which entered the psalmist's mind, probably recalling the priestly invitation to worship, and to which he responds. By v.10 his confidence seems to have been restored and he prays to be led to live a life above the reproach of those who are waiting to find fault with him (vv.11-12). His belief that he will see how good God is refers to his present life and not to any life in the hereafter.

Verse 14 is either the psalmist addressing himself or perhaps a priest encouraging him. It is by keeping our eyes open to what God is and what he is doing that we are able to face the questions and doubts which sometimes, inevitably, come into our minds.

1   The LORD is my light and my salvation;
      whom shall I fear?
   The LORD is my stronghold in life;
      whom shall I dread?

2   When evil-doers close in upon me
      like animals, to devour me,
   hostile to me they may be,
      but, without doubt, they will stumble and fall.

3   Though a whole army should make war upon me
      I shall not be afraid;
   though a battle should rage against me
      I shall still remain confident.

4   I have one request from the LORD;
      that one thing I will seek:
   to remain in the LORD's house
      all my life long,
   gazing upon the LORD's beauty
      and awaking each morning in his Temple.

5   For he will keep me safe in his shelter
      when misfortune comes;
   he will hide me under cover in his tent,
      he will set me on a rock out of danger.

6   So now I can hold my head high
      above my enemies who surround me;
   at his tent I will offer jubilant sacrifices;
      I will make music and sing psalms to the LORD.

7   Hear what I have to say, LORD;
      when I call be gracious and answer me.

8   The thought has come to me 'Come, seek my presence';
        your presence indeed I will seek, LORD.

9   Do not cease to look graciously upon me,
        do not turn away in anger.
    You have been my help;
        do not leave me, do not forsake me, my saviour God.

10 When even my father and mother have forsaken me
        then the LORD will gather me to himself.

11 LORD, teach me your way,
        lead me in the right path
        because enemies are watching out for me.

12 Do not place me in the grip of my foes,
        for lying witnesses have risen up against me
        breathing out threats of violence.

13 I firmly believe I shall see how good the LORD is
        while I am still in the land of the living.

14 Wait for the LORD!
        Take heart! Be courageous!
        Wait expectantly for the LORD!

৺ Psalm 28

This psalm begins not so much with a lament as with a prayer for help that the psalmist may be spared the just fate of the wicked who are wholly hypocritical and therefore deserve all they get (vv. 1-5). So taken up are they with the wrong they are doing that they cannot see what God is doing. As they will die for their sins the psalmist fears he may suffer a similar fate unless God hears his prayer.

Suddenly, at verse 6, there is that sudden change of mood which we have noticed in earlier psalms, a change from uncertainty and prayer to utter confidence and praise (vv.6-8). It is possible that this change comes from within as the psalmist becomes conscious that God has heard him, but it is perhaps more likely that it has been brought about by a priestly response or some other event in worship which gave him this certainty.

Verse 8 mentions both the people and the king and it is at least possible that the psalmist was none other than the king himself through whom divine strength was mediated to the nation. On the other hand the psalmist may simply extend the security he himself has come to feel to the whole people and their leader. Certainly it must have been understood in this more general sense when Israel no longer had a king.

The final verse (v.9), therefore, is a prayer for the enrichment of God's people and especially those who show they are his by the way they behave. When he prays that God may be their shepherd he is conjuring up thoughts of the divine King (cf. Psalm 23, Isaiah 40.10).

1   I call to you, LORD, my Rock;
        do not turn a deaf ear to me,
    for if you remain silent
        I shall be like a dying man.

2   Hear me when I cry out to you for help,
        raising my hands in supplication towards your holy
            shrine.

3   Do not drag me off to death with the wicked, the wrong-doers,
        who greet their neighbours with friendly words
        but intend to do them harm.

4   Repay them according to the wrongs they do,
        give them their just reward for the deeds they perform.

5   Because they cannot discern what the LORD is doing
        he will destroy them and never build them up again.

6   Blessed be the LORD,
        for he has heard my cry for help.

7   The LORD is my strong defender,
        I have put my trust in him.

For the help I have received I am overjoyed,
>   I will praise him in my song.

8   The LORD provides strength for his people,
>   security and safety for his anointed king.

9   Save your people, enrich the lives of all who belong to you;
>   be their shepherd and carry them along for ever.

ꬶ Psalm 29

This is a very powerful psalm in praise of God who is praised as the God of glory, power and holy splendour (vv. 1-2). The following verses as far as verse 9 sing of the effect of God's thunder on the world he has created. The word here translated 'thunder' often simply means 'voice' or 'sound', but generally in the Old Testament God's 'voice' is the thunder which roars from the heavens. It is the frequent repetition of this word which gives the psalm its power and vitality. The seas, in vv. 3-4, may refer to the Mediterranean but would undoubtedly call to mind the great deeps from which God separated the earth and which he keeps under his constant control (Genesis 1.2, 9; cf. Psalm 104.7-9). The cedars of Lebanon were symbols of strength and its hills were the highest around (vv. 5-6). These, and the deserts and trees (vv. 8-9), are all affected by the thunder of God. This storm language is used not infrequently to express the presence of God (Exodus 19.16-20, Psalm 18.8-16. Cf. 1 Kings 19.11-13 where Elijah is surprised that God appears to him not in these phenomena but in the 'voice of thin silence'.) Such a revelation of God evokes a one-word response, 'glory' — God's holiness, in so far as it can be seen by man, has been revealed (cf. Isaiah 6).

There had been a time, according to tradition, when God had allowed the waters of chaos their full sway and the whole earth was flooded (Genesis 6-9). The word 'flood' in this psalm (v. 10) refers to that episode and the word is found nowhere else in the Old Testament except in these two places. Then, however, he had shown his authority over the waters by making them subside and promising never to allow them to overwhelm the earth again. So this great display of power makes him sovereign and, as king, he gives strength and prosperity to his people.

Not only does this give Israel cause for praise; the very gods in heaven are called upon to do so too. The Hebrew in v.1 literally means 'sons of God' and may refer to God's court, as in Job 1. However, this has also been seen as a very old psalm because the repetition is a feature of ancient poetry, and it may therefore have as its model a Canaanite, polytheistic psalm.

It remains as a constant correction to any sentimental view of God which we may have acquired.

1 Praise the LORD, you gods;
>praise him for his glory and power,
>praise him for his renowned glory.

2 Bow down to the LORD in his holy splendour.

3 The LORD speaks in his thunder over the seas,
>the glorious God thunders,
>the LORD thunders over the oceans.

4 The LORD's thunder speaks with power,
>the LORD's thunder speaks with majesty.

5 The LORD's thunder breaks down cedars,
>the LORD smashes the cedars of Lebanon.

6 He makes the hills of Lebanon leap around like calves,
>and Mount Hermon bound like a young bull.

7 The LORD's thunder brings flashes of lightning.

8 The LORD's thunder makes the desert writhe,
>the LORD makes the desert of Kadesh writhe.

9 The LORD's thunder makes the oak trees dance around
>and strips the forests bare.

So in his Temple everyone shouts 'Glory!'

10 The LORD has been King since the Flood,
>the LORD is King for ever.

11   The LORD gives his people strength,
         the LORD enriches his people with prosperity.

❦ Psalm 30

*The mood of this psalm changes several times, passing from confidence to
an address to the psalmist's fellow-worshippers, a further appeal for help
and an expression of thanksgiving for deliverance. As in Psalm 27 this
fluctuation may be an accurate reflection of human experience.*

*As usual the difficulties from which the psalmist was delivered are not
spelled out, but enemies were involved. At their hands he was on his way to
Sheol, but so too were they on account of their wickedness. However, God
picked him out and reversed his direction so that he was no longer going
down to death but up to a full life (vv.2-4).*

*At this point he calls on his fellows to praise this God who delivers
those in distress (vv.5-6).*

*Such confidence can easily lead to complacency and self-assurance.
Then God withdraws from him and he is left again at the mercy of those
forces which were drugging him downwards towards death (vv.7-11).*

*The last two verses of the psalm make it clear that God has responded
to the psalmist's recognition of his need and has again rescued him.*

*The phrase 'you who are devoted to him' in v.5 may well refer not just
to any Israelites but to certain officials who served in the worship in the
Temple, possibly Levites (cf. Psalms 4.4, 12.2) and this may suggest that
the psalmist himself is one of them. We have already seen how they were
apparently subject to persecution by enemies (Deut. 33.11).*

*It may now, however, be the experience not only of those with respon-
sibility for worship but of all those who know the ups and downs of life,
especially the religious life.*

2   I will sing high praise to you, LORD,
         for you have hauled me out of trouble;
         you have not let my enemies gloat over me.

3   LORD, my God, I cried to you for help
      and you healed my wounds.

4   You brought me back from Sheol, LORD,
      you separated me from those on the way to the Pit
      and gave me my life again.

5   Sing praise to the LORD, you who are devoted to him,
      give him thanks for every reminder of his holiness.

6   For when he is angry there is turmoil,
      when he is pleased there is life.
  Tears in the evening persist through the night
      but morning brings a cry of joy.

7   In my complacency I said,
      'I can never be shaken,

8   It is your pleasure, LORD,
      to make me stand strong as the mountains.'
      But when you hid yourself from me I was terrified.

9   To you, LORD, I cry,
      I seek your help, my Master.

10   What is to be gained by my death,
      by my descent into the Pit?
  Can dust and ashes praise you
      or declare that you are faithful?

11   Hear me, LORD, and be kind to me,
      be my helper, LORD.

12   You have turned my mourning into dancing;
      you have stripped the sackcloth from my waist
      and put gladness in its place.

13   So I will sing praises to you with my whole being;
      I will never be silent.

LORD, my God, until my life's end
I will gratefully praise you.

❧ Psalm 31

As in some of the earlier psalms, so here there is a fluctuation of mood. The psalmist certainly has confidence in God, suggesting that he has already had experience of God's goodness. But now he finds himself in trouble once again and in need of further help (vv. 2-6). As usual it is impossible to decide what that trouble is even though he describes it in vivid language. Again, sickness and enemies seem to be involved (vv. 11-14). Whatever it is he still feels secure in God's devotion (vv. 15-21).

At verse 22 he turns and praises God to other members of the congregation, but then he turns back to God himself. Again, at verse 24 he calls upon his fellow worshippers to show similar love towards God and to take courage as they wait for the LORD to come to their aid.

The call to love the LORD is directed to his 'devoted servants' (v. 24). This is the word we have met in other psalms (Pss. 4.4, 12.1, 16.10) and I have suggested that it may well refer to some officials in the sanctuary, possibly Levites. This psalmist is probably one of them. The idea receives some support from the fact that he professes his 'hatred', his strong rejection of those in charge of useless idols, that is, the idolatrous priests (cf. the Levites in Exodus 32.25ff). The word here translated 'devoted servants' is hasid and three times already the psalmist has acknowledged and been grateful for God's devotion (hesed) in vv. 8, 17 and 22.

Now, however, the psalm encourages all those who share the singer's experience of God and at the same time the troubles of human life.

2   In you, LORD, I have trusted,
         never put me to shame.
    You always do what is right,
         so set me free.

3   Turn and listen to me,
         come quickly and deliver me;

be my rock where I can find security,
    be my fortress and save me.

4   Indeed you are my rock and my fortress;
        show that you are, by leading and guiding me.

5   Let me not be caught in the net men have spread for me;
        you are the one who gives me security.

6   I put my life in your hands,
        you, LORD, my faithful God, have set me free.

7   I hate those who are in charge of useless idols.
        I, for my part, have trusted in the LORD.

8   I, whose affliction you have seen,
        whose deep distress you know,
        I am glad and rejoice in your devotion.

9   You have not delivered me into enemy hands,
        you have given me room to walk freely.

10   Be gracious to me, LORD, for I am in trouble,
        my sight is blurred with my crying.

11   My life is ebbing away with sorrow
        and my years with sighing.
    Once strong, I now stagger under my affliction,
        my very frame crumbles away.

12   To all my enemies I am an object of derision,
        especially to those who live near me;
    I scare all my acquaintances;
        those who see me in the street run away from me.

13   I am forgotten as a dead man slips from the mind;
        I am like a needle lost in a haystack.

14   I have heard many speaking in whispers
        and I feel terror on every side.

When they sit down together to discuss me
      they plan to take my life.

15   Yet I have put my trust in you, LORD;
      I have confessed, 'You are my God.'

16   My affairs are in your hands; rescue me
      from the hands of my enemies and persecutors.

17   Be radiant with love towards me,
      in your devotion, save me.

18   LORD, give me no cause for shame
      when I call to you;
rather, may the wicked be ashamed,
      may they be motionless in Sheol!

19   May those who tell lies be struck dumb,
      those who speak of good men
      with arrogance, pride and contempt.

20   What good things you have stored up
      for those who hold you in reverence!
How much you have done in the sight of all
      for those who seek security in you!

21   You hide them away secretly in your presence
      from men who string together accusations;
you gather them safely and shelter them
      from those who attack them with words.

22   Blessed is the LORD,
      for he has shown me astonishing devotion
      when I was like a prisoner in a besieged city.

23   In my alarm I said,
      'I am cut off from your presence';
but then you heard my plea for mercy
      when I cried to you for help.

24   Love the LORD, devoted servants of his!
          The LORD keeps watch over those who are constant,
          repaying in full those who behave arrogantly.

25   Be strong! Be brave!
          All you who await the LORD's coming.

✤ Psalm 32

This psalm also calls upon 'every devoted servant' to pray to God in times of misfortune (cf. Ps. 31.24) but its chief interest lies in the remedy it offers for sin. The common view of the Old Testament is that it regards sacrifice as the essential means of gaining forgiveness, but here the psalmist makes no mention of it. God's forgiveness had come to him simply in response to his confession of sin. It ought to remind us that the idea that sacrifice can be effective without confession and repentance is an aberration, as the prophets so often reminded their hearers.

The psalmist begins with a cry of delight that he is now forgiven (vv.1-2), a cry uttered to any who will hear him. Obviously forgiveness makes a great deal of difference to his life. Then he turns to speak to God in his gratitude (vv.3-7). While his sin remained unconfessed he had felt its weight, but that weight was lifted when he confessed and received forgiveness. This is a testimony we should all heed.

This is followed by a piece of instruction. There is some doubt as to who is the 'I' who speaks and who the singular 'you' who is addressed. It may be that these are the words of God spoken through a prophet or a teaching priest, advising the one who has been forgiven as to his future behaviour. However, the references to the LORD in the third person make this less likely. Thus it would seem to be the forgiven psalmist teaching another of his friends. If the psalmist were himself a Levite encouraging other Levites, or devoted servants, to pray in confession, then it may well be to one of these that he now teaches the good way of life.

So far as the present day reader is concerned the psalm encourages us to pray for forgiveness, confessing our sins and experiencing the joy that follows, but it then reminds us of the way we ought to live our lives.

1 Happy is the man whose sin is forgiven,
  he whose waywardness is put out of sight.

2 Happy is the man whom the LORD declares not guilty,
  and not disposed to treachery.

3 When I neglected to call to you
  I wore myself out with groaning all day long.

4 For day and night I was under heavy pressure from you;
  I wilted like a tree in summer drought.

5 Then I told you of my sin
  instead of concealing my guilt,
I said, 'I confess my sins to you, LORD'
  and you waived the punishment for them.

6 Therefore let every devoted servant pray to you
  at the time when he meets crushing misfortune.
When deep waters of trouble come rushing towards him
  they will not reach him.

7 To you I can run for safety,
  you keep me safe from distress;
you surround me with your protection
  evoking joyous cries of deliverance.

8 I will instruct you and shed light on how you should behave,
  I will keep you in sight and advise you.

9 Do not be like a horse or a mule,
  they do not know which way to go;
they have to be checked with bit and bridle
  or else they will not obey you.

10 The wicked suffer great anguish,
  but as for the man who trusts in the LORD
  the LORD's devotion surrounds him.

11   Be glad that the LORD himself is with you;
         rejoice, you who do right!
         Shout for joy all who are true of purpose.

❧ Psalm 33

This is a magnificent hymn of praise to God for his faithfulness and total reliability shown in creation and in his maintenance of human life on the earth he has made.

As in the creation account in Genesis 1 God had only to say the word and the world came into being. Such a belief can only inspire reverence and awe among those whom he has made.

Although God has chosen one nation as his own, to have a special relationship with them (v.12), his concern is not limited to that nation but extends to the whole of mankind whom he has created and whose affairs he directs.

For those who do respond in reverence and awe there is complete assurance of God's devotion, his loyal, faithful care and love for those who have become his people. They can therefore rejoice whole-heartedly in him.

Of course, other psalms, as we have seen, sometimes express doubt and concern and it is true that all our different moods, based on our different experiences, may be brought before God. But in this psalm the clouds of doubt never obscure the praise and trust in God.

1   Shout, you who do right, for joy that the LORD is with you,
         praise is the lovely response of those who are sincere.

2   Express your thanks to the LORD to the music of the lyre,
         sing psalms to him to the ten-stringed lute.

3   Sing to him a new song,
         play your very best when the victory shout rings out.

4   For the LORD never deviates from what he says,
         and all he does is the outcome of his fidelity.

5   He loves to do what is right and just,
      his devotion fills the earth.

6   At a word from the LORD the heavens were made,
      the stars and planets when he breathed his command.

7   He collected the waters of the sea
      as a traveller fills his water bottle;
  he stores up the underground waters
      as a farmer gathers grain into his barn.

8   Hold the LORD in reverence, all the earth,
      stand in awe of him, all who inhabit the world.

9   For he said 'Let there be' and there was,
      he gave a command and creation appeared.

10   The LORD frustrates all the counsels of the nations,
      he brings to nothing the plans of the peoples.

11   The counsels of the LORD remain valid for ever,
      the plans he makes, from one generation to another.

12   Happy is the nation whose God is the LORD,
      the people he has chosen as his own.

13   The LORD looks down from heaven,
      he sees the whole of mankind.

14   From where he lives in heaven
      he looks closely at those who live on earth.

15   He is the one who shapes their thoughts
      and makes them discerning in all they do.

16   A king is not safe because he has a powerful army,
      a soldier does not escape danger because he is strong.

17   A horseman is deceived if he relies on his horse for safety,
      strong as it is, it cannot save him.

18 No, but the LORD protects those who hold him in reverence,
       those who believe they will see his devotion.

19 So he saves their lives when death threatens,
       and keeps them alive during famine.

20 We ourselves have waited expectantly for the LORD,
       he is our help and shield.

21 In him we are heartily glad
       for we have trusted in him whose nature is divine.

22 Look with devotion on us, LORD,
       as we have set our hopes on you.

❧ Psalm 34

This is another of those acrostic psalms, each verse beginning with a different letter of the Hebrew alphabet in alphabetical order. It shows deviations from the regular pattern similar to those in Psalm 25, since the sixth letter of the alphabet is missing and the final verse stands outside the acrostic arrangement. In spite of the restrictions this pattern imposes the psalm moves clearly forward through praise (vv.2-7), exhortation to others to trust in God (vv.8-15) to an affirmation of God's justice and faithfulness (vv.16-22).

The psalm expresses the familiar view that those who trust in God and do right will be rewarded by being rescued from trouble and kept safe, while those who behave badly will be punished with adversity. The very first psalm made this clear distinction, but we need to be reminded that although this view may serve fairly well as a general way of encouraging people to do right, it just will not do as a dogmatic theological statement. This psalm therefore needs to be balanced by others which reflect the experience of misfortune, even for those who do right, such as Psalm 39.

The closing verse, as in Psalm 25, probably indicates how the acrostic composition was taken up into Israelite worship and used there. It is a summary and a confirmation of the teaching of the psalm.

2　I will thank the LORD at all times,
　　　I will never cease to sing his praises.

3　I will speak with pride of the LORD.
　　　When the oppressed hear they will be glad.

4　Declare with me how great the LORD is,
　　　let us sing high praise to him for ever.

5　I turned to the LORD in prayer and he answered me,
　　　he set me free from all my fears.

6　Men look to him and are radiantly happy,
　　　they show no trace of embarrassment.

7　This man cried out in his trouble and the LORD heard,
　　　he saved him out of all his distress.

8　The LORD's messenger pitches his tent
　　　around those who hold him in reverence,
　　　and he comes to rescue them.

9　Try it for yourself and you will see that the LORD is good,
　　　happy is the man who looks to him for safety.

10　Hold the LORD in reverence, you who belong to him,
　　　those who do so have all they need.

11　Lions may go short of food and get hungry,
　　　but those who seek the LORD want for nothing good.

12　Come, my children, listen to him;
　　　I will teach you how to hold the LORD in reverence.

13　What kind of men enjoy life
　　　or love it because it is good to them?

14　See that you never say anything wrong;
　　　do not deceive people by telling lies.

15　Turn from bad behaviour to good,
　　　try your best to live in peace.

16   The LORD watches over those who do right
        and listens to their cries.

17   The LORD turns to punish those who do wrong
        by erasing every memory of them from the earth.

18   When men cry for help the LORD hears them
        and rescues them from all their troubles.

19   The LORD is near to those whose will is broken,
        he saves those whose spirit is crushed.

20   The man who does right may suffer many misfortunes,
        but the LORD rescues him from them all.

21   He keeps him safe from physical harm,
        not a bone of his body is broken.

22   A guilty man's crime condemns him to death,
        those who attack the innocent with hatred are punished.

23   The LORD saves his servants from death;
        no one who looks to him for safety is punished.

❧ Psalm 35

*The references in this psalm to 'witnesses' and 'the court' have suggested to
many people that it was spoken by a person falsely accused whose case had
been taken to the court of appeal in the Temple (cf. Psalm 7 and Deut. 17.1-
13). It would certainly fit such an occasion but we cannot be sure that these
references are anything more than metaphors for the trouble the psalmist is
passing through or perhaps reflections of the experiences he had previously
had in the local courts at the city gates. What is clear is that the psalmist
feels himself to be under severe attack from enemies.*

*So the psalm opens with a prayer that God will come and drive off all
his enemies (vv.1-8), followed by an expression of confidence in God (vv.9-
10). What makes matters worse for the psalmist is that he himself has*

treated well those who now attack him and all he receives in return is their antagonism (vv.11-16). Yet he can still look forward to thanking God (vv.17-18). From there he returns to complaints about his accusers and prays that God will defend him (vv.19-25). Finally he asks that those who are glad at his misfortune may suffer shame and that those who wish to see him reinstated may rejoice (vv.26-28), for this will establish God's justice.

Although the psalmist is obviously concerned for himself and for his own safety, nevertheless, in the end, what is at stake is God's justice and that is all-important to him.

1   Challenge, LORD, those who challenge me,
         fight those who fight against me.

2   Take up your weapons and armour,
         rise up to help me.

3   Lift up your spear and axe,
         come to meet my pursuers.
   Say to me, 'I am
         the one who will save you.'

4   May those who seek my life
         be ashamed and embarrassed;
   may those who plot to harm me
         retreat in confusion.

5   May they be like chaff before the wind
         as the LORD's messenger drives them off.

6   May their way be dark and dangerous
         as the LORD's messenger pursues them.

7   For no reason they set a hidden trap for me,
         for no reason they dug a pit for me to fall into.

8   May destruction take them by surprise,
         may they be caught in the trap they have hidden,
         may they fall into the pit they have dug.

9 I will be glad because the LORD is with me,
     I will rejoice because he saves me.

10 With all my being I say,
     'LORD, who is like you?
You rescue the weak from one too strong for him,
     the weak and the poor from one who plunders him.'

11 Witnesses with violence in mind rise in court,
     they question me about matters of which I am ignorant.

12 They pay me back evil for good,
     I feel like someone bereaved.

13 For when they were ill I dressed in sackcloth,
     I punished myself with fasting.

14 When my prayer returned to me unanswered,
     though offered as for a brother of mine,
I walked around like one who mourns his mother,
     I bowed down, dressed in black.

15 Yet when I was in trouble they were glad,
     they crowded round me in hostility;
when I was struck down for no apparent reason
     they roared with laughter without stopping.

16 They tried me hard with their constant jeering,
     they gnashed their teeth in anger against me.

17 LORD, how often will you see it happen?
     Save my life from those who would destroy me,
     my precious life from men fierce as lions.

18 I will thank you in a large assembly,
     where many people meet I will praise you.

19 My enemies tell lies about me,
     do not let them gloat over me;

they hate me for no reason,
>> do not let them leer at me.

20 For they give no friendly greeting,
>> they think up all kinds of lies
>> about those who are at peace with the world.

21 They make loud accusations against me,
>> saying 'Ah, we have seen what you did.'

22 You too have seen it, LORD; speak up for me,
>> stay near me, Lord.

23 Stir yourself to defend me in court,
>> my Lord and God, plead my cause.

24 You do what is right, LORD, my God,
>> give me a favourable verdict,
>> do not let them gloat over me.

25 Give them no chance to think
>> 'Ah we have what we want,
>> we have swallowed him whole!'

26 May those who are glad at my misfortune
>> be embarrassed and ashamed;
> may those who consider themselves superior to me
>> be covered with shame and disgrace.

27 May those who would like to see me acquitted
>> shout for joy and keep on saying,
> 'The LORD is great
>> he wants to see his servant prosper.'

28 Then I will declare how just you are,
>> all day long I will praise you.

🎴 Psalm 36

This psalm draws a contrast not between righteous men and wicked men, but between the wickedness of some people the psalmist knows and the righteousness of God. In some people wickedness is so deeply ingrained that they cannot help themselves from expressing it in their actions. Indeed, even in their sleep they still dream up evil schemes (vv.1-5). On the other hand, the psalmist is aware of God whose devotion is equally a part of his nature (vv.6-11) and who shows it towards everyone, human and even superhuman (v.8). But especially God acts with devotion to those who are close to him.

In the first five verses the remarks about God seem to be addressed generally to anyone who will hear, but at v.6, when the psalmist begins to praise God for his devotion, he speaks to the LORD directly. Although he mentions 'gods' in v.8 this should not be taken to mean that he actually believes in them. It is his way of saying that all beings find security with God.

At verse 12 he offers a prayer for himself that he may not be misled into wicked ways by the kind of people he has spoken of in the first five verses. Already he sees them as having fallen 'there' (v.13). It is not easy to see where he means. Perhaps he means at the point where they try to push him off course, or perhaps he has in mind the presence of God before whom the wicked cannot stand.

It is no bad thing, when our minds are full of thoughts about the evil there is in the world, to turn them to God and reflect on his goodness to all people. Such a comparison renews our confidence and enables us to go on with our living.

2 Sin has its say deep in the mind of the wicked man;
      he entertains no fear of God.

3 He thinks to flatter God,
      pretending to detect his sin and hate it.

4 His every word is wicked and deceitful,
      he lacks the wisdom to do good.

5 While he lies in bed he thinks up trouble,
    he sets out on a path which leads to evil,
    he never refuses to do a bad deed.

6 LORD, your devotion fills the heavens,
    your faithfulness reaches the skies.

7 Your righteousness is like the high mountains,
    your justice like the underground ocean,
    you help both men and beasts, LORD.

8 How precious is your devotion,
    gods and men find safety sheltered by your wings.

9 Like a generous host you give them their fill
    of good food from your larder.
  From your lovely streams which bring such pleasure
    you give them water to drink.

10 For you are the source of all life,
    bathed in your light we have light to live by.

11 Continue to show devotion to those familiar with you,
    to do what is right for those who are true of purpose.

12 Do not let an arrogant man approach me,
    do not let the wicked push me off course.

13 There they have fallen, those wicked men,
    knocked down, unable to rise.

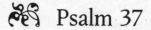 Psalm 37

*This is another acrostic psalm in which roughly speaking each pair of verses,
or the first of each group of four lines, begins with a different Hebrew letter
in alphabetical order. There is a slight dislocation of the pattern at verse 28,
but this does not affect the meaning of the psalm.*

The psalm as a whole is concerned with what happens to those who do right and to those who do wrong, to those who put their trust in God and to those who don't. We have met this concern in other psalms and it is found in all strands of Old Testament literature. The underlying purpose of this particular psalm is to warn those who listen against being jealous of wicked people who often seem to prosper, for that appearance is false. The psalmist believes it is better to be quiet and trustful, for good people will always come out of things well. Repetitive as the psalm is on account of its structure, the cumulative effect is very telling. The point has been made in connection with other psalms that this rather simplistic view of things is tenable only as a very general rule. It serves to encourage people to trust in God and probably that is what is intended, for anyone looking at human affairs realistically must have seen that the psalmist's message was not universally true. Things do not always turn out well for those who trust God. Since in the Old Testament there is no conception of any meaningful life after death, but only oblivion in Sheol, the rewards for good behaviour could not be thought of as postponed until then. Almost certainly the psalmist never intended that his words should be taken as a dogmatic theological statement. Nevertheless, the two ways of life are set clearly before people and a choice is demanded as to which one is to be followed. Seen in this light the psalm retains its value for us still.

1   Cool your jealousy of wicked men,
        do not envy wrong-doers.

2   For they quickly fade away like grass,
        and wither like green plants.

3   Trust in the LORD and do good,
        live in the land and make a secure home there.

4   Enjoy living with the LORD,
        he will give you your heart's desire.

5   Hand over your way of life to the LORD,
        trust him and he will do what you need.

6   He will make your integrity shine like light,
        and your justice like the noon-day sun.

7 Be quiet before the LORD,
  wait patiently for him.
Cool your jealousy of the man who is prosperous,
  of the man who succeeds in his wicked schemes.

8 Stop being angry; leave your fury behind;
  cool down; it leads only to disaster.

9 For the lives of wrong-doers will be cut short,
  and those who set their hopes on the LORD will live to
    inherit the land.

10 Before long the wicked will no longer be around,
  you will look hard at the place where he should be,
  but he will not be there.

11 Humble folk will live to inherit the land,
  they will enjoy untold prosperity.

12 The wicked man schemes against him who does right,
  he bares his teeth at him.

13 The LORD has the last laugh,
  for he sees that his time is coming.

14 The wicked have unsheathed their swords,
  they have bent their bows
to shoot down the poor and needy,
  to slaughter those who live honest lives.

15 Their swords will enter their own hearts
  and their bows be smashed.

16 The man who does right is better off with a little
  than those who do wrong, with all their abundance.

17 For the arms which upheld the wicked will be broken,
  and the LORD supports those who do right.

18 The LORD sees how men of integrity live,
  what they inherit will be theirs for ever.

19 They will not be disconcerted when times are bad,
    in days of famine they will have enough to eat.

20 But the wicked will perish,
    the LORD's enemies are like wood on a fire,
    they vanish! Like smoke they vanish.

21 The wicked man borrows and does not pay back,
    the good man gives and gives freely.

22 Those who are blessed by the LORD live to inherit land,
    but the lives of those who are cursed are cut off.

23 The LORD decides the way a man shall take,
    he holds him firm and is pleased with his conduct.

24 He may fall but he will not crash down headlong,
    for the LORD has hold of his hand.

25 Neither in my youth, nor now I am grown older
    have I seen a good man forsaken
    or his child begging for food.

26 Every day he gives and lends freely
    and he is blessed with children.

27 Turn away from evil and do good,
    and so live in the land for ever.

28 For the LORD loves justice
    and never abandons those devoted to him.

29 They are kept safe by him for ever,
    but the lives of the children of the wicked are cut short.

30 The man who does right always speaks wisely,
    the judgements he makes are fair.

31 He keeps God's instruction in mind,
    so he never falters on his way through life.

32 The wicked man watches for him who does right,
      and seeks to bring about his death.

33 But the LORD will not leave him in his power,
      he will not condemn him when he comes up for trial.

34 Put your hope in the LORD,
      see that you walk in his way.
For then he will give you a place of honour
      so that you live to inherit land
      and see wicked lives cut short.

35 I saw a wicked man and he was terrifying,
      bragging like a native of Canaan.

36 I passed that way again and, to my surprise, he was gone,
      I sought him but he was not to be found.

37 Take note of the man of integrity; watch the upright man;
      for the peaceable man has a good future.

38 But sinners will be completely destroyed,
      the future of the wicked will be cut short.

39 The LORD keeps safe those who do right,
      he is their refuge in times of trouble.

40 The LORD will help and deliver them,
      he will deliver them from the wicked and keep them safe,
      because they seek safety with him.

❧ Psalm 38

In many ways this psalm stands in sharp contrast to the preceding one and may very well have been put next to it for that reason. Whereas Psalm 37 is a rather cool assessment of life by someone who is comfortable, this is a passionate complaint to God about the suffering the psalmist is enduring.

It is important to recognise that, like Job (6.4), the psalmist does not hesitate from attributing his sufferings to God (vv.2-4). Regardless of the theological problems this raised for the people of the Old Testament, it could not be avoided since they believed in one God only and as far as they were concerned he controlled all things. It followed, then, that suffering must be brought about by God. One way of dealing with this dilemma of a good and all-powerful God sending suffering was to admit that it was deserved because of the sufferer's sin. The psalmist makes this confession in v.9. This was the view of Job's friends too, but Job himself was unable to accept such an explanation because he and everyone else acknowledged him to be a man of integrity who showed reverence for God. Hence his perplexity.

As in the Book of Job again, the sufferings are described in the most vivid and comprehensive terms so as to suggest the greatest possible suffering. Yet it remains impossible to diagnose any particular disease. In this way the psalm is made accessible for anyone who is passing through a difficult experience.

In the end all the psalmist can do is to seek the help of God for there is no one else to help him. This he does in the closing verses of the psalm (vv.16-17, 22-23).

2   LORD, though you are angry do not chastise me,
        though you are furious do not punish me.

3   For you have pierced me with the arrows of misfortune,
        already your punishment has fallen on me.

4   I am desperately ill because you are angry,
        my body is full of disease because I have sinned.

5   Indeed I have become submerged by my sins,
        they are a burden too heavy for me to bear.

6   My wounds fester and smell
        because I am wickedly foolish.

7   My body is twisted; I am bent double;
        all day long I go about dressed in mourning.

8   My stomach is burning with pain,
        I am desperately ill.

9   I am thoroughly numbed and crushed,
         I cry out with the pains in my heart.

10   LORD, you know all about my longings,
         my sighing is no secret to you,

11   My heart flutters, my strength has left me,
         I have almost lost my sight.

12   My friends and neighbours keep their distance from my sores,
         even my close relatives stand far apart.

13   Those who want to kill me aim blows at me,
         those who seek to hunt me threaten me with ruin,
         all day long they try by their words to betray me.

14   But I, like a deaf man, hear nothing,
         I am like a dumb man who cannot speak.

15   I am like a man who cannot hear,
         no word of rebuke passes my lips.

16   I simply place my hopes in you, LORD,
         you will answer me, Lord my God.

17   For I prayed, 'Never let them rejoice over me
         or gloat over my downfall.'

18   I am ready to drop,
         I am never free from pain.

19   Now I confess my sins,
         I am anxious because I have done wrong.

20   I have many unprovoked enemies,
         there are many who, without justice, hate me.

21   Those who repay good with evil
         are opposed to me because I do good.

22   Do not abandon me, LORD,
         my God, stay near to me.

23   Come quickly and help me,
          my Lord, who alone can save me.

🎋 Psalm 39

This is another lament from a man who is so ill that he feels his life is now coming to an end. His natural reaction to this would be to complain to God about it, but he has managed so far to hold his tongue and say nothing about it in case he should give his enemies a chance to criticise or gloat over him. Now, however, he can contain himself no longer. He must ask how much longer he has to live (vv.2-5). Of course he recognises that human life is short anyway (vv.6-7). Even so, he still will not complain; he simply asks God to do things for him. First, he asks for forgiveness for his sins which he regards as the reason for his illness; second, he prays that God will take away that illness (vv.8-11) which again he regards as chastening for sin (v.12).

The psalmist offers his prayer in the spirit of a guest. This word signifies a person who has no rights but is dependent on the hospitality of his host. It is used in books like Deuteronomy where it is often translated as 'alien' or 'stranger within the gate'. Such people are often coupled with widows and orphans as those who need the protection of the law and positive discrimination in order to ensure that they can live their lives adequately. The psalmist is happy to be in that dependent position so long as his host is God (v.13). He can only ask that God will not frown angrily upon him, but will smile so that he can smile back. This would at least ensure that he died in peace (v.14).

The Psalms seem to have an almost infinite number of variations which they can play on the theme of suffering and each one strikes a chord in our experience.

2   I said, 'I will watch how I behave
          so that I say nothing sinful;
     I will muzzle my mouth
          while wicked men are present.'

3 I spoke not a single word, not even anything good,
  yet my pain was aggravated.

4 My thoughts caught fire within me,
  as I reflected they were fanned into a blaze
  and I put them into words.

5 'Tell me LORD, when my life will end
  and how long it will be,
  that I may know how little time I have.'

6 The life you have given me spans only a few octaves!
  From your perspective I last no time at all.
All men who stand on their own two feet
  are no more than a breath of wind.

7 Yes, a man as he walks around is only a shadow,
  even when he bustles about he is nothing;
when he piles up riches
  he has no idea who will reap the benefit.

8 So now, what can I expect, LORD?
  My hopes are set on you.

9 Set me free from all my sins,
  do not leave me open to abuse by fools.

10 I am silent; I will not open my mouth;
  for it is you who have brought this upon me.

11 Take away from me the illness you have sent,
  the hostility you have shown has worn me down.

12 You reprove a man for his sin and chasten him,
  like a moth you destroy everything he enjoys;
  indeed a man is not more than a breath of wind.

13 Hear my prayer, LORD, and my cry for help,
  listen to my weeping and do not remain silent,
for I am a guest in your house,
  like my forefathers I stay with you.

14　Avert your angry looks from me that I may smile
　　　　before I go on my way and die.

🎙 Psalm 40

We have already met this kind of psalm in which thanksgiving and confidence precede a prayer for deliverance (cf. Ps. 27). This unusual order has led to the view that this psalm was originally two, a psalm of confidence in vv.2-12 and a psalm of lament in vv.13-18. This impression is deepened when we find that vv.13-17 are found again on their own in Psalm 70. Whether or not the psalm was originally two, it is necessary now to read it as a whole, for it was obviously used in this way at some stage.

The 'echoing well' from which the psalmist has been delivered is doubtless the 'well' of death. Since deliverance was God's response to his prayer he now responds in turn with a song of praise in which he feels inadequate to express all that is in his mind (vv.2-6).

The view that sacrifice is not an absolutely essential requirement (vv.7-9) may be found elsewhere in the Psalms (50.9-15, 51.18) and often in the prophetic books. This does not mean that sacrifice has no value or that there is no need ever to offer it. It rather draws attention to the need for a right attitude to God which is even more important (cf. 1 Samuel 15.22, Hosea 6.6). The offering of oneself in obedience is what is required above all else.

The first part of the psalm ends with the psalmist bearing testimony to God's help within the congregation (vv.10-12).

As the psalm now stands the plea for help which begins in v.13 is based on the confidence already expressed. It is followed by a prayer that the wicked will be ashamed and that the true worshippers will experience joy (vv.15-17). Perhaps the psalmist, having introduced his own situation in v.13, goes on to use a psalm, or a fragment of a psalm, which he already knows (Ps. 70) to express his feelings and plea for help.

2　I waited with eager expectation for the LORD;
　　　　he turned and heard my cry for help.

3 He lifted me out of the echoing well,
     from the clinging mud at the bottom.
  He set my feet on solid rock
     and gave me a firm footing.

4 He gave me a new song to sing,
     a song of praise to our God.
  Many will see all this and be awe-struck
     and so begin to trust in the LORD.

5 Happy is the man who places his confidence in the LORD
     instead of turning to proud and pretentious men.

6 You have done great things, LORD my God,
     you have carried through your marvellous plans for us;
     there is no one to compare with you.
  I would like to tell them out loud,
     but they are too many to recount.

7 Sacrifices and gifts give you no pleasure,
     but you have given me the ability to listen.

8 You do not demand whole or sin offerings,
     so I said, 'I have come myself!

9 I enjoy doing as you please, my God,
     your instruction is deep inside me.'

10 In the assembly of all your people I have proclaimed
     the good news that you have saved me,
     I will never hold my tongue, LORD, as you know.

11 I have not kept your deliverance to myself,
     I have told them you are faithful to save;
  I have not concealed your devotion and loyalty
     from the assembly of your people.

12 You, LORD, will never withhold your compassion from me,
     your devotion and loyalty will keep guard over me.

13   For misfortunes without number surround me,
             the consequences of my sin have caught up with me,
             I am blinded by them.
      There are more of them than there are hairs on my head,
             I have completely lost heart.

14   Do me a favour, LORD, and deliver me,
             come quickly, LORD, and help me.

15   May those who seek to snatch my life from me
             be covered with shame and embarrassment,
      may those who are glad at my misfortune
             be turned away in disgrace.

16   May those who gloat over me saying 'Ha, ha!'
             be appalled at the shame they suffer.

17   May all who come to worship you
             find joy and gladness in your presence;
      may those who love you because you save them
             never stop saying, 'God is great!'

18   May the LORD give thought to me,
             poor and needy as I am.
      You are my helper and rescuer,
             come, my God, without delay.

❧ Psalm 41

*This is another psalm sung by a person who is undergoing severe suffering.
He begins with the confident statement that God helps people in trouble
when they have helped others who were in trouble (vv.2-4). If the psalmist
sounds as though he advocates doing good to store up credit against a time
when he may be in need, this is not what is intended. According to the Law it
is the duty of the strong to help the weak and obedience to the Law brings*

happiness. *The person who keeps this law may therefore expect that God will also help him in his weakness and, without this being a hard and fast rule, it was seen as generally true.*

So in vv.5-10 the psalmist can spell out in prayer his distress. He admits that his present illness is due to sin (see Psalm 38.4), but what seems to distress him more than the physical illness is the attitude of other people. His enemies talk about his impending death in his hearing and then spread rumours about it far and wide. But worse still, his friends do the same.

Therefore he prays that he may live to repay his enemies and that he may live in the presence of God which is the highest blessing anyone could wish for (see Psalms 23.6, 27.8).

The final lines at the end of v.13 do not belong to this psalm at all. They are the doxology to the First Book of Psalms which comes to an end at this point. The manner in which the psalms were collected is by no means clear to us, but at some stage the whole Psalter was divided into five books, possibly on the analogy of the five books of the Law. Since the divisions do not mark a change in subject matter and do not coincide with the collections mentioned in the Psalm headings, they were probably made at a late stage in the process of collection. Nor is it clear whether the doxologies were once used in Israel's worship or whether they are simply literary conclusions.

2 Happy is the man who looks with concern on the weak,
      the LORD saves him when trouble comes.

3 The LORD protects him and lets him live,
      he makes him happy in the land,
      he does not feed him to his enemies.

4 The LORD supports him on his bed of sickness,
      when he is ill he turns his mattress over for him.

5 I said, 'LORD, be generous to me;
      heal me, for I have sinned against you.'

6 My enemies say hurtful things in my hearing,
      'How long before he dies and is forgotten?'

7   When they come to see me
        they do not mean what they say;
    they collect bad news about me
        then go out and spread it everywhere.

8   All who hate me speak together in whispers,
        thinking the worst about me.

9   'A dreadful disease grips him,
        he will never leave his bed again.'

10 Even my closest friend whom I trusted,
        the one who used to come to dinner with me,
        spreads exaggerated rumours about me.

11 But you, LORD, be generous to me,
        make me well again that I may pay them back.

12 So I shall know that you are pleased with me,
        and that my enemy will never celebrate victory over me.

13 Because of my integrity you keep firm hold of me,
        you assign me a place in your presence for ever.

                    *   *   *

    Blessed be the LORD, the God of Israel
        from one end of time to the other.
                            Amen.   Amen.

✂ Psalms 42 and 43

It is best to take these two psalms together since they were almost certainly originally one. The content is similar and the same refrain occurs at 42.6, 42.12 and 43.5. Even if they did start life separately it is sensible now to read and study them together.

In the first stanza (vv.2-5) the psalmist seems to be living so far away from Jerusalem that he cannot get to the Temple to worship God, and this distresses him greatly as he recalls how he has done so in the past. His distress, however, only evokes the taunts of people who don't understand his feelings.

In the refrain he takes himself to task for his depression and looks forward to God acting to make worship possible for him again.

The second stanza suggests that he is away in the Lebanon, to the North of Israel — unless this phrase is used simply as a metaphor for separation. He is able to sing a prayer to God but cannot share in the corporate worship in the Temple. His distress now seems to be something more than the absence from Zion. He appears to be under some sort of oppression or persecution as well.

The third stanza (43.1-5) calls on God as judge to set him free and bring him back again to the sanctuary in Jerusalem. 'Light' and 'truth' are spoken of here almost as though they were guiding angels.

The absence from Jerusalem and the sense of oppression has suggested to some that the psalm was composed during the time of the Babylonian exile. Be that as it may, the psalm continued to be read after the return to Judah when it must have been interpreted in terms of spiritual separation from God and the psalm retains its value in this sense.

2   As a deer longs for streams of water
       I long with all my heart for you, my God.

3   I thirst for God, for the living God;
       when may I come to worship him face to face?

4   I cry so much that I cannot eat,
       both day and night,
  while men say to me day-long,
       'Where is your God?'

5   I remember what happened in the past
       and am heart-broken;
  how I used to march along with the crowds,
       leading them up to God's Temple,
  a crowd on its way to the festival,
       singing and cheering and giving thanks.

6 'Why are you so downcast?' I ask myself,
        'Why are you so troubled?
        Wait for God to act!'
   Then I will praise him again,
        my God who rescues me.

7 I am so down-cast
        for I remember you
   while I am in the region of the Jordan
        near the Hermon range and Mount Mizar.

8 One ocean of trouble summons up another,
        calling with the voice of your waterfalls;
   all your waves, all your breakers
        have risen over my head.

9 Every day the LORD sends his reproach,
        every night I sing a prayer to the living God.

10 I say to God, the rock who offers me safety,
        'Why have you forgotten me?
   Why do I go about dressed in mourning
        because an enemy has oppressed me?'

11 I suffer physical persecution,
        my assailants taunt me
   and say to me all day long,
        'Where is your God?'

12 'Why are you so down-cast?' I ask myself,
        'Why are you so troubled?
        Wait for God to act!'
   Then I will praise him again,
        my God who rescues me.

1 Be my judge and try my case, God;
    set me free from people no better than foreigners,
who show no devotion to you,
    who are liars and evil men.

2 You are the God who keeps me safe,
    why have you turned me away?
Why do I go about in mourning
    because an enemy has oppressed me?

3 Send me your light and truth,
    may they be my guide,
may they lead me to your holy hill,
    to the place where you live.

4 Then I shall reach God's altar,
    and even God himself, my supreme joy.
I will praise you, accompanied by the harp,
    God, my God.

5 'Why are you so downcast?' I ask myself,
    'Why are you so troubled?
    Wait for God to act!'
Then I will praise him again,
    my God who rescues me.

🕰 Psalm 44

This is a psalm to be sung by the people, or on their behalf, at a time of national defeat and distress. It is tempting to look for an occasion in history on which the psalm may have been composed, but it is probably futile because there were many moments of military defeat. The psalmist's insist-

ence on the fact that the land of Israel was given to them (vv.2-9) and that people have been scattered abroad (v.12) suggests the exile in Babylon — and certainly the psalm would have become very meaningful then. However, the occasional use of the singular 'I' and 'my' in vv.5, 16 and 17 perhaps suggests that it was sung by the king as the representative of his people and, in this case, the psalm would almost certainly be pre-exilic.

It begins with the reminder that Israel did not conquer Canaan; it was given to them by God. The walls of Jericho fell down (Joshua 6). This activity of God on behalf of his people is clearly celebrated regularly (v.2).

The contrast in vv.10-23 could hardly be sharper. The psalmist makes no bones about it: the same God who helped them in the past has now delivered them into the hands of their enemies and brought disgrace upon them. Now normally, as we have seen in many psalms, the reason for such a change of attitude on God's part would be the people's sin. This psalmist, however, does not explain the change in this way. Indeed he cannot explain it and herein lies his problem. His claim in vv.18-23 is not that they have done no wrong but simply that they have not turned away from their special relationship with God. So they do not deserve defeat and yet God has permitted it and indeed brought it about. Moreover, it is the fact that they have remained God's people that now accounts for their suffering (v.23). So the psalmist pleads for God urgently to do something about their situation (vv.24-27).

The question of undeserved suffering is raised in many parts of the Old Testament as a protest against the view that it is always deserved (see, for example, the Book of Job). Here, though, is the recognition that suffering and hardship may come about not in spite of faithfulness but because of it. Of this the Cross of Jesus is the supreme example.

2   We have heard for ourselves, our God,
         our forefathers have told us
   all the deeds you performed in their days,
         in those days long ago.

3   It was by your power that a nation was driven out
         and our ancestors settled in the land;
   you brought disaster on their people,
         but ours flourished there.

4   Not by force of arms did they occupy the land,
        their own strength did not win it for them,
    but rather your power, your strength and light from your
          presence,
        for you were on their side.

5   You are my King and my God,
        in command at the victories won by Jacob's people.

6   By your power we will gore our enemies,
        by your authority we will trample our opponents down.

7   For I will not trust my own bow,
        my own sword will not win me victory.

8   But you will give us victory over our enemies
        and throw our foes into confusion.

9   For God's help we will sing praises all day long,
        we will give thanks to you for ever.

10   But now you have rejected us and shamed us,
        you no longer go out to battle with our armies.

11   You have made us retreat before the enemy,
        our foes have plundered us.

12   You have allowed us to be slaughtered like sheep,
        you have scattered us among foreign people.

13   You have sold your own people for next to nothing,
        you have got very little for them.

14   You have made a mockery of us before our neighbours,
        we are derided and ridiculed by all around.

15   You have made our disgrace proverbial among foreigners,
        nations shake their heads at us in disgust.

16   All day long I am aware of my disgrace;
        I am covered with shame

17 At the taunts and insults hurled at me
    by an enemy out for vengeance.

18 All this has happened to us, yet we have not forgotten you,
    we have not treated your covenant with disdain,

19 We have not wavered in our purpose,
    we have not been deflected from your way.

20 But you have crushed us; fever burns inside us;
    you have covered us over with deep darkness.

21 If we had forgotten who our God was
    and had reached out in prayer to another god,

22 Would not God have discovered it?
    For he knows what we think in secret.

23 But on your account we are being killed all the time,
    we are thought of as sheep ready for slaughter.

24 Rouse yourself, Lord; why do you sleep on?
    Wake up; do not go on rejecting us for ever.

25 Why are you facing the other way?
    Why do you ignore our suffering and distress?

26 For we lie prostrate in the dust,
    we stay prone on the ground.

27 Rise up and come to help us,
    show your devotion by setting us free.

✣ Psalm 45

Without doubt this psalm originally celebrated the marriage of the king and the accompanying translation seeks to reflect this. However, the psalm continued to be used once the Jews no longer had a king and it must then have been reinterpreted in terms of the coming Messianic king. That this was so is reflected in its use by the writer of the letter to the Hebrews as a reference to Jesus Christ (Heb. 1.8). It is quite possible that in the course of this reinterpretation slight alterations were made to the text of the psalm.

Most particularly, the first line of v.7 could hardly have referred to the king as God in the way the Letter to the Hebrews understood it, for such a view of the king was out of the question in Israel and Judah. Even the great king David is revealed as a very human figure. It is true that the king had a very special relationship with God and could be regarded as his adopted son (Psalm 2.7), but he was never seen as divine. So the translation offered here sees the verse as a reference to the continuance of the Davidic line, as promised in 2 Samuel 7 and elsewhere, its permanence being compared to the permanence of God himself.

The question may then be asked: for which royal marriage was this psalm composed? The apparent reference to the bride as a 'daughter of Tyre' (v.13) has, of course, suggested to some the marriage of Ahab to Jezebel, but Ahab was married to her before he became king and in any case it is difficult to see the psalm as referring to a Northern non-Davidic king in the light of what I have said above. Some scholars, therefore, see 'daughter of Tyre' as a reference to the people of Tyre, the phrase standing in apposition to 'the richest people' and, again, it may have been interpreted in this way at some stage.

Of course, the fact that the psalm came to be regarded as Messianic and therefore, by Christians, as referring to Jesus leaves it open to further interpretation in terms of Christ the King and his bride, the Church.

2   My mind is at work on a good idea,
        I dedicate what I produce to the king.
    My tongue finds words to speak
        as readily as the pen of a good scribe.

3   You are the most handsome man in the world,
        you always speak most graciously,
        therefore God has blessed you for ever.

4   Buckle on your sword, warrior king,

5   Be successful in your splendid, glorious armour,
        ride out in the cause of truth and right.

6   With your right hand shoot your terrible shafts,
        your sharp arrows, into the hearts of the king's enemies.
        May nations fall beneath your sway.

7   Your reign, like God himself, is eternal,
        you exercise your royal power with fairness.

8   You love what is right and hate evil.
    Therefore God, your God, has anointed you with oil,
        and with joy greater than any other king.

9   All your robes are fragrant with spices and perfumes,
        music on instruments inlaid with ivory entertains you.

10   Foreign princesses are members of your harem.
        Your consort takes her place at your right hand,
        dressed in finest gold.

11   Look and listen, daughter; listen carefully,
        forget your own people and your own family.

12   When the king desires you for your beauty
        submit to him, for he is your master.

13   Princess of Tyre, the richest people will come to you,
        they will seek your favour with a present.

14   Richly begowned is the princess within,
        her robes are woven with gold thread.

15   In her multi-coloured gown she is led to the king,
        followed by her bridesmaids,
        her companions whom she has brought with her.

16   Amid great rejoicing they are led along
        and enter the king's palace.

17   Your descendants, my king, will succeed your ancestors,
            you will make them rulers over all the earth.

18   Through them I will see that you are remembered
            by succeeding generations,
            and so the nations will praise you for ever.

❧ Psalm 46

Psalms 46, 47 and 48 belong closely together. It is likely, though not certain, that they were all used in the annual, autumnal Feast of Booths in which God was recognised as King and Jerusalem as his home, so assuring worshippers of security on account of his universal authority.

Verses 2-8 of Psalm 46 present us with a sort of 'worst case scenario'. However much the physical universe seems on the point of disintegration or nations threaten the peace of the world, God is the source of security and strength. Jerusalem his home will stand firm and his people will be safe. The city had no river, of course, (v.5); the idea of life-giving water flowing from the home of God echoes the Paradise story in Genesis 2.10-14. The refrain (v.8) which closes this opening part of the psalm reiterates what has been said in vv.2-6 — God is with us. The theme of the presence of God runs like a thread through the Bible from the promise to Moses in Exodus 3, through psalms such as this, through Isaiah 7.14 with its child named Immanuel, God with us, through the Gospels and on into Revelation. His presence may be, as here, a cause of rejoicing but for the unfaithful it may also be a cause of distress for he comes also to judge (Psalms 96.13 and 98.9).

In the second part of the psalm (vv.9-12) the psalmist recalls God's deeds in the past and on the basis of this anticipates a time of peace and security in the future which God will bring about. That, too, may seem an astonishing thing (v.9) but because it is so people may 'relax' and be free from fretting and anxiety. Finally, he repeats the refrain as the ground for such supreme confidence.

In almost any age this psalm serves to remind people where true security and hope lie. Martin Luther found it so when he used it as the basis for his hymn 'A safe stronghold our God is still' and it remains so.

Whatever the threatening circumstances God is always God, and he is with us.

2   God is the source of our security and strength.
      He is always at hand to help in trouble.

3   Therefore we shall not be afraid though the earth changes shape,
      though the mountains totter and fall into the depths of the sea.

4   Though its waters roar and foam,
      though the mountains quake with the heavy seas.

5   There is a river! Its tributaries gladden the city of God,
      the holy place where the Most High lives.

6   Since God is in the city it cannot be shaken,
      God will help it at the break of day.

7   Nations are in confusion; kingdoms on the point of collapse;
      he raises his voice; the earth melts away.

8   The LORD of hosts is with us,
      the God of Jacob our stronghold on high.

9   Come, see what the LORD has done,
      what astonishing things he has brought about on earth.

10   He puts an end to war throughout the world,
      he breaks the bow and smashes the spear,
      he burns up shields in the fire.

11   'So relax! Recognise that I am God,
      supreme among the nations, supreme in the earth.'

12   The LORD of hosts is with us,
      the God of Jacob our stronghold on high.

✌ Psalm 47

This second psalm in the group of three celebrates the kingship of the
LORD. There is some evidence to support the view that at the Feast of Booths
each year there was a ceremony in which the LORD was re-enthroned as
King. Zechariah 14.16-17 refers to the feast and associates it with the com-
ing of the autumn rains. Certain other psalms, especially 93, 95-99 belong
to this same ceremony. In all of them God who is acknowledged afresh as
King, probably in a ceremony involving the Ark which was regarded as his
throne, is also recognised as having universal authority. The psalms then
look forward to a day when all nations will understand this and submit to
his rule.

Such a psalm, however, is not simply evidence of Israel's forlorn hopes.
It remained a confident affirmation long after the actual ceremony had
ceased to be performed. God's ascension to his throne was understood not in
a literal but in a metaphorical sense, and yet his universal rule was still
acclaimed.

It is in this sense that the psalm retains its value for people today. It
serves as a reminder of the Kingdom — the Kingship — of God. The King
cares for his people; his people serve him; one day all will recognise him as
King.

2 All you peoples, clap your hands!
   Shout to God with a cry of joy!

3 For the LORD, Most High, inspires awe,
   he is a great King over all the earth.

4 He makes peoples subject to us
   and puts nations under our feet.

5 He chose for us the land we should inherit,
   the proud possession of Jacob whom he loved.

6 God has ascended his throne to a shout of acclamation,
   the LORD, to a trumpet-blast.

7   Sing praise to God, sing praises;
           sing praise to our King, sing praises,

8   For he is King over all the earth,
           sing praise to God with a skilful psalm.

9   God is King over the nations,
           he has occupied his holy throne.

10   Volunteers from the nations muster
           as the army of Abraham's God.

11   The rulers of the earth belong to God
           who is enthroned on high.

৯৯ Psalm 48

In the last of these three related psalms God and his city Jerusalem are praised (vv. 2-4). The word 'Zaphon' in v. 3 is a proper name. It may be translated 'north' but since Jerusalem can hardly be said to be in the North the psalmist is almost certainly using it as the name of the hill where the Canaanite gods were supposed to live and is applying it metaphorically to Zion, the hill where Israel's God lived.

Verses 5 and 6, 9 and 10 suggest that some activity has been seen in the Temple both by the Israelites who were present and by any foreigners who may have been represented at the Feast of Booths. We are not told what they saw and there are few, if any, clues in the rest of the Old Testament. But in view of the remarks on Psalm 47 it may have been the symbolic enthronement of the LORD as King.

The final verses, 13-15, can be understood as referring to a procession round the city and the Temple carrying the Ark (compare, e.g. Psalms 24 and 68). The 'this' of v. 15 is emphatic — almost as though the singers were pointing at something, perhaps the Ark on which the invisible God was enthroned.

So Jerusalem is to be praised, not simply because of its own beauty and strength, but much more because God the universal King has made his home there and can be encountered there by his people. In this sense the psalm continues to remind us that the Church is nothing without God, but with God living and ruling among his people it is both strong and beautiful.

2   The LORD is great and deserves high praise
        in the city of our God, his holy hill.

3   Beautiful height!
        Joy of the whole earth!
           Zion's hill!
               The very heart of Mount Zaphon!
               The Great King's city!

4   God is in her citadels,
        he is well-known as a high stronghold.

5   For see! The kings have assembled,
        they have marched in unison.

6   They themselves saw!
        As a result they were dumbfounded.

7   At that point trembling took hold of them
        like that of a woman in labour,

8   As when the east wind shatters the ships of Tarshish.

9   All we heard we have now seen
        in the city of the Lord of hosts,
        the city of our God.
   God will make it stand firm for ever.

10 We have portrayed your devotion, God,
        within your Temple.

11 As your fame is world-wide
        so men everywhere praise you.

     You hold victory in your right hand.

12 The hill of Zion is glad,
  the towns of Judah rejoice
  on account of your just rule.

13 March round Zion, all the way round her,
  count her towers.

14 Take good note of her strength,
  take account of her fortresses as you pass by
  so that you may tell them to generations to come.

15 For this is God,
  our God for ever and ever.
  He will lead us as long as we live.

✣ Psalm 49

The short refrain in vv.13 and 21 of this psalm summarises its teaching. Life is short and death comes to all. The teaching is offered in the style of the Wisdom teacher, much of the language bearing strong resemblance to that found in Proverbs and Ecclesiastes. The psalm is not addressed to God and there is no element of praise or thanksgiving in it or even lament over the sufferings of the righteous. The only hint that it was meant to be used in worship is the reference to the harp accompaniment in v.5. Since this 'wisdom' teaching is common to all cultures it is here addressed to all people everywhere (v.2).

* Verses 6-13 indicate the psalmist is troubled by foolish people who put their trust in wealth. It is not wealth itself which he criticises but reliance on it. It was possible to 'redeem' an animal and more especially a first-born son by paying money instead of offering it as a sacrifice or by substituting a less valuable animal (Exodus 13.13-16, 34. 18-20). It was also possible to set free a slave by buying him from his master (Leviticus 25.25-55). But there is no way in which a man can buy himself immunity from death.*

* Verses 14-21 speak of the foolish who in the Old Testament are morally blameworthy because they refuse to respect and obey God. They die and there is no hope of any return from Sheol, the place where all the dead go. It*

*is a dark, empty place and the very negation of life. Verse 16 is a crucial verse.
It need mean nothing more than that when the psalmist's life is declining
and he looks like dying God will save him from death. This would be in line
with the Wisdom teaching and with the Old Testament in general. The
phrase 'he will take me up', however, is used to mark the end of the life of
Enoch and Elijah, neither of whom are actually said to have died. So it is just
possible that it expresses some hope of a continuing life after death. Even if
this is so the thought is not developed and the psalmist returns to the fate of
the foolish and the rich.*

*The time came when certain of the Jews came to believe in resurrec-
tion, not immortality (Daniel 12 and the Pharisees of the New Testament),
and Christians have to read this psalm in the light of the resurrection of
Jesus and all that means for his followers. The folly of trusting in wealth and
material prosperity remains as a warning wholly in line with the teaching of
Jesus.*

2 Hear this, all you nations,
       listen, all people everywhere,

3 All mankind of every class,
       rich and poor alike.

4 The words I speak are wise,
       the thoughts I consider are discerning.

5 I listen carefully to a puzzling saying
       and elucidate its meaning to the music of the harp.

6 Why am I afraid in times of trouble,
       when assailants take advantage of me on all sides,

7 Who trust in their wealth to help them
       and boast about how rich they are?

8 But no man can possibly redeem himself,
       he cannot buy from God his freedom.

9 The price he would pay for his life is too great,
       he could never afford what it would cost

10   For him to go on living for ever
          and not set eyes on the Pit for the dead.

11   But he will see wise men who die,
          while fools and brutes are wiped out together;
          they leave their wealth for others to enjoy.

12   Their graves become their eternal home
          where they stay for all time to come,
          claiming those plots of ground as their own.

13   Men are like oxen who do not live long
          like animals whom death soon silences.

14   This is the fate of the foolish,
          those who come after them will express their pleasure.

15   Like a flock of sheep they are herded to Sheol,
          death acting as their shepherd.
    Good men dominated them in the morning
          and consigned them to waste away in Sheol
          with no chance of rising from there.

16   But God will loose me from the grip of Sheol,
          for he will take me up.

17   Do not be afraid when a man makes money
          and his family grows richer and richer,

18   For he will take nothing with him when he dies,
          his wealth will not accompany him.

19   Though he congratulates himself during his lifetime
          and is honoured because he does well for himself

20   He will join the company of his ancestors
          who will never again see the light of life.

21   Men are like oxen who do not live long,
          like animals whom death soon silences.

৭৪৬ Psalm 50

The whole of this psalm has to be seen against the background of a case at law. Verses 2-6 portray the arrival of God the judge in Zion accompanied, as usual, by fire (compare Psalm 18). Verse 5 is usually taken to refer to faithful Israelites but the phrase 'devoted servants' has been met already in Psalms 4.4, 16.10 etc. and the suggestion has been made that it refers to some officials, possibly Levites or prophets. Here they are called on to state God's case against his people, a typically prophetic task.

The charge is set out in vv.7-15, but the precise nature of it is held back until vv.14-15. It is not sacrifice itself which God, through his 'devoted servant', reprimands but rather the offering of sacrifice as though it were something he needed to sustain his own life. The true motive for sacrifice ought to be gratitude (v.14) or humble petition (v.15).

The verdict of guilty is assumed to have been given on some and they are further addressed in vv.16-23. The charge against them now is that they are prepared to recite the laws but not obey them. God has been patient with them but now he can be so no longer and must take them to task. It is just possible, though less likely, that it is the sacrificial laws which are in mind here rather than the moral law, in which case the criticism would be that sacrifice without moral behaviour is abhorrent to God (compare Amos 5.21-24). In any case the final verse returns to the theme of sacrifice intended as a way of expressing thanks which are sincerely felt.

The whole psalm, therefore, accords well with the teaching of Jesus for whom adherence to ritual and to moral law was good, but only when accompanied by genuine inner motives.

2 The Supreme God, the LORD, has spoken,
>   he has summoned the world
>   from eastern sunrise to western sunset.
> From Zion, city of perfect beauty,
>   God shines like the sun.

3 Our God is coming,
>   he will not stay silent.
> Fire consumes all before him,
>   and rages fiercely all around him.

4   He summons the heavens and the earth
        to his lawsuit with his people.

5   'Gather to me my devoted servants
        who seal my covenant with sacrifice.'

6   The heavens announce that he is just
        and that God's court is now in session.

7   'Listen to me, my people, I will speak to you,
        Israel, I will bring a charge against you;
        I am God, your God.

8   It is not for your sacrifices that I reprimand you,
        nor for your burnt-offerings which you are always
            bringing to me.

9   I do not accept a bull from your stall
        or goats from your fold

10 Because every beast in the forest belongs to me,
        the cattle on a thousand hills.

11 I know every bird on the mountains,
        the wild life also is mine.

12 If I were hungry I would not tell you
        for the world and everything in it is mine.

13 Do I eat meat from bulls
        or drink blood from goats?

14 So sacrifice to God to express your thanks,
        to the Most High to fulfil your solemn promises.

15 Call on me in times of trouble;
        when I rescue you, honour me with sacrifice.'

16 To whoever he finds guilty God says,
        'What right have you to recite my decree
        and take my covenant laws upon your lips?

17 You, you hate it when I correct you,
        you fling my words behind you.

18 If you see a thief you make friends with him,
        you keep company with adulterers.

19 You despatch your words with evil intent,
        you string together lies.

20 You sit down with your brother but speak against him;
        you make false allegations against your own family.

21 Such things you do and I have kept quiet;
        you thought I was a man like you;
    but now I reprove you,
        I list them for you to see.

22 Take note of this, you who ignore God,
        or like a lion I will tear you in pieces
        and there will be no one to rescue you.

23 Whoever offers a sacrifice to say thank you honours me;
        whoever approaches me in this way,
        I will see that he enjoys God's salvation.'

✿ Psalm 51

*This confession of sin and prayer for forgiveness has provided the words
needed by men and women over the centuries as they have sought to express
their own thoughts and feelings to God. The psalmist is able to seek forgiveness partly on the ground of his confession, but more particularly because
he is convinced of God's devotion to him and to all his people (v.3). It is this
above all else which makes both the confession and the prayer possible.*

*Verse 7 has sometimes been used as evidence for a doctrine of original
sin, or for the sinful nature of sexual relations, but all it really means is that
man is born into a world permeated by sin and therefore there was no time*

when he could be regarded as innocent. Later Jewish theologians believed that human beings were born with an inherent 'tendency to sin' though it is doubtful whether even that is meant here. The psalmist simply wishes to say that his sin is long-standing and deep-seated.

Verse 8 is difficult to translate. It seems to mark the transition from confession to prayer in which the psalmist recognises God's desire for truth and sincerity even when it is obscured by sin. Further he is aware of his own need of God to show him how to conduct his own life in the future since wisdom is given to people only if they stand in awe of God (compare Job 28).

In verse 18 the psalmist seems to advocate a purely spiritual and non-sacrificial worship. We saw in Psalm 50, however, that, strong as this expression is, it means not a complete repudiation of sacrifice but an insistence that sacrifice without confession and penitence is offensive to God. It is a complete misunderstanding of God's true nature.

It is almost universally agreed that the final two verses (20-21) were added to the psalm when it was sung during the exile in Babylon. They were intended to correct any possible misunderstanding of the previous verses, that sacrifice was no longer necessary at all.

It remains true, however, that in these days when sacrifice is no longer offered by Jews and when Christians believe that the one final sacrifice has been offered by Jesus, those who confess their sin and are penitent may rely on the grace and constancy of God for forgiveness.

3   Be kind to me, God, as your devotion demands,
         in your deep compassion cancel my sin.

4   Wash away all my guilt,
         make me clean from my sin.

5   For I am well aware of my sin
         and dwell upon my errors.

6   Against you, you alone, I have sinned,
         I have done what you count as wrong.
     So you are right when you pass sentence,
         you are justified in condemning me.

7   I have been guilty since birth,
         sinful since my mother conceived me.

8   Truth is what you want though it be obscured;
      you make me recognise wisdom where it is not obvious.

9   Remove my sin as with a sprig of hyssop that I may be clean,
      wash me that I may be whiter than snow.

10   Let me hear again the sounds of happy rejoicing,
      let me be glad, though you crushed the life out of me.

11   Turn your back on my sin,
      cancel all my guilty deeds.

12   Create for me, God, a pure conscience,
      give me a fresh and firm will to obey it.

13   Do not banish me from your presence
      nor withdraw from me your divine power.

14   Give me back the joy which is found in your deliverance,
      may I be upheld by a will freely surrendered to yours.

15   I will teach wrong-doers how you act,
      and sinners will return to you.

16   You, God, are my deliverer; save me from violence;
      I will sing aloud that you always do right.

17   Lord, unseal my lips
      and I will speak openly in praise of you.

18   For sacrifice gives you no pleasure;
      if I were to make a burnt offering you would not accept it.

19   My sacrifice is a broken self-will;
      you will not disdain one so broken and crushed.

20   Be pleased to do good to Zion,
      rebuild the walls of Jerusalem.

21   Then, at that time, you will be pleased with proper sacrifices,
      with an offering burnt or wholly consumed,
      then bulls will be offered on your altar.

❧ Psalm 52

The fact that this psalm is spoken by one individual against another and not against wicked men in general has led to the conclusion that its background may be a law case heard in the Temple (see Psalm 7). The confident condemnation of the man is reminiscent of the words of the prophets and may suggest that a prophet working in the Temple, or perhaps a Levite, is complaining about the behaviour of one of his fellows. The fact that at the end he offers his praise in the presence of 'devoted servants' (v.11) may support this suggestion (see Psalms 4, 12, 50 etc.), but we cannot be sure.

The psalm begins by setting side by side God's never-failing devotion and the wickedness of the person of whom the psalmist speaks (v.3). The wickedness consists largely of slander and lies (vv.4-6). Quite often, especially in books like Proverbs, the use of the tongue is a matter of great concern. So, in v.7, he threatens him with the judgement of God.

The reactions of those who see this judgement will be two-fold; they will be over-awed by the power and justice of God and they will laugh at the one who is being punished. What they say about the wicked man differs from what the psalmist had complained of. Their criticism concerns his wealth not his words, though it is not the wealth itself which they condemn but his trust in it instead of in God (see Psalm 49.7).

By contrast the psalmist will find himself permitted to go on worshipping and praising God in the Temple. The use of the metaphor of an olive tree reminds us of Psalm 1.3. There he will join other 'devoted servants'.

Whatever specific situation produced this psalm it is still a reminder to us of the dangers of misusing words to damage other people and of the joy that comes in worship for those who seek to do right.

3 Why do you boast about being evil, proud man?
    God's devotion never fails.

4 You plan to ruin people with your tongue,
    it is as sharp as a razor, telling cutting lies.

5 You love evil more than good,
    you prefer telling lies to speaking the truth.

6   You love every word that engulfs others in misery,
       all conversation which slanders them.

7   God, for his part, will leave you shattered for ever,
       he will scatter you and make you homeless,
       uprooted from the land of the living.

8   Those who do right will see it and be overawed,
       they will laugh at him,

9   'Look at the man who does not depend on God for safety,
       he put his trust in his great wealth,
       he sought safety in what he himself wanted.'

10   But I am like an olive tree flourishing in God's Temple,
       I have trusted in God's eternal devotion.

11   I will praise you for ever, for you have made me so;
       I will pronounce your name for you are good;
       I will do so in the presence of your devoted servants.

ॐ Psalm 53

This psalm is virtually identical with Psalm 14.

2   The fool says to himself,
       'God is irrelevant.'
  Such men are destructive; they commit abominable evil,
       no one does anything good.

3   God looks down from heaven
       on men everywhere,
  to see if there is a prudent man
       who seeks God in worship.

4   They have all proved faithless and are corrupt,
        no one does anything good,
        not a single one of them.

5   'Do they not know what will happen, those wicked men,
        who devour my people as readily as food,
        who never call me God?'

6   They will stand there in great terror
        such as has never been before;
    for God has scattered godless people,
        he has made them ashamed and rejected them.

7   If only Israel's deliverance would come from Zion!
        When God restores his people's fortunes
        Jacob will rejoice, Israel will be glad.

🙦 Psalm 54

This brief psalm needs little by way of introduction or explanation. It falls into three parts. The first (vv.3-5) is the psalmist's prayer to be rescued from the actions of ruthless people who threaten him. In the second (vv.6-7) he recalls God's ability and readiness to help him by repaying his enemies for their wickedness. Finally, in vv.8-9, he declares his willingness to make a thank-offering because he has now been rescued. The use of the past tense here may simply indicate that he is so sure of God's help that he can speak as though he had already received it, a way of speaking sometimes used by the prophets. On the other hand it may be another instance of the psalmist hearing words of assurance from a priest or enjoying some other experience which had the same effect (see Psalm 3.8 etc.).

The 'gloating over his enemies' sounds very harsh to us these days but, however much it may need to be modified by the New Testament injunction to love our enemies, we ought not to lose sight of the fact that evil is evil and its defeat is something to be glad about.

3   Save me, God, by your own power,
        give judgement in my favour by your might.

4   Hear my prayer, God,
        listen to what I say.

5   For insolent men have risen against me,
        ruthless people seek my life;
        they do not keep their minds on God.

6   But God is my helper,
        the Lord is with those who support me.

7   Repay my enemies with disaster,
        keep your promise and put an end to them.

8   Freely I will offer sacrifices to you,
        I will praise you for you are good.

9   For you have rescued me from every trouble,
        and so I gloat over my enemies.

✁ Psalm 55

It has to be said that the Hebrew text of this psalm is, in places, so difficult and uncertain that translators cannot be wholly confident that they have been able to represent accurately what the psalmist actually said. However, though we may be unsure about details, the general meaning of the psalm can be discerned.

Verses 2-12 describe in the most graphic terms the fear and anguish which the psalmist's enemies cause him. How much he would love to run away from it all. Moreover, their activities do not seem to be restricted to him but to extend throughout the city.

There is still worse to come, however. The psalmist may just be able to put up with attacks from enemies; the trouble is though that they are led by his intimate friend, with whom he had gone to worship and whom he now addresses directly (vv. 13-15). The psalmist then calls down threats on them all (v. 16).

In the second half of the psalm his thoughts alternate between his own feelings about his erstwhile friend and his trust in God (vv. 17-22). His friend is thoroughly hypocritical and has broken any bond between them; God is utterly reliable and faithful to his promise.

Verse 23 seems to be spoken by someone else and so we must assume either that the psalmist is quoting to himself a text which he has learned from his worship or that these are the words of a priest reassuring him (see Psalm 54.9, etc.). In any case the words allow him to become confident that God will deal effectively with his enemies.

Anyone who has been betrayed by a close friend will be able to identify with this psalmist. In such circumstances we do well to recall the faithful-ness of God, as he did, for God is a friend who will never betray our trust.

2   Listen to my prayer, God,
      do not hide when I ask a favour.

3   Give me your attention and answer me,
      I am restless with anxiety.

4   I am panic-stricken at the threats of my enemies,
      at the pressure wicked men put on me;
for they bring trouble on me like a land-slide,
      and in their anger treat me with hostility.

5   My mental anguish is profound,
      the dread of death has come over me.

6   I live in fear and trembling,
      I shudder all over.

7   I said, 'If only I had wings like a dove
      I would fly away to roost;

8   Yes, I would fly far away
      and settle in the desert.

9   I would speed to a place of safety
      from the raging wind and storm.'

10 Confound and confuse what they say, Lord,
        for I see violence and fighting in the city.

11 Day and night they walk around on its walls,
        causing trouble and making mischief in it.

12 Destruction is everywhere,
        malicious damage is never absent from its streets.

13 It is not just an enemy who taunts me
        or I might tolerate it.
    It is not an antagonist who gloats over me
        or I might hide from him.

14 But no, you are a man of my own class,
        my intimate friend and companion.

15 We used to have deep and enjoyable conversations together,
        we used to walk among the crowds in the Temple.

16 Desolations be upon them!
        Let them go down to Sheol alive!
        Misfortunes will cause terror among them, I swear!

17 As for me, I will call to God
        and the LORD will save me.

18 Morning, noon and night
        I moan and groan,

19 But when he hears my voice
        he rescues me and saves my life
    from him who is my closest friend,
        for he was among many who attacked me.

20 God who has reigned from the beginning
        will hear me and humiliate them.
    God never changes,
        yet they have no reverence for him.

21 My friend raised his hand against me,
        he broke the bond between us.

22 Words poured from his mouth like cream,
        yet his thoughts were hostile;
    they were more soothing than oil,
        but they were as cutting as swords.

23 Entrust your fortunes to the LORD,
        he will support you;
    he will never let you be shaken
        if you do what is right.

24 You, God, will despatch them
        down into the pit of destruction.
    Those violent and malicious men
        will not live out half their lives.
    But, for my part, I will trust in you.

🙞🙜 Psalm 56

*As with the previous psalm so here again the Hebrew text presents many
difficulties which affect the meaning of certain details, but not the general
interpretation of the psalm.*

*It is divided into three sections by the refrain found in vv. 5 and 11.
Verses 2-5 appeal to God for help and define the psalmist's difficulty. As is
often the case he is persecuted by enemies, who remain unidentified. The
refrain asserts his confidence in the face of such hardships, confidence in the
nature of God and his promises.*

*Verses 6-10 continue to describe the attacks of the psalmist's enemies
but move on to speak of their inevitable defeat because God who has seen
his sufferings is on his side. This leads into the refrain again.*

*The final part of the psalm assumes the psalmist has now been rescued
and is ready to make his thank-offering in fulfilment of a vow he had made*

when he was in trouble. Once more he may have received some assurance in worship that his troubles were over (see Psalms 54 and 55).

The psalm, like so many others, is a reminder to us that we may speak to God in worship without inhibition, telling him of our troubles, and may receive, in the context of that worship, a renewal of hope and confidence which enables us to face the future without fear.

2   Be kind to me, God, for men are persecuting me,
        continually assailants oppress me.

3   My adversaries persecute me all day long,
        indeed those who attack me are many.

4   Though each day I am afraid of fierce enemies
        still I put my trust in you.

5   I praise God for his promises,
        I trust in him and have no fear;
        what can mere man do to me?

6   All day long they damage my affairs,
        they plan how best to harm me.

7   They band together to spy on me,
        they watch every step I take
        as they wait to kill me.

8   For them, however, there is no escape;
        cast down such people, God, in anger.

9   You have kept count of my sleepless nights,
        collect my tears in your water-skin;
        have you not entered them in your book?

10 Then my enemies will retreat from me
        on the day I call to you;
        this I know — God is mine!

11   I praise God for his promises,
         I trust in him and have no fear;
         what can man do to me?

12   I made solemn promises to you, God;
         I will keep them with a thank-offering to you.

13   For you have rescued me from death,
         you have saved me from stumbling
     so that I may walk freely in your divine presence,
         my life bathed in its light.

❧ Psalm 57

This is yet another psalm in which the psalmist is in trouble but has confidence in God and knows it will pass. It pays less attention to the attacks made on him than does Psalm 56, for instance, though they are mentioned in vv.4, 5 and 7. The main emphasis, however, is on his confidence in God.

The refrain in vv.6 and 12 divides the psalm into two parts. In vv.2-6 the psalmist asserts his belief that his troubles will be short-lived because God will deliver him. The refrain is a call to God to show that he is mighty and is the God of the whole universe.

The second half of the psalm begins by referring to the enemies but quickly moves on to a hymn of praise. Thus the pattern is similar to that in Psalm 56, but the 'feel' of the psalm is different. The dominant note here is one of praise to God and of testifying to his grace and power before the whole world.

2   Be kind to me, God, be kind to me,
        for to you I have looked for safety;
    I seek safety in the shadow of your wings
        until the storms are passed.

3   I call to God, Most High,
       to God who brings them to an end for me.

4   He will send messengers from heaven to save me,
       bringing disgrace upon those who crush me.
       God will send devotion and faithfulness.

5   I lie down among man-eating lions,
       with teeth like spears and arrows
       and a tongue like a sharp sword.

6   Rise high, God, above the heavens,
       show your glory over all the earth.

7   They prepared a net to catch me as I walked by,
       I ducked underneath it!
   They dug a pit in my path,
       but fell into it themselves!

8   I have made up my mind, God,
       my purpose is fixed;
       I will sing you songs of praise.

9   Awake, my inmost being!
       Awake, lute and lyre!
       I will awaken the new day.

10   I will confess you among the people, Lord,
       I will sing your praise among the nations.

11   For your devotion fills the heavens,
       your faithfulness reaches the skies.

12   Rise high, God, above the heavens,
       show your glory over all the earth.

❧ Psalm 58

This psalm is addressed directly to wicked people and bears some resemblance to the prophets' attacks on evil. It may therefore have been spoken or sung by a Temple prophet or a Levite responsible for teaching the law of God. It is in some ways similar to Psalm 52, though it is addressed not to one person but to a group who are in authority, either priests or nobles. The word used in v.2 may even mean 'gods' but if so it is certainly used in a sarcastic way.

After speaking to them directly in vv.2 and 3 the psalmist proceeds to describe them in the third person. They are sinful from birth (see Psalm 51.7) but there is no hint of remorse or repentance (vv.4-6).

In a series of vivid pictures (vv.7-10) the psalmist calls down the judgement of God on them. This takes the form of a series of 'curses'. They are not curses in the sense of evil spells, the very uttering of which brings them about; they are rather strong threats that God's vengeance upon the wicked is certain. The idea of blessings for those who are obedient and curses for those who are not is common enough in the Old Testament (see Deuteronomy 27 and 28).

In the last two verses the psalmist pictures those who do right as being glad at the downfall of the wicked (see the 'gloating' in Psalm 54.9), but this joy is in the fact, now demonstrated beyond doubt by the vengeance which God takes, that God is just. 'Vengeance' is a strong word but it does indicate the just judgement upon evil.

Again the psalm may leave the modern reader feeling uncomfortable because of the intensity of its passion against wicked men, but nevertheless it saves us from regarding evil as something merely inconvenient. For Christians evil was so potent that it could only be dealt with and overcome through the crucifixion of the one who was completely innocent of it.

2   You men in authority, are your pronouncements just?
    Do you judge your fellow-men fairly?

3   Indeed not! You plan all kinds of evil in the mind;
    you dispense violence in the land.

4 Wicked, they have been alienated from birth,
      liars, they have wandered from the truth since life began.

5 They are every bit as venomous as snakes,
      deaf as a cobra which stops its ears

6 And so does not hear the music of the charmer
      or the cunning weaver of spells.

7 God, break their teeth in their mouths;
      LORD, smash the fangs of these 'lions'.

8 Let them evaporate like the water they go looking for,
      let them disappear like an arrow shot by an archer.

9 Let them be like a flowing stream which runs dry,
      like a still-born child which never sees the sun.

10 Let them be like a thorn bush, cut down before they realise it,
      like a live animal which the morrow sweeps away.

11 A man who does right will be glad when he sees vengeance
            taken,
      he will wash his feet in the blood of the wicked.

12 Men will say, 'So there is a reward, then, for the man who does
            right;
      so there is a God who dispenses justice in the earth.'

🦋 Psalm 59

*Like many others this psalm begins with a description of enemies who are
attacking the psalmist, but as it proceeds it calls on Israel's God, as God of
hosts, to punish nations (v.6). The nations are mentioned again in v.9. In
v.12 the attack is on 'my people' and God is 'our' protector, while in v.14
their defeat will let men everywhere know that God is Jacob's ruler. All this*

points up the difficulty of the psalm. Much of it reads like a personal song, of which we have had many examples, but there are words and phrases which seem to suggest that it is the community and not an individual who is threatened. The difficulty may be resolved by regarding the psalm as one sung by the king and therefore using the imagery of the individual song, but sung by the king as representative of the people (compare Psalm 44 which is clearly a community psalm but which occasionally uses the singular 'I'). This then allows us to see vv.4, 6-9, 15 as an attack on the capital city, even though the king is unaware that he or his people have done anything to warrant such an attack (v.5). As in Psalm 2.4 God holds the threatening nations in derision.

It is futile to ask which king sang the psalm and on what occasion. Indeed it was most likely used on more than one occasion or it would not have been preserved. Certainly we can see that the description of the troubles the king and his nation are in are confessed to God against a background of supreme confidence in the future of the city, which is reminiscent of Psalms 46-48.

Such confidence in God's protection was sometimes so great that the Israelites could not conceive the possibility of defeat and capture even when they had sinned and deserved it. This was true at the time just before the exile in Babylon, as Jeremiah and others were quick to point out. Yet the psalm reminds us that such confidence is well-placed when government and people — or Church — trust God and seek humbly to obey his commands, when they really are his people and he is their God.

2   Deliver me from my enemies, my God,
        raise me to safety above my assailants.

3   Deliver me from evil-doers,
        save me from violent men.

4   For here they are, lying in wait for me;
        fierce men gather round to attack me.

5   Though I am innocent they are quick to prepare a case against
        me.
        Awake when I call to you, and see it.

6 You, LORD, are God of hosts, Israel's God.
        Awake to punish all the nations;
        have no mercy on those who deal in treachery.

7 Each evening they come back like dogs,
        they growl and prowl round the city.

8 Speech comes tumbling out of their mouths,
        cutting words are on their lips.
        'Who can hear us?', they say.

9 But you laugh at them, LORD,
        you hold all the nations in derision.

10 My Strength, I will sing psalms to you,
        for you, God, are my high stronghold.

11 In his devotion my God will go before me,
        he will point out to me those who are watching with
            hostile intent.

12 Kill them, God, lest they deceive my people;
        scatter them and cast them down with your power,
        our Protector and Lord.

13 The very words they speak are sinful;
        so may they be caught by their own pride,
        because of the curses and lies they repeat.

14 Finish them off in your anger,
        finish them off till they cease to be,
    that men all over the earth may know
        that God is ruler in Jacob.

15 Each evening they come back again like dogs
        growling and prowling round the city,

16 Roaming about looking for something to eat,
        complaining if they cannot get enough.

17   For my part, I will sing about your strength,
            each morning I will sing aloud of your devotion,
        for you are a high stronghold for me,
            and a place of safety at times when I am in trouble.

18   My Strength, I will sing psalms to you,
            for you, God, are my high stronghold,
            a God devoted to me.

✽✽ Psalm 60

*Like Psalm 59 this psalm was sung in response to some acute difficulty
which was facing the nation. If we are to understand verses 3-6 partially
literally and not wholly metaphorically then it would seem that the enemy
has made serious inroads into Israelite territory and the whole people are
under severe threat. As is usually the case there is insufficient precise information to enable us to pin-point the historical occasion and the fact that it
has been preserved in the Book of Psalms suggests that it was used more
than once on different occasions.*

*The prayer for deliverance in v.7 is based on the promise of God in
vv.8-10. This section is found also in Psalm 108 and it may be that both
psalms are quoting a well-known saying about the distribution of the land
when the Israelites entered Canaan. In the tradition concerning those early
days not only were the Canaanites dispossessed and the land shared out
between the Israelite tribes, but Israel was also given power over the other
small nations like Moab and Edom and was able to defeat the mighty Philistines. Since it was customary to seek advice from a prophet before embark-
ing on military action (see 1 Kings 22) this promise may have been quoted
by a Temple prophet when the psalm was being sung there.*

*Although this is a national psalm singular pronouns are used in v.11
and this probably means that it was sung by the king on behalf of his people
(see Psalms 44 and 59). Verses 11-14 show that king and people felt that
God had deserted them. It was important that he should go into battle with
them as in the early days (see 1 Samuel 4) for he alone could give them
victory.*

What is happening to them now is seen as a sign of God's anger and

132

consequent rejection of them, but there is neither any complaint in this psalm that it was undeserved, nor is there any expression of penitence.

What the psalm says most clearly is that neither self-help nor any other human help is of any use in desperate situations. Only God can save and his promises and power to do so may be trusted.

3   God, you have rejected us, broken through our defences;
        you have been angry. May you now restore us.

4   You have made the earth quake, have split it open.
        Mend its cracks, for it is falling apart.

5   You have made your people face terrible hardship;
        you have made us drink wine and sent us reeling.

6   You have given a signal to your true worshippers
        to take flight before the enemy archers.

7   Save us by your powerful right hand; answer our prayers,
        so that those whom you love may be delivered.

8   God has promised — and he is holy,
        'I will triumph; I will share out Shechem,
        I will measure out territories in the valley of Succoth.

9   Gilead belongs to me; so does Manasseh.
        Ephraim is my helmet and Judah my sceptre.

10 Moab will be my wash bowl,
        over Edom I will fling my sandal,
        Philistia will be smashed to pieces against me.'

11 Who will lead me as far as Edom?
        Who will guide me to its fortified city?

12 Surely, God, you have deserted us,
        you no longer go out to battle with our armies.

13 Help us out of our distress,
        for human help is useless.

14　With God's help we shall fight with courage,
　　　though it is he who will overrun our enemies.

✤ Psalm 61

There are two possible ways of understanding the original setting of this psalm. First it may have been sung by some individual who felt himself alienated from God and who prayed for restoration and security. Since his security was bound up with that of the whole nation he prayed for the king's security as well. Second, it may have been the king himself who felt alienated and in need of security. In verses 7 and 8 the people joined their prayers for his well-being and in the final verse the king promised to fulfil his vow by praising God.

The phrase 'wherever I may be' in v.3 has led some to think the psalmist was away from Jerusalem but this is not necessarily so. It is simply a recognition that in any place and at any time he may call on God.

The verses which refer specifically to the king (7-8) recall the promise made to David in 2 Samuel 7.15. The divine qualities of devotion and faithfulness are here personified as guardian angels (see Psalm 57.4).

Whoever the psalmist was he appears to have been in some danger and has made a solemn promise to God, possibly of a thank-offering sacrifice, which he will fulfil not just once but frequently.

The psalm may still stimulate confidence in the power and love of God in people who find themselves in danger and it also provides a vehicle for their prayers.

2　My God, hear my cry,
　　　listen to my prayer.

3　Wherever I may be I will call to you
　　　when my courage fails;
　　　lead me up, on to a rock which is higher than I.

4　For you provide me with shelter,
　　　you are a tower of strength against my enemy.

5   Let me be a guest in your tent for ever,
        let me find shelter, hidden beneath your wings,

6   For you, God, have heard my vows,
        you have given me what men possess if they hold you in
            reverence.

7   Add year after year to the king's life,
        may his years be as many generations.

8   Let him live in God's presence for ever,
        appoint devotion and faithfulness as his guardians.

9   So will I always praise you in song
        as I fulfil my vows day after day.

❦ Psalm 62

*This psalm is not addressed directly to God but is a testimony offered to
other people about God's ability to provide security. Verses 4 and 5 seem to
indicate that among those whom the psalmist addresses are people who
threaten him and others like him. They may also suggest that the psalmist
holds a prominent position in the community. The focus of the psalm shifts
quickly from these people to God in whom alone men have confidence.*

*The opening verses are repeated in vv.6-7 with a slight difference.
Whereas v.2 speaks of 'help' coming from God, v.6 speaks of 'hope' coming
from him. The psalmist's trust in God saves him both from external trouble
and from the inner despair which such trouble may engender.*

*On the basis of his own confidence he can call on his fellows to share it
(vv.9-11). Human help may promise much but achieve little (v.10). Wealth
is no guarantee, particularly if it is ill-gotten (v.11).*

*The 'numerical saying' in vv.12 and 13 is a fairly common form of
speech (see Amos 1 and 2, Proverbs 30). Usually the higher number controls
the saying and so here the two things which give the psalmist confidence are
God's power and God's devotion. In the very last verse, almost as though he*

cannot help himself any longer, he speaks directly to God in the presence of his audience.

If God is powerful, if he is also devoted to his people (that is, loves them with unending loyalty) then, come what may, there is nothing to fear. The psalmist is certain that God is like this and many throughout the ages have added their own testimony. All this should give us not only help but hope.

2   I leave myself quietly in God's hands,
       my help comes from him alone.

3   He alone is the Rock where I find safety,
       my tower of strength.
       Nothing can shake me.

4   How long will you people attack a man?
       How long will you all commit murder
  so that he leans like a wall
       or is pushed over like a fence?

5   People look for ways of driving him out of high office;
       they do not mind telling lies,
       they speak words of blessing, but inwardly they curse.

6   I leave myself quietly in God's hands,
       my hope comes from him alone.

7   He alone is the Rock where I find safety,
       my tower of strength.
       Nothing can shake me.

8   My safety and my honour rest with God,
       he is my Rock where I find shelter.

9   Trust in him at all times, my people,
       pour out your thoughts before him.
       God provides me with shelter.

10   People count for nothing more than a breath of wind,
       human beings are deceptive;

place them in the scales all together
and they are lighter than air!

11 Do not trust in what you may gain by extortion,
nor be inflated with the spoils of robbery;
though wealth seems to generate wealth
do not set your heart on it.

12 One word God has spoken;
nay, two things I have understood:
that power belongs to God

13 And devotion to you, Lord,
that you are the one who rewards a man
according to what he does.

৯৯ Psalm 63

*As in Psalm 61 there is nothing to suggest that the psalmist is anything
other than an ordinary Israelite worshipper until we come to the final verse
and find a sudden, brief reference to the king. Since the last two lines of v. 12
are parallel, contrasting those who make a vow in God's name with those
who make false promises, the line about the king stands out even more awkwardly and some have been led to regard it as an intrusion. Even if this is so
we should still have to ask what was meant by inserting it at this point. It is
possible, of course, that the psalmist is the king and that he reveals his identity at this point (see Psalm 61). Or it may be that the psalmist sees his own
security is made more certain if the whole community, of which the king is
both head and representative, is committed to God.*

*For this psalmist, whoever he may be, worship with its constant re-
minders of God's devotion and assurances of his presence has fulfilled
all his hopes and longings and so, when he meets trouble again from
'enemies' (once more undefined) he has confidence in God. He who in time
of trouble has made a vow to God sincerely, not taking the name of the
LORD in vain, will be proud as he fulfils it, unlike those who made their*

*promises without any sincere intention of fulfilling them who will be
excluded from the singing of praise to God.*

*For such Israelites worship was not just a matter of 'going to church'.
They expected to meet God and the worship offered provided them with the
assurance of his presence which they needed in daily life with all its difficulties and dangers. Psalms such as this should make us reflect about our own
worship.*

2   God, you are my God, eagerly will I seek you.
        I long for you like a thirsty man for water,
        like one who has grown gaunt
    in a land stricken with drought and dying for lack of water.

3   At such times I have looked on you in the sanctuary
        and have seen your power and glory.

4   Because your devotion is better than life itself
        I will sing your praises.

5   So I will live in adoration of you,
        I will lift my hands in prayer to you.

6   My longing will be satisfied as with rich and luscious food
        and I will praise you with joyful songs.

7   I call you to mind as I lay in bed
        and think of you through the night hours,

8   How you have always helped me
        and sheltered me safely beneath your wings.

9   Then I have followed closely where you have led,
        and your strong right hand has supported me.

10   There are those who seek to destroy me,
        but they will go to places deep under ground.

11   They will live for ever on the fringes of the waste lands
        and become food for jackals.

12   The king will be glad God is his God.
            Whoever makes a vow in God's name will be proud to
                sing his praises,
            but those who make false promises will be silenced.

🎵 Psalm 64

There is no doubt about the trouble this psalmist is in, nor about his under-lying belief in God's justice. He is scared stiff (v.2) because of his enemies. The picture of his enemies is indeed a frightening one. They huddle together hatching plots to destroy him with slander. The 'arrows' and the 'shooting' are, of course, metaphorical. The Hebrew text of the psalm is difficult to translate at several points and may have become damaged through copying, but the terrifying scene of secret meetings in which the enemies plot how to trap the unwary and so destroy him is clear enough.

In verses 8-9, however, the psalmist claims that though they may be acting in secret they cannot hide either their schemes or themselves from God and he will pay them back in their own coin.

Other people looking on will realise that what happens to the secret plotters is the operation of God's justice and they themselves will be afraid of him (v.10). But those who do right have nothing to fear and every reason to be glad (v.11).

The 'eye for an eye' justice attributed to God in this psalm may be dis-turbing to many of us, but the psalm reminds us again to take evil seriously. We are aware too that any divine judgement on the wicked does not always act as a deterrent and that those who do right are not always kept safe. But the psalm is not setting out a scheme of doctrine; it is a response to a particu-lar situation. The preceding psalms have emphasised God's devotion; this prevents us from forgetting that he is just.

2   God, hear my voice, raised in lament,
            save my life when I am scared of my enemy.

3   Hide me away from the society of bad men,
            from gangs of evil-doers,

4   Who sharpen their tongues like swords
        and aim cruel words like arrows,

5   Shooting people of integrity from ambush,
        shooting suddenly, but keeping out of sight.

6   They encourage themselves with wicked words,
        they tell in secret where their traps are laid;
        they say, 'Who can see them?'

7   They have thought up all kinds of injustice.
        'We have made our plans perfectly', they think.
        Their intentions are hidden deep inside them.

8   But suddenly God shoots them,
        they are wounded by his arrow.

9   He turns their own words against them and makes them fall,
        all who see what happens to them tremble.

10 People everywhere are afraid;
        they declare it to be God's work
        and grasp that he has done it.

11 Those who do right are glad and find security in God,
        men of true purpose are proud to sing his praise.

❧ Psalm 65

The second half of this psalm (vv. 10-14) suggests that it was probably sung at the spring harvest when the corn crops were gathered. The first fruits of these crops were offered at the Feast of Unleavened Bread and this psalm would be an appropriate accompaniment to the offering. It celebrates the fact that it is God who provides the rains which in the autumn have made possible the sowing and which in the spring have caused the grain to swell so that the harvest may now be reaped.

The first part of the psalm (vv. 2-5) with its reminder of the obligation to fulfil vows and its confession of sin may well indicate that the psalm was first sung following a period of drought, which people had seen as a punishment for sin, and during which they had promised an offering if God ended the drought and sent rain.

The intermediate verses (vv. 6-9) bridge the gap between the readiness to fulfil the vow and the harvest thanksgiving with a passage in praise of the creator God. The verses use some of the language which may have been used by the Canaanites to describe Baal the conqueror of the sea and the rain-giver. For the psalmist these attributes are now claimed uniquely for the LORD.

No doubt the psalm continued to be used in Israel's worship even when there had been no drought. It remained a reminder of the proper human response of thanksgiving and thank-offering to the powerful God of creation who provides for all material needs. It still calls us to be grateful and to show our gratitude in worship for all his goodness, not least for all those things which sustain human life.

2   Your people ought to praise you, God, in Zion,
        they should fulfil their vows to you.

3   You listen to their prayers,
        and so everyone comes to you.

4   You forgive us our guilty words
        and blot out our rebellious deeds.

5   Happy the man you choose to accept!
        He will live in your courts.
   Let us be filled with good things in your house,
        in your holy Temple.

6   With awe-inspiring deeds you rightly respond to us,
        God, our Saviour.
   All over the earth to the distant seas
        men put their trust in you,

7   The God who has planted the mountains in his power,
        who is equipped with might,

8   Who calms the raging of the seas, the roar of the waves,
          and quietens the uproar of the peoples.

9   Those who live at the earth's margins
          stand in awe at your signs;
          from farthest east and west you evoke cries of joy.

10   You care for the earth and make it fruitful,
          you enrich it greatly.
     There is ample water in your heavenly streams;
          you make it ready to grow corn.
          This is how you make it ready:

11   You saturate its furrows, you smooth out its ridges,
          you soften it with showers, you make its plants multiply.

12   You crown the year's labours with good harvests,
          the juice drips from your loaded carts.

13   You water the dried up pastures,
          the hills are encircled with joy.

14   The meadows are clothed with sheep,
          the valleys attired in corn.
          They shout and sing for joy.

❧❧ Psalm 66

So marked is the difference between the first half of this psalm (vv. 1-12) and the second (vv. 13-20) that some scholars consider them to be two separate psalms, the first a hymn of praise by the whole community for God's past dealings with them and the second a psalm to accompany the fulfilment of a vow by a single individual. Others have seen the switch from the plural 'we' to the singular 'I' as evidence that the psalm is really a national thanksgiving sung by the king as the people's representative (see Psalms 59, 60 and 61). It is equally possible, however, to see the second half as a personal prayer accompanying a thank-offering set within the context of the worship of the whole community.

So the psalm opens with a call to all men to praise God (vv. 1-4). In particular it recalls the great events which marked the birth of Israel: the crossing of the Sea at the Exodus from Egypt and the crossing of the Jordan at the entry into the promised land (vv. 5-7). Almost sacramentally the singers feel themselves to have been 'there' with their forefathers with whom they were one. Verses 8-12 are a reminder of the way in which the chosen people have been tested, kept under oppression and set free. If any specific incident was in mind here we can no longer know what it was. Possibly it is simply a general summary of Israel's experience.

It is in the context of this corporate thanksgiving that the psalmist can now offer his own personal thanksgiving for deliverance. All we are told is that he had been 'in trouble' and had promised a sacrificial thank-offering if God should deliver him. This was in no sense a bribe offered to God. His prayer has been heard not because of his promise but because of his sincerity. So now he will fulfil his promise.

There is an insight into the nature of worship in the very structure of this psalm. For Christians there must always be corporate thanksgiving for what Christ has done for all men and in that context each individual may bring his own thanks for what Christ has done for him personally.

1   Shout for joy to God, all the earth!

2   Sing aloud that he is glorious,
        praise him for his glory.

3   Say to God, 'What awe-inspiring things you do!
        So great is your power that your enemies cower before
            you.

4   Everyone on earth pays homage to you,
        they sing you psalms, psalms to you personally.'

5   Come and see what God has done,
        his activities fill people with awe.

6   He turned the sea into dry land,
        our forefathers crossed the river on foot;
        there we were glad he was our God.

7   In his might he rules for ever;
        he keeps a close watch on the nations,
        the rebellious had better not rise against him.

8   Bow in adoration, you peoples, to our God,
        make your voices heard in prayer to him,

9   To him who has set us on life's path
        and does not allow our feet to slip.

10 For you have tested us, God,
        you have refined us like silver.

11 You got us entangled in a hunter's net,
        you almost squeezed the life out of us.

12 You allowed horsemen to ride all over us,
        we have been through fire and water
        but you have brought us out into the open again.

13 I will enter your house with sacrifices,
        I will fulfil the vows I made to you,

14 The vows I swore, the promises I made
        when I was in trouble.

15 I will offer you choice animals in sacrifice
        and the aroma of burnt rams;
        I will bring bulls and goats.

16 Come and hear, all you who worship God,
        I will tell you what he has done for me.

17 I cried aloud to him,
        I sent up a prayer in my fear;

18 If I had been harbouring wicked thoughts
        the Lord would not have heard me.

19 But God has heard me, of that I am sure,
        he has paid attention as I have prayed.

20   Thanks be to God who has set aside
                  neither my prayer to him
                  nor his devotion to me.

✦ Psalm 67

*Though this psalm mentions the harvest in v.7 this is not the dominant
theme and is insufficient ground for regarding it as a harvest psalm. The
overall theme is one of prayer for a universal recognition of Israel's God.*

*Verses 2-3 and 8 form a framework in which the psalmist prays that
God's acts towards Israel may become the ground on which all other people
may come to acknowledge him as their God. Such an idea is not uncommon
in the Old Testament (see Isaiah 40, for example) but it crops up more frequently in the later books. The 'refrain' in vv.4-6 introduces two reasons
why they should do so; first his just rule over the whole world and second his
general provision of natural resources.*

*It is worth reminding ourselves, though sometimes Israel forgot it,
that, according to tradition, God's choice of Abraham (Genesis 12.1-3), his
choice of Israel in Egypt (Exodus 19.5-7) was not solely for Israel's benefit.
They were to be a 'light to the nations' drawing all men to God (Isaiah 42.6-
7, 49.6). This is always at least a part of the function of the people of God, to
be living evidence for the gracious activity of God among men, evidence
which just by being there will convince men that God is God.*

2   May God be gracious and enrich our lives,
                  may he radiate kindness to us,

3   So that people everywhere may know what you do
                  and all nations recognise your power to save.

4   May the peoples praise you, God,
                  may they all praise you.

5   May the nations be glad and shout for joy
          because you rule the peoples fairly
          and guide the nations in world affairs.

6   May the peoples praise you, God,
          may they all praise you.

7   Earth has yielded its harvest;
          God, our God, enriches us.

8   May God enrich our lives
          that people everywhere may worship him.

❦ Psalm 68

This is one of the most difficult psalms to understand. It is hard to detect any developing theme, so much so that some have despairingly regarded it as an 'Index of first lines' such as we find in our hymn books! However, we ought to make some attempt to interpret it as a unity and perhaps it is as well to begin with vv. 25-36 which seem to suggest a procession carrying the Ark, the chariot-throne of the invisible God (see Psalm 24), entering the Temple where the LORD was acclaimed king of the whole earth.

Once this is seen, then v.2 which speaks of God 'arising' can be taken as a recollection of the words reported to have been used when, after the events at Mount Sinai, the Israelites moved off with the LORD, invisible upon the Ark, at their head (Numbers 10.35-36). So the first verses of the psalm may anticipate the procession by looking back to that time in the wilderness (v.5). It was there that the LORD entered into covenant with them, an idea reflected in v.6, setting his people free. We have no reference to God sending rain when he appeared on Mount Sinai, but there was thunder and cloud (Exodus 19.16-25). This God of Sinai is now God of Israel, who again provides rain for his people in the promised land. The LORD does this, not Baal whom the Canaanites regarded as the rain-giver and king (see 1 Kings 18 as a contest between the LORD and Baal about the ability to end the drought).

Verses 12-15 then promise victory in much the same way as the pres-

ence of the LORD on the Ark was expected to against the Philistines (1 Samuel 4). Verses 16-24 probably recall the capture of Jerusalem, followed by the bringing of the Ark into the city by David and the LORD's enthronement there (1 Samuel 5-7) which involved the defeat of enemies like the Philistines.

So now the procession celebrating these events can move off (vv. 25-29). The references to Zebulun and Naphtali in the procession may suggest a date before the Northern tribes seceded on the death of Solomon, unless it is simply an echo of what happened in the first procession. The kings bearing gifts suggests that the LORD is the great King to whom others bring tribute (30-32). The psalm ends with a hymn of praise (vv. 33-36).

Interpreted in this way the psalm indicates the need felt by the Israelites for activities in worship which were accompanied by words which reminded the people of what they were celebrating and why, and which allowed them to share, in a sense, in the events which they recalled.

The actions and the words of the Eucharist perform a similar function for Christians today.

2   When God arises his enemies will scatter.
    Those who hate him will run away from him.

3   Like smoke driven by the wind,
    like wax melting before a fire,
    so the wicked will perish before God.

4   But those who do right will be happy;
    they will rejoice in God's presence,
    they will overflow with happiness.

5   Sing to God, sing psalms to him;
    make way for him who rides through the deserts.
    Be glad and rejoice in the LORD's presence.

6   A father to orphans, defender of widows,
    so is God in the holy place where he lives.

7   God provides the lonely with a home,
    he sets prisoners free and makes them prosperous;
    but those who rebel against him live in a scorched land.

8   God, when you went out at the head of your people,
         when you marched through the waste lands,

9   The earth shook, the heavens opened with rain
         at the presence of God, the God of Sinai,
         at the presence of God, the God of Israel.

10   Generously you provide rain, God,
         for your own land when it is parched,
         the land which you made your own.

11   Those to whom you gave life are settled in it;
         in your goodness, God, you provide for the poor.

12   The Lord himself makes a promise,
         'The women will bring news of a great army.

13   The kings and their armies are in full flight,
         housewives will share out the spoil

14   Though they lie among their hearth stones
         — a dove with wings overlaid with silver
         and feathers of pale green and gold —

15   When the Almighty scatters kings
         like a snowfall on Mount Zalmon.'

16   How high is the mountain of Bashan!
         How many are its peaks!

17   Why do you look down,
         you many peaks of Bashan,
     on the mountain where God is pleased to live,
         where indeed the LORD will reside for ever?

18   God's chariots number twice ten thousand,
         thousands upon thousands;
         with them you came from Sinai on your holy throne.

19   You went up on the high hill; you took many captives;
         you received tribute from men,

you went to live there, LORD God,
>   while rebels were angry.

20   Thanks be to the Lord every day!
>   He bears our burdens;
>   God is the one who saves us.

21   God is good who acts to save us,
>   death's extremities belong to the LORD, our God.

22   Surely God will crush the heads of his enemies,
>   the crowns of those who strut about in their sin.

23   The Lord said, 'From as far as Bashan I will bring them back,
>   I will bring them back from the depths of the sea,

24   So that you may trample them to death
>   and dogs, with their tongues out, thirst for their blood.'

25   They see your processions, God,
>   the processions of my God, my King, into the sanctuary.

26   Singers lead the way, followed by musicians,
>   and between them, girls playing cymbals.

27   In the assembled throng they praise God,
>   the LORD who comes from Israel's fountain.

28   There is Benjamin, a small tribe,
>   in command at their head,
>   with the princes of Judah, full of excitement,
>   and the princes of Zebulun and Naphtali.

29   He has given orders concerning your 'Strength', God,
>   your mighty Ark which you made for us.

30   Because of your Temple high in Jerusalem
>   kings are bearing gifts to you.

31   Rebuke the cattle of the marsh,
>   the herd of bulls with their calves,

which stampeded into the Sea of Reeds.
        Scatter the nations which enjoy war.

32   Tribute will come quickly from Egypt,
        Ethiopia will speedily pay his dues.

33   Sing to God, you kingdoms of the earth,
        sing psalms to the Lord,

34   To him who rides through the highest and most ancient
            heavens.
        Listen! He speaks in his mighty thunder.

35   Praise God for his strength;
        his might extends over all Israel,
        his strength over the clouds in the sky.

36   Reverence for God is due from his sanctuary;
        it is Israel's God who gives superhuman strength and
            power.
    Thanks be to God!

Psalm 69

*This rather long psalm is yet another complaint from an individual
followed by an expression of praise once he feels assured of deliverance. His
present troubles are described in rich metaphors which suggest that he feels
he has almost reached the point of death (vv. 2-4), but it is people's attitude
towards him which causes him even greater distress (vv. 5-13). His prayer
that others may not be involved in his shame and his assertion that he is in
disgrace on account of God (vv. 7-8) probably shows that the psalmist held
some high position in society, though we cannot know what it was. At this
point it is not so much enemies who bother him; it is the attitude of friends
and relations (vv. 9-13). The prayer for deliverance which follows is possible
because he still believes in God's devotion (vv. 14-19).*

At v.20, however, he does turn to his 'enemies'. These verses (20-29) are probably not directed against his relations and close friends. Yet, as we have seen in other psalms, the enemies cannot be identified beyond saying that they were fellow-Israelites from whom he expected something better (v.21). Consequently the divine judgement which he calls down upon them is extremely severe. It consists of complete deprivation, even of life itself (vv.23-29).

Briefly in v.30 he returns to his own complaint and prayer. As in many other psalms the change of mood to one of confidence in God and praise (v.31ff.) is sudden and may have been brought about by some act or word giving him assurance. At any rate his thanks will be expressed in song and this genuine response is better than, but not necessarily a substitute for, sacrifice (vv.31-32. See also Psalms 50 and 51). His own deliverance is an encouragement to others who are in distress (vv.33-34).

The closing verses of the psalm (35-37) suggest that the people are now exiled and the cities in ruins. It seems likely that when this psalm was sung during the exile in Babylon these verses were added to ensure its relevance for these new circumstances. Not only does God restore individuals who call to him; he also restores the whole community. Verse 34 favours such an interpretation, as poverty and imprisonment can be seen as metaphors describing the Exile.

We have discussed this attitude of vengeance towards enemies in connection with previous psalms (see, for example, Psalms 5 and 54). But here we find again that belief in the grace and goodness of God which enables a person not only to endure, but to come through hardship triumphantly.

2   Save me, God!
      For the waters have reached up to my neck.

3   I have sunk in deep mud
      where there is no firm ground;
   my way has taken me into deep water
      where the current has swept over me.

4   I am tired out with calling to you,
      my throat burns like a fire,
   my eyes are worn out
      with watching for you.

5 There are more people who hate me without reason
        than I have hairs on my head.
All too many would like to do away with me;
        they are my enemies and would like to do away with me.
Can I possibly pay back
        what I have not stolen?

6 God, you know how foolish I have been;
        I cannot hide my guilty actions from you.

7 Let no one who waits for you be ashamed because of me, LORD
        of hosts;
        let no one who seeks you ever be disgraced by me.

8 For it is on your account that I have borne disgrace
        and my face has been covered with shame.

9 I have become a stranger to my family,
        a foreigner to my own brothers.

10 The jealousy of those in your family has consumed me,
        the insults of those who insult you have fallen on me.

11 I wept and fasted for all I was worth
        but all I received was insults.

12 I used sackcloth for my clothing
        and became a laughing stock to them.

13 Men sit just inside the gate talking about me,
        when they have had a few drinks they make up songs
        about me.

14 For my part, I will offer my prayer to you, LORD,
        at a time you approve, God.
Great is your devotion! Answer me!
        Certain is your deliverance.

15 Rescue me from the mud; keep me from sinking in it.
        Let me be rescued from those who hate me,
        and from the deep waters.

16 Prevent the current from sweeping over me,
  the deep water from engulfing me,
  the pit of death from closing its mouth over me.

17 Answer me, LORD, so rich is your devotion;
  so great is your compassion, turn to me!

18 Do not hide your face from me,
  I am in such distress, answer me quickly!

19 Draw near to me, save my life;
  to confound my enemies, rescue me.

20 You know the insults I have to bear,
  my shame and my disgrace;
  you are aware of all my difficulties.

21 Insults have left me a broken man,
  I am sick with fear;
 I looked for someone to sympathise,
  but there was no one,
 for some who would comfort me,
  but I found none.

22 They gave me poison for food
  and vinegar to drink to quench my thirst.

23 May they be caught up in disaster through the food they eat,
  may they be lured on by their sacred feasts.

24 May no light enter their eyes; stop them from seeing,
  give them continual pain; make them collapse.

25 Pour out your indignation on them,
  may your rage catch up with them.

26 May their home become like a deserted camp,
  like tents with no one to live in them.

27 They never leave alone those you have struck down,
       they keep on talking about the pain of those you have
         wounded.

28 Pass sentence on them for their sins,
       exclude them from your verdict of innocence.

29 Erase their names from the record of those who are to live,
       do not list them among the innocent.

30 As for me, I am in trouble and pain;
       you can save me, God; lift me up to safety.

31 I will praise God with a song,
       I will make known his greatness in my praise.

32 The LORD will prefer this to an ox
       or a bull complete with horns and hooves.

33 Because of what they have seen
       those who are oppressed can be glad;
     as for those who seek God in worship,
       their courage will be revived.

34 For the LORD listens to those living in poverty,
       and does not disregard those in prison.

35 Let heaven and earth praise him,
       the seas and all that swim in them.

36 For God will save Zion,
       he will rebuild the cities of Judah,
         his people will live there and take possession.

37 His servants' children will inherit the land
       and those who love him will live there.

✑ Psalm 70

This short psalm was included as part of Psalm 40 (vv. 14-18) and comments were offered on it at that point.

2 Do me a favour, God, and deliver me,
  come quickly, LORD, and help me.

3 May those who seek my life
  be covered with shame and embarrassment.
May those who are glad at my misfortune
  be turned away in disgrace.

4 May those who gloat over me, saying 'Ha, ha!'
  be appalled at the shame they suffer.

5 May all who come to worship you
  find joy and gladness in your presence.
May those who love you because you save them
  never stop saying 'God is great'.

6 May God come quickly to me
  poor and needy as I am.
You are my helper and my rescuer;
  come, LORD, without delay.

✑ Psalm 71

This is the psalm of an older man (vv. 9 and 18) who has learned to trust and be confident in God in spite of all the difficulties that life brings. He uses words at the beginning which strongly resemble those of Psalm 31. Although at this point in his life he is in some trouble (vv. 9-12) it is not the trouble which dominates the psalm nor the prayers for help; it is his confi-

dence in God which has come through constant reflection on the words used in worship (vv.1-3), as well as through his own past experience (vv.5-7). Indeed his life so far has been a 'sign' to others of God's power (v.7).

Now other people may taunt him by suggesting that God has abandoned him (v.11), but he prays that those who seek to add to his troubles in this way may be put to shame when they discover how wrong they were (vv.12-13).

At v.14 he turns away from his own troubles and from his enemies towards God, remembering all that he has done. He has both learned (v.17) and retold (vv.15-16) the story of God's faithfulness to his people. Even in older age and during difficulty he will go on doing so (v.18). So confidence in the present circumstances breaks out again and turns into a song of praise (vv.19-24).

The psalm, then, reminds us of three great truths. First, what we hear and learn in worship about the things God has done, whether it be in the Exodus or in Christ, stands us in good stead when trouble comes. Second, as age creeps on we are the more able to look back on our own experience and trace the hand of God at work in it. Third, even as we get older we can still bear our testimony to God through the confidence we show in adversity and through the words we sing to God and speak to others.

1   I find my security in you, LORD,
          never let me be covered with shame.

2   You always do what is right,
          so rescue me and set me free.
          Listen attentively to me and save me.

3   Be my rock where I can find security,
          be my fortress and save me;
          indeed you are my rock and fortress.

4   My God, set me free from the power of the wicked,
          from the grasp of unjust and cruel men.

5   For you alone give me hope, LORD,
          I have trusted in you since my early days.

6   I have leaned on you since birth,
          when you delivered me from my mother's womb.
          I praise you continually.

7 For many years my life has been a sign of your power,
         you shelter me with your strength.

8 I am full of praise for you all day long
         and tell how magnificent you are.

9 Do not throw me aside in old age,
         do not abandon me when my strength has gone,

10 For my enemies talk about me,
         those who are out to kill me discuss how to do it,

11 Saying, 'God has abandoned him;
         chase him and catch hold of him,
         for there is no one to rescue him from us.'

12 God, do not stand at a distance from me,
         my God, help me quickly.

13 Let them be covered with shame and embarrassment
         who threaten my life,
     Let them be enveloped in reproach and disgrace
         who seek to harm me.

14 I will always wait expectantly for you
         and offer you praise again and again.

15 Daily I will retell the story of your deeds,
         how you have done what is right and saved us,
         though I do not know all you have done.

16 I will come with the mighty acts of the Lord GOD on my lips,
         I will remind people that you alone do what is right.

17 You have taught me, God, from my early days,
         up to this very moment I have told how magnificent you
             are.

18 So now that I am old and my hair is grey
         do not abandon me, God,
     as long as I proclaim your strength to my peers,
         your power to everyone who enters your house.

19   Your goodness to us, God, knows no bounds,
         you have done great things.
         Who is like you, God?

20   You have made me see much terrible trouble
         but you will revive me.
     From the deep underground waters
         you will lift me up again.

21   You will make me greater than ever
         and surround me with your comfort.

22   I will praise you on the lute
         for your faithfulness, God;
     I will sing you psalms to the harp,
         Holy One of Israel.

23   I will shout for joy as I play for you,
         I myself whom you have rescued.

24   All day long I will sing of your goodness to me,
         for those who seek to harm me are ashamed,
         yes, they stand disgraced.

✤ Psalm 72

The whole of this psalm is a prayer for the king, not so much for his personal well-being, but that he may rule in such a way as to bring prosperity to the whole nation. The first two verses set out clearly what this means. The king is responsible for seeing that justice prevails in his kingdom. This means more than keeping an eye on the law courts; it means ensuring that social life is ordered in such a way that no one is neglected, oppressed or deprived. So there is a special mention of the poor both at the outset and again in vv. 4, 12-14. It is recognised, however, that the ability to rule like this is a gift from God and the opening lines are a prayer that this gift may be given to the king. In Isaiah 11, similarly, the coming king's just rule is dependent on the gift of the spirit of God, the divine endowment and power. In the psalm the justice which the king is to exercise is measured against the justice of God himself. It is this divine justice which the king, as God's adopted son (see Psalm 2.7), must maintain.

When this is done then prosperity will come to the land (again see Isaiah 11) and its influence in the international sphere will be great (vv.8-11, 15).

Of course, Judah never had such a king but it was a hope and a prayer expressed at the coronation of each new monarch. When, during the exile in Babylon, the monarchy ceased then the hope of a future king remained and the psalm became 'messianic'. Not unnaturally Christians have seen the rule of Christ reflected here, believing that in him the Messianic king has come.

The final verses attached to this psalm (vv.18-20) are the doxology which closes the Second Book of the Psalms (see Psalm 41.13).

1   God, endow the king with justice like yours,
        the royal son with your concern for the right,

2   So that he may judge your people rightly,
        and secure justice for your poor.

3   Then the mountains will hold prosperity
        and the hills be nourished by your goodness.

4   May he secure justice for the poor among his people,
        may he give help to those who are needy,
        may he crush the oppressor.

5   May he live long alongside the sun
        and in the presence of the moon for ever.

6   May he be like rain which falls on the grass,
        like heavy showers which water the ground.

7   May goodness flourish throughout his lifetime,
        and great prosperity until the moon wears out.

8   May his rule extend from sea to sea,
        from the river to the ends of the earth.

9 May desert peoples bow low before him,
        may his enemies lick the dust.

10 May the kings of Tarshish and the coastlands bring gifts,
        may the kings of Sheba and Seba present their tribute.

11 May every king make obeisance to him,
        may every nation become subject to him.

12 May he rescue the poor who cry for help
        and the distressed who have no helper.

13 May he have pity on the poor and needy
        and save the lives of those in need.

14 May he free them from oppression and violence,
        may he regard their lives as precious.

15 Long may he live!
        May he receive gifts of gold from Sheba,
  may prayers be offered for him continually,
        may blessing be sought for him all day long.

16 May there be an abundance of corn in the land,
        may it wave in the wind on the hill tops,
  may its ears be as heavy as those on Lebanon,
        may its sheaves stand as thick as grass in the field.

17 May his fame last for ever,
        may it spread everywhere openly,
  may people wish for each other prosperity like his,
        may all nations call him happy.

              *   *   *

18 Thanks be to the Lord GOD, the God of Israel,
        for he alone does marvellous things.

19 Thanks be to the glorious name of God for ever,
        his glory fills the earth.
  Amen and Amen.

20 The end of the prayers of David, son of Jesse.

🎐 Psalm 73

This psalm is composed by a realist who looks honestly at his own and other people's experience of life and finds that what he sees does not correspond with what he has been brought up to believe. The view that those who do right prosper and those who do wrong suffer is common enough in the Old Testament and it may have served to encourage good behaviour, but sometimes it became elevated into a doctrinal statement regarded as universally true.

This psalmist, however, has seen the prosperity of the wicked and has even become jealous of it (vv.2-12), especially since he has sought to do right and finds himself at a disadvantage (vv.13-15). Why this should be he cannot understand — until he goes to worship (vv.16-17). There something happens which changes his perception. It is true that the wicked do get their deserts in due course and their present prosperity is transitory (vv.18-20). Without any belief in life beyond this present one God's justice can only be vindicated if the wicked do eventually suffer in this life. To this extent the psalmist doesn't press the issue as far as the writers of Job and Ecclesiastes who recognise that there are some wicked people who never do get their deserts. On the other hand through worship, if not through reason, he comes to understand that the highest good is to know oneself to be in the presence of God and that this can be the experience even of those dogged by misfortune.

Some interpreters see v.24 as at least opening up the possibility of life beyond death (see Psalm 49.16). They understand the Hebrew word here translated as 'place of honour' as meaning 'glory', as it often does, and take this to refer to some after-life. Far more likely the psalmist is concerned with this life in which closeness to God (v.28) is worth more than all the apparent prosperity of the wicked.

Of course, Christians, whose belief in a life after death is based on the promise and the resurrection of Jesus, may say that living in the presence of God here and now leads on to living in his presence hereafter, since 'nothing can separate us. . . .' (Romans 8.38-39).

1 God is good indeed to Israel,
     to those whose intentions are honourable.

2 I was deflected from my path a little,
      I was beginning to wander off it;

3 For I became jealous of those who had so much to boast about
      when I saw how well the wicked get on.

4 They never have any pain,
      they are fully fit and prosperous-looking.

5 They escape the trouble that comes to others,
      they do not fall ill like the rest of mankind.

6 Therefore they wear their pride like a necklace,
      they put on violence like a robe.

7 Their eyes bulge at the thought of food
      as visions of it pass before them.

8 They make fun of people and slander them;
      from their exalted position they threaten with oppression.

9 They speak their words for the heavens to hear,
      they parade their mocking throughout the earth.

10 So they swear they will never know pain
      but will meet with days of plenty.

11 They say, 'How can God know?
      The Most High knows nothing!'

12 See how wicked these men are!
      Yet, always comfortable, they grow still richer.

13 I have kept my thoughts free from evil,
      I have washed my hands to show my innocence,
      but all to no avail.

14 I am struck down all day long,
      every morning my punishment awaits me.

15 If I had said, 'Let me go on talking in this vein'
      why, I should have been a traitor to the rest of your
            family.

16 When I think, 'I will get to the bottom of this'
  it seems too difficult for me

17 Until I enter God's sacred courts,
  then I understand what will happen to the wicked.

18 Surely you will ruin them with their empty promises,
  and overthrow them with their beguiling words.

19 How suddenly they are consigned to destruction,
  swept away and finally destroyed

20 As a dream disappears, Lord, at the moment of waking,
  as visions are dismissed when sleepers are roused.

21 But my thoughts have become embittered,
  and I am hurt through and through.

22 All unawares, I too have become boorish,
  in your presence I am like stupid cattle.

23 Yet I am always with you,
  you have grasped me firmly with your hand.

24 You give me good advice and lead me on,
  and in the end you will conduct me to a place of honour.

25 Who else is there in heaven to help me?
  When I am with you I have all I could wish for.

26 My whole being pines for you,
  the Rock on which I can rest my mind.
  You have given yourself to me, God, for ever.

27 Now see! Those who keep their distance from you will perish,
  you will destroy all who are faithless to you.

28 For my part, I like to be close to God,
  I take refuge in the LORD, my God,
  so that I may tell all you have done.

❧ Psalm 74

In this psalm we have a description of the troubles which have befallen Judah and Jerusalem and this makes it virtually certain that it was sung after the Fall of Jerusalem in 587 BC, possibly on the site of the ruined Temple. There is no mention of the fact that some people have been taken into exile. It is acknowledged that the devastation (vv.3-8) is due to God's anger and rejection of the people he had once chosen (v.1). The call to re-member (v.2) is an appeal to God not only to recall that he had chosen them but to act now on the basis of that. Yet there is nothing and no one to indicate how long this devastation will last (v.9) and how long God will seem to be utterly powerless (vv.10-11).

Not that the psalmist thinks he is powerless. Using the imagery of popu-lar mythology he proclaims God as King (v.12), Creator (vv.13-14) and sustainer of the world (vv.15-17). But since the powerful conquerors now make fun of God he pleads with God to prove them wrong by restoring his people (vv.18-23).

We must assume, however, that the psalm was used also on other occasions of national disaster and particularly in the 2nd century at the time of the Maccabaean revolt when Jerusalem was again destroyed.

Prophets like Amos (3.2) had said that the fact that Israel was the chosen people of God would not guarantee them security but would, in fact, make punishment more certain if they turned their backs on God. Jeremiah had declared that Jerusalem was no guarantee of security either (7.4) and like his predecessor Micah predicted the fall of the city (26.18). Yet this psalm shows no recognition that what has now happened is a judgement on Judah for sin.

It is worth remarking, however, that even in the face of such adversity God's power and justice are never questioned.

1   Why, O God? Have you rejected us for ever?
      Why does your rage smoulder against your own flock?

2   Remember the company you assembled long ago,
      whom you redeemed to be your own special tribe.
      Remember Mount Zion where you have lived.

3 Pick your way through never ending ruins,
      all the damage the enemy has caused in the sanctuary.

4 Within your meeting place your foes have cheered their
          victory,
      they have set up their standards as signs of it.

5 They broke down the door leading to the stairs,
      its interwoven timbers they cut with axes.

6 They tore out the carvings completely
      and smashed them with hatchet and pick-axe.

7 They sent your sanctuary up in flames,
      they profaned the place where you meet us.

8 They said to themselves, 'We will stamp them out completely',
      so they burned all those whom God appointed in the
          land.

9 We can see no sign; there are no prophets left;
      we have no one who knows how long this will last.

10 How long, God, will the enemy make fun of you?
      Will he offer you personal insults for ever?

11 Why do you restrain your hand?
      Why do you keep it firmly behind your back?

12 But you, God, have been my king from the first,
      winning victories throughout the earth.

13 You, by your strength, split the sea-god in two,
      you smashed the heads of the sea-dragon.

14 You crushed the heads of Leviathan
      and gave him as food to sailors.

15 You opened up springs and streams,
      you dried up rivers which never run dry.

16   Both day and night are in your power,
          you set in place both moon and sun.

17   You decided where the earth should end,
          you made both summer and winter.

18   Remember this, LORD; enemies make fun of you,
          senseless people offer you personal insults.

19   Do not leave your 'dove' to the wild beasts,
          never forget your persecuted people.

20   Attend to those who feed on oppression;
          violence lurks in every dark corner of the land.

21   Let your oppressed people no longer feel ashamed,
          let the poor and needy praise you.

22   Arise, God, and prosecute your case,
          remember how senscless people make fun of you.

23   No longer ignore the noise your opponents make,
          the ceaseless shouting of those hostile to you.

⁊ Psalm 75

This psalm is best understood as a liturgical piece in which more than one person share. The opening verse (2) sets the scene in worship offered by the community where the congregation reminds itself of God's past actions on its behalf.

Verses 3-9 are spoken by a prophet working in the Temple who begins by passing on a message from God himself (vv. 3-5). The message is that God is in charge of all things, chooses the right time to act and makes sure that justice is done. The temptation is for men to think this is their prerogative. The prophet then follows this with his own comments, reinforcing the message (vv.6-9).

Either the prophet or another of the worshippers then declares his

166

intention to continue his praise and proclamation (v.10) and the psalm concludes with another word of God, presumably coming from the prophet, assuring that right and wrong will be appropriately rewarded.

The psalm therefore makes comparison between God and men which puts human beings in their proper place and forbids them from taking to themselves those tasks and responsibilities which rightly belong to God (see also Psalm 8).

2   We praise you, God, we praise you,
      you are near to us when your wonderful deeds are recited.

3   'I will take advantage of the time appointed,
      I myself will administer justice fairly.

4   When the earth, with its inhabitants, is collapsing
      it is I who hold firm the pillars it rests on.

5   I said to those who boast, "Stop boasting",
      and to the wicked, "Do not overestimate yourselves".'

6   Do not estimate yourselves so highly,
      do not speak with such arrogance,

7   For nothing from the East or the West,
      nothing from the desert can make men important,

8   But only God, who is judge,
      who humbles one and makes another important.

9   For the LORD holds a cup in his hand,
      full of fermented wine, well-spiced.
   He will pour it out for all the wicked in the land,
      and they will drink it to the dregs.

10   As for me, my proclamation will never cease,
      I will sing psalms to the God of Jacob.

11   I will reduce the wicked to nothing
        while those who do right will reach the
        heights

ꙮ Psalm 76

The obvious themes of this psalm are the majesty and power of God and his authority to judge all peoples. It seems to have in mind the traditions about the capture of Jerusalem (2 Samuel 5 and 6). Salem is an abbreviated form found only here and in Genesis 14.18. The word suggests peace or prosperity, but may possibly have been a title for the Canaanite god of the city prior to its capture by David. In any case Jerusalem is the place where God now lives, his earthly headquarters, though his real home is in heaven (v.9).

It is difficult to pin-point the occasion for which the psalm was written. It may have been as a thanksgiving for some deliverance of the city from enemy attack. On the other hand some see behind it a dramatic representation in worship of the LORD's victory over foreign gods and peoples, perhaps associated with his kingship (see Psalm 47).

The first three and last two verses speak of God in the third person and are therefore addressed to the people generally. Verses 5-11 are addressed directly to God, though they continue the sense of vv.2-4. It may be, therefore, that this change of person is of the kind which can and frequently does occur in prayer and not too much should be made of it. Verses 12-13 are quite clearly a call to all nations to make an appropriate response to God who has been characterised as universal King and Judge in Jerusalem.

The description of God in such war-like language may be something of an embarrassment to us today. For the people of Old Testament days it simply emphasised his power and greatness and it should now be seen in that light. It is worth noticing that when God is depicted as Judge his judgement is in favour of those who are humiliated (v.11). In the Old Testament, as in the New, God is seen as the helper of the poor and oppressed.

2   God is famous in Judah,
        in Israel his renown is great.

3 He came to live in Salem
  and made his home in Zion.

4 There he broke the flashing arrows,
  shields and swords, weapons of war.

5 You are bathed in light and majesty,
  coming from the hills where you caught your prey.

6 Resolute soldiers were despoiled,
  they sank to their final sleep;
  the elite troops were left powerless.

7 By your stern command, God of Jacob,
  both horse and rider were stunned.

8 You, God, how awesome you are!
  Who can hold his ground before you
  when your anger is so fierce?

9 When you announced your verdict from heaven
  earth was afraid and silent,

10 When you rose to pass judgement, God,
  in favour of those humiliated on earth.

11 Human wrath will itself confess your greatness,
  whoever survives divine wrath you will wear as your belt.

12 Fulfil the vows you have made to the LORD, your God;
  from all sides let men bring gifts in awe.

13 He cuts princes down to size
  and inspires awe among the kings of the earth.

✵ Psalm 77

Once more we find a psalmist who is in deep distress, though we are not told its nature. It may be some personal trouble, in which case the psalmist finds confidence by reflecting on God's dealings with the whole people of Israel. Alternatively it may be that the psalmist is a representative figure, the king or some leader of the worshipping community, who is expressing both his own and his people's distress. The most troublesome thing about his situation was that it seemed to contradict the understanding of God he had gained from his knowledge of the past (v.6). He had come to believe in a God who was present, whose devotion was constant, whose promises were trustworthy (vv.7-11). So his concern is not so much with his outward circumstances as with the inner doubts which are raised about his understanding of God. It is, we may say, a theological problem.

All this, however, was in the past. Set over against these doubts are the great acts of God which he and his people recall in worship. It is here that reflection on the nation's past and God's part in it stimulates confidence and faith. So vv.12-22 recall, first in general terms (vv.12-15) and then in terms of the Exodus and the crossing of the sea, the miraculous power of God exercised on behalf of his people. The language he uses to describe these events is highly imaginative. In v.17 the waters may be either the waters of the Red Sea or the waters of chaos which God subdued. Verses 18-19 use the traditional language used to describe the appearing of God (see Exodus 19.16-18, Psalm 18.7-16). Verses 20-21 clearly refer to the Exodus and the wilderness wanderings. Here, although God was at work, 'his footsteps could not be seen' and his people had to follow in trust as sheep follow a shepherd.

So in his doubts about the presence of God the psalmist has learned to trust where he cannot see. Again, then, the psalm reminds us of the importance of reflecting in worship on those events which are the basis of our faith. This enables us to continue to believe in spite of our doubts and fears.

2   I raise my voice and cry to God,
        I raise my voice and he hears me.

3   When I was in distress I sought the Lord;
        my hand reached out to him all night long,
        without ever going numb;
    my inmost being refused to be comforted.

4 I called to God and sighed,
> I thought about him and my spirits drooped.

5 I kept my eyes tightly closed
> and was too troubled to speak.

6 I thought back to the olden days,
> I recalled bygone years.

7 In the night I plucked the strings of my mind,
> I thought deeply and searched for an answer.

8 'Will the Lord turn his back on me for ever?
> Will he go on being displeased with me?

9 Has his devotion come to an end for good?
> Has his promise failed for all time?

10 Has God forgotten how to be gracious?
> In his anger has he withheld his mercies?'

11 I thought, 'Is it meant to wound me?
> Is the Most High using his power in a new way?'

12 I will remember what the LORD has done,
> yes, I will remember your marvellous deeds in days gone by.

13 I will call to mind all you have done,
> I will think deeply about your achievements.

14 All you do, God, is done because you are holy;
> who is a great god like God?

15 You are the God who works wonders,
> you show your power among the peoples.

16 You set your people free, using your strong arm,
> the descendants of Jacob and Joseph.

17 The waters saw you, God,
> the waters saw you and became agitated,
> the very ocean depths boiled up.

18 Rain poured from the clouds,
   the skies crashed with thunder,
   your lightning zig-zagged across the sky.

19 The crash of your thunder rolled round,
   lightning lit up the whole world,
   the earth trembled and shook.

20 You made your way through the sea,
   you followed your path through the deep waters,
   yet your footsteps could not be seen.

21 You led your people like a flock of sheep
   with Moses and Aaron in charge.

❧ Psalm 78

The purpose of this psalm is clearly set out in the first seven verses. It is to teach each generation what God has done for Israel and how Israel responded with disobedience so that they may now make the correct response of obedience. Exodus 13.11-16 (also Deut. 6.20-25) lays down that such teaching should be passed on from father to son at the Feast of Unleavened Bread. After 621 BC when King Josiah laid down that no sacrifice could be made outside Jerusalem, Passover was combined with this feast and the practice of retelling the events of the Exodus from Egypt has continued at Passover ever since. Much of the language of the psalm is reminiscent of that of Deuteronomy and it may well be that the psalm was used at the joint Feast after 621, since Josiah's reforms seem to have been based upon a book found in the Temple which many think was at least part of Deuteronomy.

The 'riddle' for the psalmist is why Israel should have been so disobedient in the face of all that God had done. He refers to the Exodus events in vv.8-16 and to Israel's rebellion in vv.17-19. Then, when God provided water from the rock in the desert they couldn't trust him to provide food (v.20). He gave it to them anyway (vv.21-29), but they still were not satisfied (v.30). His punishment (vv.31-33) brought about a change of heart but only temporarily. *Still God forgave them (vv.34-39). So the psalmist takes them back again through the plagues in Egypt, the Exodus, the wanderings, the entry into Canaan (vv.40-55). Still they were rebellious (vv.56-58) and so the sanctuary at Shiloh was destroyed and the Ark captured (vv.60-64 — see also 1 Samuel 3-4). The rejection of Joseph and Ephraim (v.67) refers either to the rejection of Saul as king (1 Samuel 15.26, 16.13-14) — although he was actually a Benjaminite — or to the secession of the Northern Kingdom of Israel in 922 BC and its destruction in 722 BC. The concluding verses are a reminder of how Judah and Jerusalem were chosen with David as King.*

The failure to respond in trust and obedience to what God has done, either in Exodus or in Christ, remains a riddle. The psalm teaches us about the patience of God and the need for us to offer the proper response to his grace and goodness.

1   Listen, my people, to my teaching,
      pay attention to what I say.

2   I will tell you a story from tradition,
      I will speak about the riddles of the past.

3   We have heard and known of them
      because our fathers told them to us.

4   We will not hide them from our children,
      but will pass on to coming generations
   the mighty deeds of the LORD, for which he is to be praised,
      and all the wonders he has performed.

5   He laid down rules for those in Jacob
      and set out his law in Israel;
   he gave orders to our fathers
      to teach them to their children

6   So that the next generation might know them,
      children yet to be born,
   and they in turn might tell them to their children

7   Who may then have confidence in God,
      not forgetting what he has done,
      but rather keeping his commandments.

8   Then they will not be like their fathers,
        a generation both stubborn and rebellious,
  a generation which lost its grip
        and became unfaithful to God.

9   The Ephraimites, who fought with bow and arrow,
        turned tail when war broke out.

10   They did not keep God's covenant,
        but refused to live by his law.

11   They forgot what he had done,
        the miracles he had shown them.

12   Before their fathers' very eyes he had performed a miracle
        in the land of Egypt, in the plains of Zoan.

13   He divided the sea and led them through it,
        piling up the waters on either side of them.

14   He guided them by a cloud in the daytime,
        and throughout the night by a fire-like light.

15   He split open rocks in the desert,
        providing them with water as plentiful as the
            underground seas.

16   He made streams emerge from the rock,
        causing them to flow down like rivers.

17   But they sinned against him yet again,
        rebelling against the Most High in the desert.

18   They wilfully threw out a challenge to God,
        demanding food to satisfy their appetites.

19   They spoke out in opposition to God,
        'Can God lay a table in the desert?

20   Admittedly, when he struck the rock
        water gushed out in torrents,

but can he also give bread?
>And can he provide meat for his people?'

21 So, when the LORD heard them he was furious,
>his anger flared like a fire against Jacob,
>his fury mounted against Israel,

22 Because they did not rely on God
>and had no faith in his power to save them.

23 Then he gave orders to the sky above
>and opened the doors of heaven.

24 He made it rain 'Manna' upon them
>and gave them heaven-sent corn.

25 So human beings ate the food of angels;
>God sent them as much as they could eat.

26 He made the East wind get up in the sky,
>he propelled the South wind by his power.

27 He rained down on them meat like a dust-storm,
>birds on the wing like sand on the sea-shore.

28 He made them settle inside the camp,
>all round where they were living.

29 They ate until they could eat no more,
>as much as they wanted he sent them.

30 But when they went on craving for more
>while their food was still in their mouths

31 God's anger welled up against them;
>he killed off their most vigorous men
>and laid low the Israelite elite.

32 In spite of all this they still sinned again,
>and would not believe he could work such wonders.

33 So he brought their lives to a fruitless end,
        and their years to a fearful finish.

34 As he killed some, others sought to worship him;
        they turned and looked to God eagerly.

35 They remembered that God had made them safe,
        that God Most High had set them free.

36 They addressed him with flattery
        and lied when they spoke to him.

37 They were not constant in their loyalty to him,
        nor were they faithful to his covenant.

38 Yet God had mercy on them;
        he forgave their sin and did not destroy them,
    he restrained his anger many times
        and kept his fury under full control.

39 He remembered that they were only men,
        like wind which goes on its way and does not return.

40 How often they defied him in the desert,
        and hurt him in the wasteland.

41 They challenged God again and again
        and pained the Holy One of Israel.

42 They did not remember the power he displayed
        when he set them free from a hostile people,

43 How he showed signs of his power in Egypt
        and demonstrated it in the plains of Zoan.

44 He turned their rivers into blood
        and made their streams undrinkable.

45 He sent swarms of flies which bit them badly
        and frogs which ruined them.

46 He handed their harvest over to the locusts,
       their produce to swarms of them.

47 He killed their vines with hail
       and their fig trees with frost.

48 He surrendered their cattle to the hail
       and their flocks to the thunder flash.

49 He let loose his blazing anger upon them,
       wrath, fury and hostility,
       sending these as messengers of disaster.

50 He removed all obstacles to his anger,
       he did not keep them back from death
       but surrendered their lives to the plague.

51 He struck down all the eldest sons in Egypt,
       the first fruits of virility in the Hamite homes.

52 He led out his people like sheep
       and guided them like a flock in the desert.

53 He led them safely and unafraid
       while the sea overwhelmed their enemies.

54 He brought them over the border of his holy land,
       to this mountain which he gained by his own power.

55 He drove out the other nations before them
       and shared out the territory they should possess,
       settling the tribes of Israel in their homes.

56 Still they challenged God Most High,
       they rebelled and would not obey his decrees.

57 They were disobedient and treacherous like their ancestors,
       they were as perverse as a faulty bow.

58 They aroused his anger with their heathen shrines,
       his jealousy with their images.

59 When he heard them he was furious
   and rejected Israel completely.

60 He left his home in Shiloh,
   the tent where he lived among men.

61 He allowed the symbol of his power to be captured,
   his glorious Ark to fall into enemy hands.

62 He was so furious with his people
   that he surrendered them to the enemy sword.

63 Young men in their prime were burnt to death,
   girls had no one to sing their praises.

64 Priests were killed by enemy swords,
   widows could no longer weep.

65 Then the LORD arose, like a sleeper at dawn,
   like a warrior made noisy by wine.

66 He afflicted his enemies on the back-side
   and made them ashamed ever after.

67 But he rejected the family of Joseph,
   he did not choose the tribe of Ephraim;

68 Instead he chose the tribe of Judah   ·
   and Mount Zion which he loved.

69 He built his sanctuary as high as the heavens
   on foundations as long-lasting as the earth's.

70 He chose David as his servant
   and took him from the sheepfolds.

71 He brought him from tending the ewes
   to shepherd his people Jacob,
   Israel his chosen possession.

72 David devoted himself fully to his task
   and guided them with skillful hands.

❧ Psalm 79

It may be that the juxtaposition of this psalm with Psalm 78 is not just an accident. Psalm 78 tells of the choice of Jerusalem after all the sins of former generations. This one contains a plea that the sins of former generations should not be held against them (v.8).

Although we cannot identify any particular event with certainty it seems likely that the destruction of Jerusalem referred to was that of 587 BC by the Babylonians. The psalmist recognises, however, that the tragedy was due to God's anger (v.5) and he prays that this may now be turned against the invaders (vv.6-7). There is a hint that the psalmist attributes God's anger to the sins of former generations and we are reminded of the proverb which was quoted by Jeremiah (31.29) and Ezekiel (18.2) which was apparently being used about this time — 'The fathers have eaten sour grapes, and the children's teeth are set on edge.' The psalmist does however go on to seek forgiveness of 'our sins' too (v.9) and to ask that Israel may be rescued so that God's honour may be maintained.

No doubt there is more than a little human vindictiveness in vv.10-12 which fiercely seek vengeance seven times over on the enemies, but v.12 claims that it is because the insults are directed against God. This mixture of motives is not surprising and we have noticed before the passion with which such prayers may be expressed (see Psalms 5, 54, 69) and the concern for God's honour.

Finally, (v.13), there comes a vow to thank God once the divine vengeance has been taken.

If this psalm was composed to mourn the 587 BC disaster it was almost certainly used again on similar occasions, especially in 167 BC when the Temple and city were defiled again by Antiochus Epiphanes and in AD 70 when they were destroyed by the Romans. It may not be easy to go on using the psalm today except as a reminder of the seriousness of sin and its consequences and of the need for the honour of God to be preserved.

1   God, foreigners have invaded the land which belongs to you;
      they have defiled your holy Temple,
        they have turned Jerusalem into a heap of ruins.

2   They have thrown out the corpses of your servants
      as food for the birds of the air,

and the bodies of those devoted to you
for the wild beasts to eat.

3 They have made their blood flow like water
all round Jerusalem, and there is no one to bury them.

4 We have become objects of ridicule to our neighbours,
of derision and mockery to those around us.

5 How long will it go on, LORD?
Are you going to be angry for ever?
Must your anger burn like a fire?

6 Give vent to your fury
against the foreigners who are strangers to you,
against the kingdoms who never utter your name.

7 For they have consumed Jacob
and devastated his homeland.

8 Do not hold against us the wrongs of earlier generations,
but let your mercy soon come to meet us,
for we are reduced to helplessness.

9 Help us, God who rescued us,
so that you may be held in honour;
set us free and forgive our sins,
so that you may be renowned.

10 Why should foreigners ask,
'Where is their god?'
Let us see your vengeance falling on them
for shedding the blood of your servants.

11 Let the groans of the prisoners reach your ears,
reach out in power to preserve those condemned to death.

12 Fling back in their faces seven times over, Lord,
the insults our neighbours have hurled against you.

13   Then we your people, the flock you feed,
         will go on thanking you for ever,
         and singing your praises to generations to come.

৯৯ Psalm 80

It is highly likely that this psalm was placed after Psalm 79 because the latter ends with a reference to Israel as God's flock and this one begins with a reference to God as shepherd. The references to Joseph and his two sons Ephraim and Manasseh and to his brother Benjamin all indicate that the psalm was composed for use in the Northern Kingdom where these tribes traditionally settled. They seceded from Judah in 922 BC on the death of Solomon, they were overrun by the Assyrians in 732 when the Galilean area was annexed and were finally brought to an end in 722 BC when the central area of Ephraim itself was occupied.

The psalm is divided into four stanzas each ending with a refrain (vv. 4, 8, 15, 20), the third one being slightly different. The first stanza (vv. 2-4) is a prayer for salvation and restoration using language which conjures up the thought of the Exodus from Egypt. The psalmist still has faith in the God who delivered them then. The second stanza (vv. 5-8) puts the present difficulties down to God's anger. Their sorrow is increased by the fact that their enemies mock them. The third stanza is slightly longer (vv. 9-15). Using the metaphor of the vine it briefly describes the Exodus and the occupation of Canaan, all of which were due to the activity of God. It is therefore all the more difficult for the psalmist to understand why God has now exposed them to invasion. The same metaphor is found in Isaiah 5.1-7 and in Hosea 10.1 and Jeremiah 2.21. The fourth stanza is again a prayer for deliverance and in v.18 prays for power for the king, the 'right hand man' of God, a play on the name Benjamin which means 'son of the right hand'.

The psalm continued to be used in the Southern Kingdom, probably at a time when there were those who looked for the restoration of the Northern Kingdom at some point in the future (Jeremiah 31.31, Ezekiel 37.15-23).

The vine is, of course, a familiar metaphor for the Church in the New Testament (John 15) and this makes the psalm more readily accessible. By recalling God's grace in the past we may find faith and hope rekindled in the present.

181

2   Shepherd of Israel, listen to us.
         You who lead Joseph's people like a flock of sheep,
         you who sit enthroned on the cherubim,
         beam brightly upon us.

3   Before Ephraim, Benjamin and Manasseh
         summon up your power
         and come to save us.

4   Our God, restore us!
         Make your face light up that we may be saved!

5   LORD, God of hosts,
         how long will you be angry with your people's prayer?

6   Sorrow you have given them for food,
         three-fold tears you have given them to drink.

7   You have made us a bone of contention to our neighbours,
         our enemies mock us to their hearts' content.

8   God of hosts, restore us!
         Make your face light up that we may be saved!

9   A vine you brought out of Egypt;
         you planted it where you had driven out foreign nations.

10   You cleared them out before it,
         it made deep roots and filled the land.

11   The mountains were covered by its shade,
         the branches overshadowed the mighty cedars.

12   It spread out its branches as far as the Mediterranean,
         and its shoots as far as the Euphrates.

13   Why have you broken down the walls surrounding it?
         Now passers-by pluck fruit from it.

14   Wild boars from the wood gnaw at it,
         swarms of insects feed on it.

15 God of heaven, turn towards us again,
        look down from heaven and see us.

16 Come and save this vine,
        this stock which you firmly planted.

17 It is set on fire; it is cut down.
        May those responsible perish when you look in anger on
            them!

18 May your power rest upon your right hand man,
        upon the man you have strengthened for service.

19 We will never turn away from you again;
        only let us live and we will call to you by name.

20 LORD, God of hosts, restore us!
        Make your face light up that we may be saved!

🍃 Psalm 81

*This psalm was probably intended for use in the great autumn Feast of
Tabernacles where, among other things, the Law was read (Deut. 31.9-13)
and people pledged their obedience to it. This accounts for the fact that
it begins with a call to praise the LORD (vv.2-6) which is followed by a
prophetic oracle. In this God speaks to his people through the prophet
(vv.7-17).*

*The call to worship is based on the fact that observation of the Feast is
enjoined by law, as one of the three great festivals which the Israelites were
to attend: Unleavened Bread and Weeks in the spring and Tabernacles in
the autumn (Exodus 23.14-17, Leviticus 23, Deut. 16.1-17). The mention
of Joseph and Egypt in v.6 indicates that the Law was already regarded as
ancient and going back to the time of the Exodus.*

*So the prophetic oracle begins with a reminder of the way in which
God had heard their cry in Egypt and set them free (v.7). He tested them at
Meribah (Exodus 17.1-7; see Psalm 95.7-8). There then follows a warning*

(again see Psalm 95). The first commandment (v.10) probably stands for all Ten. The opening words of the Decalogue (v.11; see Exodus 20.2, Deut. 5.6) are combined with a promise of provision. The refusal to listen (vv.12-15) refers not only to the rebellion in the desert but also to the continuing disbelief and distrust, down to the present day. In the final verses the prophet makes his own comments before returning to the word of God in the very last line.

In the Old Testament the Law is not the condition for becoming the people of God. They become that by an act of grace on God's part (see Deut. 7.6-11), but then the response of obedience is expected from them and the Law is given to help them. That this is not forthcoming is a mark of ingratitude and selfishness. Those who today believe that God's grace has been shown in Jesus Christ need to make this response of obedience. They need to hear in worship the rebuke and challenge that this psalm gives.

2   Sing out to the LORD our strength,
          shout with joy to the God of Jacob.

3   Start the music, strike the tambourine,
          play a tune on the lute and harp.

4   Sound the trumpet at new moon,
          and at full moon, on our festival day.

5   For it is a regulation for Israel
          by order of the God of Jacob.

6   He made it a rule among Joseph's people
          when he went to war against Egypt.

7   'I lightened the load on his shoulders,
          his hands let go of the bricklayer's hod.

8   You cried out in distress and I rescued you,
          though unfamiliar with the voice I heard.
    Hidden in the thundercloud I answered you,
          and tested you at the waters of Meribah.

9   Listen, my people, I solemnly warn you;
          Israel, you had better listen to me.

10   There must be no other god among you,
          you must not bow down to a foreign god.

11   I, the LORD, am your God,
          who brought you out of the land of Egypt.
          Open your mouth wide and I will fill it with food.

12   But my people would not listen to me,
          Israel would not say yes to me.

13   So I let them go, with their minds made up,
          to follow their own advice.

14   If only my people would listen to me!
          If only Israel would do as I wish!

15   In a moment I would bring their enemies to their knees,
          I would turn my hand against those hostile to them.'

16   Those who hate the LORD would cringe before him,
          their moment of humiliation would last for ever.

17   But the LORD would feed Israel with the finest wheat.

        'Yes, I would satisfy you with wild rock honey.'

ॐ Psalm 82

*At first it seems as though the people addressed in this psalm are human
judges, as in Psalm 58, but then vv.6-7 make it clear that the psalmist is
thinking about the lesser superhuman beings who apparently make up the
LORD's court. This raises questions about the existence of other gods.
According to much of the Old Testament the Israelites did not deny the
existence of other gods, at least not until after the Babylonian exile. What
they did deny was that these gods had any relevance for Israel. For instance,
Deuteronomy 6.4 said that Israel was to worship, serve and obey only one*

God, the God who had brought them out of Egypt, but in v. 14 of the same chapter the existence of the gods of other nations is recognised.

In the present psalm, then, God is seen as supreme over all other gods (see Psalm 95.3) who are reduced to the status of vassals. As a human king was responsible for justice in his land so also the God who stood behind him was similarly responsible for seeing that justice was maintained. Here God's universal Kingship was acknowledged, possibly within the Feast of Tabernacles (see Psalms 47, 93, 95-99). He is seen as presiding over a court and calling to account those lesser gods of other nations who have failed in their responsibilities. This failure means that, although they may be gods, they will perish like men. Such is the authority of Israel's divine King.

The first and last verses provide a frame for this picture which was perhaps represented dramatically in Israel's worship. They acknowledge God as judge — and the word often conveys the idea of 'ruler' as well — and recognise that though other nations may have their own gods whom they worship their destiny is really in the hands of the LORD.

Such beliefs, held by a relatively small and weak nation, are astonishing. They are a challenge to modern Jews and Christians to make the same leap of faith in proclaiming our God to be the God of all creation and the God of all nations.

1   God takes his place in the heavenly court,
        he is judge in the divine assembly.

2   'How long will you reach unjust verdicts
        and pronounce the guilty innocent?

3   See that justice is done to the weak and the orphan,
        assert the innocence of the helpless and the poor.

4   Set free the weak and the poor,
        rescue them from the clutches of the guilty.

5   — They are both ignorant and stupid,
        they grope about in darkness
        while earth's foundations are shaking —

6   I thought you were gods,
        all sons of the Most High,

7 But in fact you will die as men die,
you will fall like any soldier prince.'

8 Rise up, God, and be judge in the world,
for all the nations belong to you alone.

Psalm 83

If Psalm 82 speaks about other nations' gods this psalm speaks of God's power over those other nations themselves and comes to a similar conclusion that the LORD is in control of all the world. This similarity may suggest that Psalm 83 has its setting in the Feast of Tabernacles too and that the alliance of hostile nations is symbolic rather than historical. Indeed we know of no historical occasion when all these nations lined themselves up against Israel. The difficulty is shown by the fact that dates from the 9th to the 2nd century have been suggested.

It is worth drawing attention to the fact that these peoples are seen primarily as enemies of God and only secondarily as enemies of Israel. This perhaps makes slightly less difficult for us the prayers for them to become terrified and ashamed. The difficulty is further alleviated by the fact that in the final verse all this activity against them is directed towards showing them that the LORD is the God who controls them and all things. Only those who fail to recognise this will be destroyed.

The psalm may still be used as a prayer that God will thwart everyone who opposes him so that they may learn of him and his universal kingdom.

2 God, do not remain silent,
do not be quiet or still, God.

3 See how your enemies are getting worked up,
those who hate you are becoming defiant.

4 They make clever plans against your people,
they conspire together against those you hold dear.

5   They say, 'Come, let us wipe them out as a nation;
       the name Israel shall be remembered no longer.'

6   They are of one mind about their plans,
       they form an alliance against you,

7   The Edomites and the Ishmaelites,
       the Moabites and the Hagrites,

8   Gebal, Ammon and Amalek,
       Philistines and the people of Tyre.

9   Assyria also has joined them
       to give support to the children of Lot.

10   Do to them as you did to the Midianites
       (and to Sisera and Jabin at the river Kishon):

11   They were wiped out at Endor
       and spread like dung on the ground.

12   Treat their nobles as you did Oreb and Zeeb,
       and their princes like Zeba and Zalmunnah

13   Who said, 'Let us take into our possession
       "God's Meadows".'

14   My God, send them swirling away like dust,
       like chaff driven by the wind,

15   Like a fire which burns up the forest,
       as a flame which sets the hill-side ablaze.

16   Chase them away with your storm winds
       and terrify them with your gales.

17   Turn their faces crimson with shame
       so that they come to worship you alone, LORD.

18   Let them be ashamed and live in fear for ever,
       then let them die in disgrace.

19   So may they discover that you,
          no other than the LORD himself,
          are Most High, in control of all the world.

ॐ Psalm 84

It is tempting to think that this psalm, like Psalms 81-83, was used at the Feast of Tabernacles and was an expression of the joy which was a feature of that festival. It is tempting, too, to see the psalmist as one who was on pilgrimage to the festival, though it cannot be shown for certain that this was the original setting. If it was then the psalmist, catching sight of the Temple on the crest of the hill of Zion, sings of his longing to be there (vv.2-4) and of his envy, not in a bad sense, of those who live and work there.

The pilgrims themselves are happy enough. They experience the beginnings of the autumn rains (v.7), they anticipate becoming aware of the presence of God (v.8), they pray for the king (v.10), all things which were connected with the Feast of Tabernacles (see Zechariah 14.16-18). Finally, the psalmist longs to be in the Temple, or even at the entrance to it, because he knows God as his Protector and Provider (vv.11-13).

Even if the psalm did arise as a pilgrim song of this kind it certainly came to be used much more generally as an expression of the desire for and the joy in worship, even when, in the Babylonian exile, pilgrimages to Zion were no longer possible. It is in this sense that the psalm may still be used. The joyous anticipation of worship is not always a feature of Christian experience today. Is this perhaps because we have been too concerned to say that we can meet God anywhere and have forgotten, as those who sang this psalm never did, that worship is a rendezvous with his people which God always keeps?

2   How dearly I love your house,
          LORD of hosts.

3   I long, yes, I pine
          for the courts of the LORD's Temple.

joyously to sing with heart and soul
    to the living God.

4   The sparrow, too, has found a home there,
    the swallow has built herself a nest;
they rear their young near your altars,
    LORD of hosts, my God and my King.

5   Happy are those who live in your house
    and may sing your praises again and again.

6   Happy are those who find their strength in you,
    who are set on taking the road to Zion.

7   By travelling through the dry valley
    they turn it into a spring,
    they are blessed with drenching rain.

8   They go from strength to strength on their journey
    and God will appear to them in Zion.

9   LORD, God of hosts, hear my prayer,
    listen, God of Jacob.

10   Take care of our 'protector', God,
    look kindly on him you anointed.

11   One day in your Temple courts
    is better than a thousand elsewhere;
I prefer to stand on the threshold of God's house
    than to go and live in the homes of the wicked.

12   For the LORD God is both Sun and Shield to me;
    the LORD makes men gracious and glorious,
    he withholds no good gift from those who live in
       integrity.

13   LORD of hosts,
    happy are those who trust in you!

ॐ Psalm 85

This psalm must have been sung at a time of national misfortune (vv. 5-8). It begins by looking back to a previous act of deliverance on God's part (vv. 2-4) and ends with a promise by either a priest or a prophet of salvation (vv. 9-14). The past act of deliverance is described in terms which suggest the return from the Babylonian exile and if this is what is meant then the psalm must have been used on some occasion subsequent to that. This was possibly a time of drought and famine which they saw as due to God's anger.

The priestly or prophetic promise is interesting. The qualities of 'devotion' and 'justice' are personified as attributes of God coming down to earth, while 'fidelity' and 'peace' are personified as the nature of the human response and consequence. So the psalmist looks forward to a time when the two pairs meet and ideal conditions may be found on earth (v. 13).

The final verse shows that these personified qualities are simply the 'outriders' of God himself and, as he himself comes, peace and prosperity will follow.

We have already met more than once psalms in which present distress seems to be eased and hope renewed by looking back to what God has done in the past. We have noted also sudden changes of mood which may have been due to a word of assurance from some Temple official. Here we have an example of both.

It is not surprising that the future hopes and ideals set out here in vv. 9-14 have been seen as referring to a time when God comes, or comes again, in Christ to establish his Kingdom.

2   You looked with favour on your land, LORD,
        you restored good fortune to Jacob.

3   You forgave your people's wrong-doing,
        you put all their sin out of sight.

4   You called back all your anger,
        you cooled off your rage against them.

5   Restore us, God our Saviour,
        put a stop to your displeasure.

6 Will you be angry with us for ever?
        Will you prolong your anger for all generations?

7 Will you not make life good again?
        Then your people will be happy, knowing you.

8 Show us how devoted you are, LORD,
        give us your help and save us.

9 Let me hear what the LORD God is saying;
        he is promising peace to his people and his devoted
                servants,
        so let them not be foolish again.

10 Surely he is at hand to save his worshippers
        so that he, in all his glory, may live in the land.

11 Devotion and fidelity will meet,
        justice and peace will embrace.

12 Fidelity will sprout from the earth,
        justice will look down from heaven.

13 So the LORD will give us prosperity
        and our land will yield a rich harvest.

14 Justice will walk ahead of him
        and peace will follow in his footsteps.

✦ Psalm 86

*This psalmist who tells his troubles to God describes himself as a 'devoted
servant' (see Psalms 4.4, 12.1, 16.10) and a 'slave girl's son' (see Psalm
116.16). These are the only two places in the Old Testament where this
latter phrase is found. In 1 Samuel 1.11, however, Hannah calls herself
'your slave girl' and her son Samuel is described as a Levite. There are some*

grounds, therefore, for thinking that the psalmist was a Levite undergoing some persecution, if that is not too strong a word, at the hands of ruthless people (v.14, see Deuteronomy 33.8-11).

In the psalm the psalmist expresses his own deep devotion to God and his awareness of God's devotion to him. Out of this relationship there comes the confidence to pray to God for help. The prayer that he may be single-minded in his respect for God reminds us again of the demands made upon the Levites in Exodus 32.25-29. The psalm ends with a prayer (vv.16-17) that God may make him prosperous not simply for his own sake but so that this may be a sign to his opponents of God's ability to help his servants, a sign which will make them ashamed.

Even if the original singer was a Levite doubtless the psalm came to be used by other loyal Israelites as well, and it may still be used as a confession of our own commitment to God and of our belief in God's devotion, out of which may spring our prayer for help and deliverance from any adversity that may befall us.

1   Turn your attention to me, LORD, and answer me,
   for I am weak and poor.

2   Keep me safe for I am your devoted servant,
   save me, for I trust in you.

3   You are my God, be kind to me,
   for I cry out to you all day long.

4   Make your servant happy, Lord,
   for I long to be near you.

5   You are good and forgiving, Lord,
   deeply devoted to those who seek your help.

6   Listen to my prayer, LORD,
   take notice of the pleas I make.

7   I appeal to you in times of trouble
   because you answer me.

8   There is no other God like you, Lord,
   none who can do what you do.

9   And the nations you have brought into being
        will come and bow down to you,
        they will honour you as the LORD.

10 For you are great; you do marvellous things,
        you are God, you alone.

11 Teach me, LORD, what you want me to do;
        I will be faithful to you in all I do,
        make me single-minded in my respect for you.

12 Lord, my God, I will acknowledge you whole-heartedly,
        I will always hold you in honour,

13 For the devotion you show to me is great
        and you rescued me from Sheol below.

14 My God, insolent people have risen to attack me,
        a ruthless mob seek my life,
        people who have no regard for you.

15 You, Lord, are a merciful and gracious God,
        your anger is not quickly roused,
        your devotion and fidelity are abundant.

16 Turn to me and be gracious;
        grant your strength to me, your servant,
        save me, your slave-girl's son.

17 Perform some sign of prosperity on me
        so that those who hate me may see it and be ashamed.
        For you are the LORD; you have helped and comforted me.

🕸 Psalm 87

Unfortunately the meaning of this psalm is very uncertain indeed. Translators have sometimes changed the order of the verses and suggested changes in the Hebrew text in order to make some logical sense of it for the present day reader. This translation retains the order in the Hebrew Bible but has, in one or two places, resorted to textual emendations.

It can be said with certainty that the psalm is sung in praise of Zion and there may be some contrast with the Northern sanctuary at Bethel behind the words 'any other abode in Jacob' (v.2). As translated here the psalmist asserts that he will remind worshippers of the origin of other peoples including Egypt, for which Rahab is a nickname, and Babylon. This may suggest a date later than the Exile (v.4). Because God has founded Zion then it, as mother (see Isaiah 49.14, 50.1), produces plenty of people to worship him (v.5). So in their worship they confess that the God who is to be found there is the source of their joy.

So understood, the psalm is another reminder that God who is all-knowing is aware of the background of other nations and by choosing Zion he has assured for himself a succession of worshippers. That succession has continued not only in the Jewish community but in the Christian Church.

2　The LORD founded Zion on the holy hill.
　　　　He loves its very gates
　　　　more than any other abode in Jacob.

3　Weighty pronouncements he makes in you,
　　　　great city of God.

4　I will remind my own people of Rahab and Babylon,
　　　　yes, and Philistia too, along with Tyre and Ethiopia,
　　　　where each had its birth.

5　But of Zion people will say,
　　　　'She gives birth to one after another
　　　　and he, the Most High, is her founder.'

6　The LORD records in his list of peoples
　　　　where each had its birth.

7   So singers and dancers alike declare,
        'All the springs of my delight are in you.'

৵৪ Psalm 88

*This is an unusual psalm, not because it complains of hardship and diffi-
culty — many psalms do that — but because it offers no hope of relief. We
have seen several psalms in which the mood of doubt and gloom changes to
one of hope and confidence. Here the gloom persists right to the very last
words.*

*As usual we cannot say what the troubles are. It seems as though
they were connected with physical suffering but we cannot rule out the
possibility that the psalmist is using strong metaphors. His trouble is all
the greater because of the view held by most people in Old Testament times
that death was the end and whatever existence there might be in Sheol was
totally meaningless (vv.11-13), since those who depart there are cut off
from God (vv.6-7). The psalmist does not hesitate to hold God responsible
for his troubles (vv.8-9).*

*Yet he still goes on praying even though God seems to take no notice
(vv.14-15) and in spite of the fact that his sufferings have plagued him all his
life (v.16), separating him from his friends (v.19).*

*It is useful to have in our psalter what may be called a negative psalm.
It allows us to admit without shame that there are some people who, for no
obvious reason, suffer all through their lives. This remains a mystery, but
the psalmist encourages us not to stop praying. Two other points are worth
making. First the psalm should not be seen in isolation. Other psalms
indicate that there are other things to be said about suffering. Second, for
Christians as well as for some Jews, there is a hope of life beyond death
of which this psalmist knew nothing. There what is now hidden may be
made clear to us.*

2   O LORD, my God, I cry for help in the day-time
        and call to you in the night.

3   Let my prayer reach you;
        open your ears to my cries.

4   For my life is full of trouble,
          I am on the point of entering Sheol.

5   My name is on the list of those descending to the Pit,
          I am now a man beyond help.

6   Among the dead my ties with life are severed too,
          among those killed who lie in the grave,
     whom you remember no longer
          for they are cut off from your care.

7   You have sent me to the bottom of the Pit,
          to regions dark and deep.

8   Your anger rests heavily upon me,
          you overwhelm me with waves of wrath.

9   You have separated me from my friends,
          you make me detestable to them.
          Shut in, I have no way out.

10   I cannot see for my tears.
     I have called to you, LORD, every day
          and stretched out my hands to you in prayer.

11   Do you perform miracles for the dead?
          Do dead men get up and praise you?

12   Is the story of your devotion recited in the grave?
          Or your faithfulness in Abaddon?

13   Is your marvellous deed known in the darkness of death?
          Or your victory in the land of forgetfulness?

14   But I, LORD, have cried to you for help,
          each morning my prayer reaches you.

15   Why, LORD, will you have nothing to do with me?
          Why do you turn your back on me?

16   Since childhood I have been afflicted and dying,
          I have put up with your torment helplessly,

17 Your fury has swept over me in waves,
        your fearful assaults have finished me.

18 They come like water round an island,
        all day long they completely surround me.

19 You have separated me from my dearest friends
        who were my companions.

What a dark place!

❧ Psalm 89

This lengthy psalm is important because of its reference to God's promise to David as described in 2 Samuel 7. If the psalm originally had a historical setting then it can be seen as wrestling with the question as to why this promise was apparently broken. This would suggest a date during the Exile but the only king then was Jehoiakin and it is hard to see in what circumstances he might have sung such a psalm in Babylon. The alternative is to see it not as historical but as part of that ritual, sometimes assumed but not proven, in which the king, representing his people, went through a symbolic death when the land was dried up during the summer drought, later to be restored by God as he sent the autumn rains (see notes on Psalm 18).

The psalm begins (vv.2-5) with a hymn of praise to God for his devotion which leads him to make the promise to David of a permanent dynasty. The next section (vv.6-19) consists of praise to God for his power which sets him above all gods (see Psalm 82). Rahab in this psalm, unlike Psalm 87, refers to the female deity who, according to ancient Near Eastern mythology, was split in two by the creator god in order to make the earth and the heavens from her body. Of course the psalmist is using this mythological language only as a metaphor.

Verse 19 provides a transition to the next section (vv.20-38) which tells of the promise to David of a permanent dynasty, though individual kings will be punished for disobedience. Verses 39-46 now speak of the renunciation by God of his promise by removing the king's symbols of authority. The final verses seem to be spoken by the king himself as he laments his debased condition. If a ritual interpretation is correct then we should have to say that God's raising and exaltation of the king must have followed, even though we now have no text for it.

The psalm reaffirms the greatness of God and his authority to judge those who are disobedient, especially those who, like the king, stand in close relationship with him. As it stands therefore it acts as a warning against relying on God's promises without accepting the responsibility of obeying him.

2 I will sing of your devotion for ever, LORD,
      I will proclaim your faithfulness to successive generations.

3 My claim has been
      that devotion always has its basis in heaven,
      your faithfulness has its foundation there.

4 'I have made a covenant with my chosen one,
      I have promised on oath to David my servant,

5 "I will found for you a dynasty that will be permanent,
      I will give your throne a firm basis through successive
         generations." '

6 Your wonders are praised in heaven, LORD,
      your faithfulness in the divine assembly.

7 For who in the skies can be set alongside the LORD?
      Who in the court of heaven can compare with him,

8 A God before whom the divine council trembles,
      inspiring great awe in those who surround him?

9 LORD, God of hosts, who is like you,
      powerful as you are and surrounded by your faithfulness?

10 You are the ruler of the proud sea;
      when its waves mount up you still them.

11 You crushed Rahab to powder and left her for dead,
      you struck your enemies and sent them flying.

12   The heavens are yours; so too is the earth.
           You founded the world and everything in it.

13   You created holy mountains in the North and South,
           Mounts Tabor and Hermon shout your name with joy.

14   You are powerful and mighty,
           your hand is strong, your right hand supreme.

15   Your rule is founded on right and justice,
           your presence is marked by devotion and fidelity.

16   Happy are the people familiar with the royal acclamation,
           who walk through life on paths lit by your presence.

17   All day long they rejoice that they know you by name,
           because you do what is right for them their prestige rises.

18   For you provide them with strength to boast of,
           because of your goodwill we can hold our heads high.

19   For our royal protector is the LORD's own man,
           our king belongs to the Holy One of Israel.

20   Once you spoke in a vision
           to your devoted servant; you said,
    'I have placed a crown on a soldier's head,
           I have elevated one I chose from the people.

21   I came across David, my servant,
           I anointed him with my holy oil.

22   I will keep a firm hold on him,
           my power will make him strong.

23   No enemy shall ever make demands on him,
           no one steeped in evil shall ever humiliate him.

24   I will remove his foes and crush them,
           I will strike down those who hate him.

25 My faithfulness and devotion shall accompany him,
        because of me he shall hold his head high.

26 I will extend his authority as far as the sea,
        his power as far as the rivers.

27 He will cry to me, "You are my father,
        my God, the Rock where I find safety."

28 Yes, I will adopt him as my eldest son,
        "Most High", as far as the kings of the earth are concerned.

29 I will maintain my devotion to him for ever,
        my covenant with him will be permanent.

30 I will found his dynasty for all time,
        and his life shall last as long as the heavens themselves.

31 If his children turn their backs on my law
        and cease to live as I have laid down,

32 If they violate my decrees
        and fail to keep my commandments,

33 Then I will beat them for their rebellion
        and whip them for doing wrong.

34 But I will not nullify my devotion to their father,
        I will not go back on my faithfulness.

35 I will not violate my covenant,
        I will not alter a word that has passed my lips.

36 Once and for all I swore,
        "Let me cease to be a holy God
        if ever I lie to David."

37 His dynasty shall last for ever,
        his life shall remain before me as long as the sun,

38 As long as the moon, set there for ever,
        a faithful witness in the sky.'

39 But now you have rejected him you anointed,
     in your fury you have cast him away from you.

40 You have renounced the covenant you made with your servant,
     you have thrown his crown dishonoured to the ground.

41 You have breached the walls that protect him,
     you have left his fortifications in ruins.

42 All who cross his path rob him,
     those who live near taunt him.

43 You have made his opponents more powerful,
     and made his enemies glad.

44 Yes, you have blunted his sharp sword,
     and prevented him from standing firm in battle.

45 You have removed the sceptre from his hand
     and hurled his throne to the ground.

46 You have made him old before his time,
     you have covered him with shame.

47 How long, LORD? Will you go into hiding for ever?
     Will your anger burn like a fire?

48 I am reminded how short life is,
     how you have created all mankind to no purpose.

49 Can a man live without also dying?
     Can he save himself from the power of Sheol?

50 You used to show devotion, Lord,
     where are the signs of it now?
     You promised it faithfully to David.

51 Remember, Lord, my disgrace though I am your servant,
     I carry in my heart all people's insults.

52 Insults which your enemies hurl at me LORD,
     which dog the footsteps of your anointed.

*   *   *

Blessed be the LORD for ever.
Amen!   Amen!

❦ Psalm 90

*This well-known psalm contrasts the power of God with the transitoriness
of human life. There is no indication of the kind of situation in which it was
first used.*

*It opens by addressing God as the one who has always been God and
who has the authority to end human life as he began it (vv.1-3). From
this divine perspective what seems a very long time to human beings is
exceedingly short (vv.4-6). Moreover it is not just the brevity of human life
which is apparent, but its sinfulness as well (vv.7-9). By keeping these two
things in mind people may approach God in a proper spirit of humility
(vv.10-12).*

*The cry of lament, 'How long?' (v.13), seems to suggest a time of diffi-
culty for the whole people, but the remainder of the psalm does not dwell on
this; instead vv.14-17 are a prayer, spoken with confidence, for a return to a
happiness once known.*

*In no way does the psalm intend to belittle human kind. Rather it seeks
to emphasise the greatness of God and his ability to help those who are in
trouble.*

1   You, Lord, have been our home
          through successive generations.

2   Before the mountains were born,
          before the world was delivered in labour,
    from one end of time to the other
          you are God.

3   You can turn men back to dust
          and say 'Turn back, sons of Adam'.

4 The way you see things
     a thousand years have passed just like yesterday.

5 They are last night's watch; you have swept them away;
     they are like sleep which in the morning fades like grass.

6 In the morning it blossoms and is renewed,
     in the evening it withers and dies.

7 For when you are angry we come to an end,
     when you are furious we are terrified.

8 You have placed our wrong-doings where you can see them,
     our hidden sins are brought to light in your presence.

9 For all our life passes by under your fury,
     our years come to an end like a sigh.

10 Our span of life is seventy years,
     or eighty if you give us strength.
   It rushes by in trouble and sorrow,
     it passes quickly and we are gone.

11 Who feels the force of your anger,
     who feels your wrath like your worshippers?

12 Teach us to count our days like this
     that we may approach you with understanding minds.

13 Turn back to us, LORD. How long?
     Take pity on us, your servants.

14 Each morning satisfy our needs with your devotion
     that we may sing aloud and be glad all our lives.

15 Give us as much happiness as you gave us suffering
     in the years when we experienced hardship.

16 Let it become clear to us that you are at work,
     and let our children see how splendid you are.

17   Make our experience delightful, Lord our God.
       Make what we do of lasting worth,
       for us make it of lasting worth.

ஜ Psalm 91

The first part of this psalm is spoken by one of the religious officials in the Temple (vv.1-13), either a priest or a Levite. He begins by speaking of his own confidence in God, as one who spends his time in God's presence (vv.1-2). Then he turns to some individual and from his own experience seeks to reassure him (vv.3-13). These assurances must not he understood absolutely. There is plenty of human experience to show that even those who do seek the LORD are assailed by troubles. Probably there is behind the psalm some specific situation in which the person addressed finds himself, but we can never know what it was because we are not told.

From v.14 onwards, however, the official speaks not his own word but a word which God has spoken to him about the person needing encouragement. In this indirect way the one who has come to the Temple seeking help is assured that he will receive it.

The psalm, then, has something to say to those whose task it is to give leadership in worship or to offer pastoral advice. To speak from one's own experience can be useful, but it becomes even more useful when supported by a word of acceptance and assurance from God himself.

1   As one who lives in the shelter of the Most High,
       who rests in the shadow of the Almighty,

2   I say to the LORD, 'My refuge and my stronghold,
       my God, I put my trust in you.'

3   Surely he will save you from the hunter's trap,
       from the destroying plague.

4 He will cover you as a bird does her young,
          under his wings you will be safe;
          his faithfulness is like a shield and a belt.

5 Do not be afraid of the nocturnal terror,
          nor of the arrow which flies in the day time,

6 Nor of the plague which travels in the dark,
          nor of the destruction which devastates at noon.

7 A regiment may fall at your side,
          a battalion at your right hand;
          but to you it shall not come near.

8 With your own eyes you will look on
          and see how the wicked are rewarded.

9 For the LORD is your refuge, too,
          you have made the Most High your home.

10 No disaster will meet you,
          no stroke of misfortune will come near your family,

11 For on your behalf he has ordered his messengers
          to protect you wherever you go.

12 They will support you with their hands
          for fear you trip over a stone.

13 You will tread upon lions and adders,
          and trample on lion cubs and snakes.

14 Because he loves me I will set him free,
          I will lift him to safety because he knows my name.

15 When he calls me I will respond to him,
          I will be with him in his trouble,
          I will rescue him and give him a place of honour.

16 I will give him as long a life as he could wish for
          so that I may go on showing him my saving power.

❦ Psalm 92

Here we have a psalm which is devoted wholly to praise and thanksgiving, in contrast to Psalm 88 which was devoted wholly to lament. In this way the Psalms cover the whole range of human experience.

Verses 2-6 tell of the happiness the psalmist feels at being able to sing his praise to God for what he has done. This may refer to the things which God had done for his people Israel as a whole, but bearing in mind what comes after, the psalmist is probably also referring to what God has done in his own life.

The fool or moron, that is, the person who has wilfully refused the offer of divine wisdom and has been faithless and disobedient, does not realise that he and those like him will be brought to nought by God (vv.7-10).

In contrast the psalmist himself has had his strength renewed and so can gloat over his enemies (vv.11-12; see also Psalms 5, 54, 69, 79 etc.). The description of those who do right as flourishing trees in the Temple courtyard (vv.13-15) reminds us of Psalm 1.3 and is a symbol of the psalmist's prosperity.

The psalm opens with a call to praise God and ends by making the point that what happens to the psalmist will itself bear witness to God's justice (v.16). His own experience, therefore, is set in the context of praise of and witness to God. So should all our worship be God-centred and all our experience viewed in the light of him and his eternal purposes.

2   It is good to praise the LORD,
        to sing psalms in your honour, Most High,

3   To tell out your devotion in the morning,
        your faithfulness each night,

4   Accompanied by a ten-stringed lute
        and the playing of a harp.

5   For you have made me glad, LORD, by what you have done,
        I sing for joy at your activity.

6   How great are your deeds, LORD!
        How profound is your purpose!

7   A moron is unaware of this,
        a fool does not understand it —

8   That wicked men are like growing grass
        and all those who do wrong flourish

9   Only to be destroyed for ever;
        while you, LORD, are supreme for ever.

10 But look, LORD, at your enemies!
        Look, your enemies are perishing,
        all who do evil are being scattered.

11 You have made me as vigorous as a wild ox;
        worn out, you have refreshed me with oil.

12 I have gloated over my enemies,
        I have heard the cries of those who rise against me.

13 Those who do right flourish like a palm tree,
        they grow like the cedars of Lebanon,

14 They are planted in the sanctuary of the LORD,
        they flourish in the courts of our God.

15 In old age they will be like fruiting trees,
        green and luxuriant,

16 So telling out that the LORD is just,
        my Rock, in whom there is no injustice.

🎶 Psalm 93

*We now come to a group of psalms (93 and 95-99, along with 47) which
celebrate the Kingship of the LORD and his authority over the whole earth.
Several of them contain the words 'The LORD is King' (93.1, 96.10, 97.1,
99.1) and the interpretation we give to these words will influence our view*

as to how the psalms were first used. The phrase may simply be a statement about God's authority which could be used on any occasion. However, the fact that it is similar to the acclamation made at the coronation of two human kings, Absalom (2 Samuel 15.10) and Jehu (2 Kings 9.13), has led many to the conclusion that there was a ceremony as part of the Feast of Tabernacles in which the LORD'S Kingship was reasserted each year (Zechariah 14.16). Indeed the phrase could well be translated 'The LORD has become King'. This would not imply that he had never been King before but that his status as King was being reaffirmed, possibly in some ritual action which made use of his throne, the Ark (see Psalms 24.7, 69.24). The order of the two Hebrew words here is reversed as compared with 2 Samuel 15.10 and 2 Kings 9.13, emphasising that it is the LORD and no other, human or divine, who is King (see Psalm 82).

If this ritual interpretation is correct, and although it cannot be proved it seems likely, then the affirmation of Kingship is based upon the fact that it was God who created the world (vv.1-2). Part of this act of creation was the subduing of the 'great deep' (see Genesis 1.2, 6-10) here described as the underground currents. Some therefore think that the Kingship ritual contained an act which symbolised God's victory over the waters. Whether this is so or not the present psalm sees the currents as powerful not only in the past, but in the present as well (v.3). Yet God is far more powerful as he reigns over them (v.4). The decrees may be the natural laws by which God now keeps the waters in check, but the word is often used of the Ten Commandments. Since these were apparently stored in the Ark (Exodus 25.16, 21, Deut. 10.1-5) and since the Ark was God's throne, we may perhaps think of this holy object being placed again in the Temple.

Interesting as this original context may be the psalm certainly came to be used more generally, as did Psalm 24. It became an act of praise to God the King who reigns supreme over all and whose presence beautifies all it touches. In this sense the psalm may still be used in worship as a celebration of the nature of God.

1   The LORD is King!
         He has put on his robes of majesty.
     The LORD has put on robes of strength,
         he has put on his belt of wrath.
     The world is firmly founded
         and cannot be moved.

2　Your throne has been firm from the start,
　　　　you have been there from the beginning of time.

3　The underground currents have shouted, LORD,
　　　　the underground currents have shouted out loud,
　　the underground currents still shout,
　　　　making a crashing sound.

4　But greater than the sound of much water,
　　　　more majestic than the breakers of the sea,
　　　　supremely majestic is the LORD.

5　Your decrees are unchanging;
　　　　holiness is an adornment for your Temple,
　　　　LORD, as long as time shall last.

❧ Psalm 94

This psalm breaks the sequence of 'Kingship' psalms and the reason for this is by no means clear. Perhaps it is placed here to underline the difference between the divine and the human kings, both of whom, in their own ways, were responsible for justice. The fact that the LORD is addressed as Judge simply draws attention to this aspect of his rule (see Psalm 96.10, 13, 98.9). In those two psalms the Judge had authority over other nations and it may be that the wicked who are described in vv.3-8, 16 and 20-21 are foreign kings. However, it seems rather more likely that the psalmist had in mind Judah's kings, some of whom seem to have disregarded God. The prophets had to complain about kings who devised policy on purely human considerations instead of on the word of God (see Isaiah 7.1-17) and these verses portray a similar attitude. The behaviour mentioned in verse 6 in particular is a sure breach of Israelite law (see Exodus 22.21-22 etc.), but even worse they regard God as impotent to do anything about it. The psalmist himself is clear that God's knowledge and wisdom in all matters is far superior to man's (vv.9-11) and therefore the person who allows himself to be instructed by God will prosper (vv.12-14). So the judgement of the wicked and the success of those who do right will demonstrate the fairness of divine justice (v.15).

At this point the psalmist appears to recall instances in the past when God has helped him. Has he himself perhaps suffered from his ruler's injustice (vv.16-19)? In a question which clearly expects a negative answer he is convinced that God will not be party to the evils they do (vv.20-21), but will grant him safety and punish those who have treated him and others unjustly (vv.22-23).

The clash between political power exercised on the basis of expediency and pragmatism and the divine will is not limited to a person in Judah in some remote past. Earthly rulers today may be ordained by God (Romans 13.1) but if they are foolish enough and wicked enough to flout God's law or his will, then they can expect only retribution while those who suffer as a result of their actions may be assured that God is on their side.

1   The LORD is a God who demands vindication.
       God of vindication, appear in brightness.

2   Arise, Judge of the earth,
       repay the proud in full.

3   How long, LORD, will the wicked rejoice?
       How long will they rejoice in their success?

4   They babble on, pouring out words without restraint,
       all the wrong-doers boast to one another.

5   They crush your people, LORD,
       they oppress those who belong to you.

6   They kill widows and aliens
       and murder orphans.

7   They say, 'The LORD cannot see,
       the God of Jacob takes no notice.'

8   Take notice yourselves, you morons among the people;
       when will you learn some sense, you fools?

9   Is he who gave us ears unable to hear?
       Is he who shaped the eye unable to see?

10   Will he who instructs nations not also chastise them?
    Does he who teaches mankind himself lack knowledge?

11   The LORD knows the schemes men devise,
    that they are futile.

12   Happy is the man you school, LORD,
    the one you teach from your law,

13   Giving him rest from his days of trouble
    until a pit is dug for the wicked to fall into.

14   For the LORD will not forsake his people,
    nor desert those who are his own.

15   For justice will again be seen to be fair,
    and all men of good intent will pursue it.

16   Who will stand up for me against the wicked?
    Who will take my side against wrong-doers?

17   If the LORD had not given me help
    I should soon have gone to live in the silent grave.

18   If I thought, 'My foot has slipped'
    then your devotion has always held me up.

19   When I harbour a multitude of anxious thoughts
    your consolations bring me delight.

20   Do you associate with judges out to destroy,
    who make trouble as they administer the law?

21   They make attacks on the life of those in the right
    and condemn the innocent to death.

22   But the LORD is like a strong tower to me,
    my God is a Rock where I can find safety.

23   He repays them for all their wrongs,
    for their evil deeds he will put an end to them,
    the LORD our God will put an end to them.

ᏬᎦ Psalm 95

The first half of this psalm is very familiar to Christians since it is often used as a call to worship. The second half is usually conveniently overlooked! There are, in fact, two calls to worship. The first in vv.1-5 invites people to praise God on the ground that he is a Great King. In human terms this means a king who has several vassal kings serving him. So the gods of other nations are now merely God's servants (see Psalms 48.3 and 82). His Kingship is based on the fact that he is the creator of the world (see Psalm 93). All is his because he made it. But God is not only creator of the world; he is also the 'creator' of the Israelites as a people and so the second call to worship (vv.6-7) is based on this. They are the people of the shepherd King (see Psalm 80.2). It has been suggested that the first invitation was given at the entrance to the outer court of the Temple and the second at the entrance to the inner court, into which only Israelites were allowed.

Then there comes a very sudden change. Someone, presumably a Temple prophet, perhaps a Levite, calls them to hear a word of God warning them against lack of trust in the divine King. This he does by recalling traditions about Massah and Meribah which we can now read, for example, in Exodus 17.1-17 and Deut. 33.8 (see also Psalm 81.8), when the Israelites rebelled by doubting God's ability to provide water. They are urged not to do so again, and we remember that the Feast of Tabernacles was the occasion when the King was acknowledged and rain was expected. In Deut. 33.8 this tradition is associated with the Levites and it would be appropriate if one of them were to remind the people of it now.

It is right to use the opening verses as a call to worship, but we should do well also to use the warning as a reminder that to worship the King involves trust and obedience to him, and if these are not forthcoming then those who go through the motions of worship are in danger of losing their way in life completely and missing the 'rest' which God would give them.

1   Come, let us make our voices ring out to the LORD,
        let us shout in triumph to the Rock who keeps us safe.

2   Let us come into his presence with praise,
        let us sing out psalms in triumph.

3　For the LORD is a great God,
　　　　　a great King above all the gods.

4　The unexplored parts of the earth are in his power,
　　　　　the mountain ranges belong to him.

5　The sea belongs to him; he made it;
　　　　　his hands shaped the dry land.

6　Come, let us make obeisance, let us bow down,
　　　　　let us kneel before the LORD, our Maker;

7　For he is our God,
　　　　　we are the people he looks after,
　　　　　the flock he tends.

　　　If only today you would listen to what he says!

8　Do not be stubborn as you were at Meribah,
　　　　　as you were at Massah, that day in the desert,

9　When your ancestors tested me,
　　　　　when they made trial of me;
　　　　　then they saw what I could do.

10　For forty years I could not stand the sight of those people,
　　　　　I said, 'They are a people who wilfully go astray,
　　　　　they disregard the path I have chosen for them.'

11　I was so angry with them that I swore,
　　　　　'You will never enter the land where I was going to settle
　　　　　you.'

Psalm 96

*When the Chronicler was writing his account of David's bringing the Ark
into Jerusalem he put this psalm on the lips of the Temple singers (1 Chron.*

16.23-33). This may support the suggestion made in the introduction to Psalm 93 that these psalms were used in the Temple after the procession of the Ark at the Feast of Tabernacles. In any case this psalm is a call both to Israelites and to other nations and to the whole created world to praise God as King.

The first six verses call on Israel to praise the LORD for all that he has done. Whether the reference to the 'new song' means the first time the psalm was used or whether it was a new song because it marked the coming of the New Year, we cannot be sure. Again, the LORD's supremacy over other gods is shown by the fact that he created heaven and earth.

In vv.7-10 the call is to other nations to recognise and acknowledge the glory, the honour, the holiness of God. The offering they are to bring is a kind of tribute money by which they confess themselves to be his servants. Moreover, they are now to bear witness everywhere to his Kingship and his fair administration of justice. Metaphorically the created world itself is invited to share in the joy of the occasion (vv.11-12).

The occasion is the 'coming' of the LORD. Perhaps this refers to his coming into his Temple again to take up his throne from which he will exercise his just rule over the whole world.

Again, whatever its original setting the psalm came to be used in an anticipatory sense, for the other nations did not acknowledge God as King or bear witness to his rule. It came therefore to have this forward look and it is in this sense that it can still be used today, for even if we accept that the Kingdom came in Christ we are aware that its culmination lies ahead. We wait to see the consequences of his just rule.

1   Sing to the LORD a new song,
       sing to the LORD, all the earth.

2   Sing to the LORD; praise him for all he is.
       From day to day tell out the good news that he has
           saved us.

3   Recite his glorious deeds among the nations,
       his wonderful acts among all peoples.

4   For the LORD is great; he deserves all our praise,
       he inspires awe more than any other god.

5   For the nations' gods are worthless,
          whereas the LORD made the heavens.

6   Majesty and splendour are his courtiers,
          strength and beauty stand in his sanctuary.

7   Attribute to the LORD, you families of nations,
          attribute to the LORD glory and strength,

8   Attribute to the LORD the glory which is due to him,
          bring an offering and come into his courts.

9   Make obeisance to the LORD in his holy splendour,
          dance, all the earth, in his honour.

10   Say among the nations, 'The LORD is King!
          The world is firmly founded and cannot be moved,
          he will judge the nations fairly.'

11   Let the heavens be glad, let the earth rejoice,
          let the sea roar and all that lives in it,

12   Let the fields and all their crops exult,
          let all the trees in the forest sing aloud

13   In the presence of the LORD. For he comes,
          yes, he comes to set up his just rule on earth.
     He will rule the world properly
          and govern the people faithfully.

❧ Psalm 97

This is another psalm celebrating the LORD's Kingship. The cloud, fire and lightning (vv.2-5) are symbols of his holiness, his divine nature, but they are also often used to speak of his appearing to men. They are found in passages like Exodus 19.16-19 and Psalm 18.8-16. Elijah expected to find God in them but didn't (1 Kings 19.11-12). Here they are signs of his kingly rule which is founded on justice. As in the other kingship psalms the 'other gods' have become his servants (v.7). The sentence he has passed (v.8) may refer to his judgement over these other gods as in Psalm 82. Consequently other nations will be ashamed but Zion, representing the people of Judah, will rejoice.

Verses 10-12 are words of encouragement to loyal Israelites. They may have been spoken by a Temple prophet. Perhaps 'those devoted to him' means any Israelite, though as we have noticed in earlier psalms (4, 16, 89 etc.) it does sometimes seem to be used to describe the Levites or Temple prophets and it may be that v.10 picks out this group in particular who seem to have been vulnerable to persecution (see Deut. 33.8-11) before promising joy to all who do right.

Holy as God is, supreme as he is over heaven and earth, he still comes to the people he has made. He comes demanding loyalty and promising joy.

1   The LORD is King! Let the earth rejoice,
        let all the coastlands be glad.

2   Cloud and heavy mist envelop him,
        his rule is founded on right and justice.

3   Fire goes before him
        and he sets his enemies ablaze on every side.

4   His lightning has lit up the whole world,
        the earth has seen it and squirmed.

5   The mountains melted away like wax in his presence,
        in the presence of the Lord of all the earth.

6   The heavens declared his victory,
        and the people saw him to be glorious.

7   All those who worship images will become ashamed,
        those who boast in worthless idols;
        all other gods will make obeisance to him.

8   Zion has heard and is glad,
        its daughter towns in Judah rejoiced
        at the sentences you passed, LORD.

9   For you, LORD, are Most High, over all the earth,
        exalted far above all gods.

10   You who love the LORD, hate evil.
        He preserves the lives of those devoted to him,
        he saves them from the power of wicked men.

11   Light is scattered like seed for those who do right,
        and gladness for men of good intent.

12   Rejoice, you who do right, in the LORD;
        praise him for all that reminds us of his holiness.

ॐ Psalm 98

*In many ways, especially towards the end, this psalm is similar to Psalm 96.
Like that psalm it too begins with a call to sing a new song and the ground
for the people's praise is to be God's actions on Israel's behalf (vv. 1-2). We
cannot be sure what acts the psalmist had in mind, but it may very well be
the Exodus from Egypt and the settlement in Canaan. Since God's victory
has been seen by all peoples (vv. 2-3) so all peoples are now called to join in
the hymn of praise (vv. 4-6). Verse 6 shows that we are dealing with the
theme of the LORD's Kingship and his coming to exercise his just rule over all
the earth (v. 9).*

1   Sing to the LORD a new song,
        for he has done wonderful things.
    He gained victory by his own power,
        and by his holy strength.

2   The LORD has shown his power to save,
        he has revealed that he does right for all nations to see.

3   He has borne in mind his devotion and faithfulness
        to the household of Israel.

218

People at the ends of the earth
    have seen the victory of our God.

4 Raise your voices to the LORD, all the earth,
    burst into loud singing and psalms.

5 Sing psalms to the LORD accompanied by the harp,
    by the harp and the sound of music.

6 With trumpets and horns
    raise a joyful shout in the presence of the King, the LORD.

7 Let the sea roar and all that lives in it,
    the world and those who inhabit it.

8 Let the rivers clap their hands,
    let the mountains cry out together in joy

9 In the presence of the LORD, for he comes
    to set up his just rule on earth.
   He will rule the world properly
    and govern the peoples fairly.

❧ Psalm 99

The three stanzas of this psalm each end with a refrain declaring the holiness of God the King. Holiness is not just another characteristic alongside righteousness, love etc. It expresses the very nature of God, what he is in essence. It is what makes him God. It therefore demands that people approach him in awe and reverence (v.3), but yet they can approach him and find him near. The vision described in Isaiah 6 demonstrates well the meaning of holiness. It causes Isaiah to fall prostrate confessing his humanity and his sinfulness, but he is nevertheless addressed and commissioned by the Holy One, the King.

It is generally believed that Isaiah's vision was occasioned by the experience or the recollection of some ceremony in worship involving the Ark, perhaps such a ceremony as has been envisaged in Psalms 95-98.

This psalm too apparently contains allusions to the Ark, the throne of the invisible God over which were ranged the cherubim.

The first stanza (vv. 1-3) refers to these cherubim and envisages God enthroned there. This evokes the confession that he is awe-inspiring and holy. The second (vv. 4-5) speaks about the just rule of the King. The word 'strength' possibly contains an allusion to the Ark which can also be regarded as his footstool (v. 5) since he sits enthroned on it. The third stanza (vv. 6-9) speaks of those people who have the twin responsibilities of making known God's will through the Law and of making intercession for the people. Moses, Aaron and Samuel are examples and they were all closely associated with the Ark. Such people are the priests. Thus all three stanzas contribute to the picture of God as the Holy King.

If we fail to recognise the holiness of God as it is shown to us in this psalm our worship will be impoverished. Here are held together certain vital truths about God. Being the Holy King he can be approached only with great respect, his rule is just and fair, his will is made known and is meant to be obeyed, his forgiveness is offered to the penitent but his punishment threatens those who persist in sin. As usual Christians will want to add another dimension to this in so far as they see Jesus as the great High Priest and King. It complements those pictures of the gentle Jesus.

1 The LORD is King, the peoples tremble;
      he is enthroned on the cherubim, the earth quakes.

2 The LORD in Zion is great,
      he is exalted over all peoples.

3 They confess, 'You are great and inspire awe in us.'
      Holy is he!

4 A King's strength lies in his love of justice,
      you have established your fair rule;
   whatever is just and right
      you have done in Jacob.

5 Exalt the LORD our God,
      make obeisance at his footstool.
      Holy is he!

6   Moses and Aaron are among his priests,
        Samuel is one of those who invoke him by name.
    They were people who called to the LORD
        and he himself answered them.

7   In a column of smoke he used to speak to them;
        they fulfilled his instructions
        and the decrees which he gave them.

8   LORD, our God, you yourself answered them.
        For them you were a God who forgave sins
        as well as one who punished their misdeeds.

9   Exalt the LORD, our God,
        make obeisance on his holy hill.
        For holy is the LORD our God!

❧ Psalm 100

This summons to worship God is similar to the second call to worship in Psalm 95.6-7. The basis for the call is the fact that God has made Israel his own people. Since the psalm follows a group of psalms which have spoken of the LORD as King the phrase 'the flock he feeds' recalls that God is their Shepherd-King (v.3). In the last line of this verse there is a clear recognition that Israel's status as the people of God is due solely to God's grace (see Deuteronomy 7.6-11). Therefore devotion and faithfulness will always be shown by him (v.5).

   This is a fitting invitation to worship reminding worshippers of their true relationship to the God they come to worship. Christians will be reminded of the words of Jesus: 'You have not chosen me, but I have chosen you and appointed you. . . .' (John 15.16). This is the true spirit of joyous worship.

1   Raise a shout to the LORD, all the earth!

2   Worship the LORD in joy,
        come before him with a joyous shout.

3   Recognise that it is the LORD who is God,
        he is the one who made us
    to be his own people and the flock he feeds;
        we did not do it ourselves.

4   Pass through the gates of his Temple with thanks,
        come into his courts with praise.
        Praise him and thank him,

5   For the LORD is good, his devotion lasts for ever,
        and his faithfulness to one generation after another.

❧ Psalm 101

This is an unusual psalm in that it consists almost entirely of pledges or vows made concerning future behaviour. Verses 2-4 are promises to live a life of integrity. Verses 5-8 pledge short shrift for those who fail to live up to this standard. Clearly the singer is one who is in a position to carry out the threats of these latter verses and it is usual to assume that it was the king. We know from 1 Samuel 10.25 that the rights and duties of the king were laid out before him, at least in some period of Israel's history, and it could well be that the present psalm is his own acceptance of these at his coronation.

We have seen, too, that it was part of the king's duty to establish and maintain justice in his kingdom (see Psalm 72) and this he will do by excluding from his court all who do not practise it. The aim will be to keep Jerusalem free from evil since it is God's city.

The opening verse clearly sets the psalm in the context of worship to the LORD and the promises are therefore all the more serious for having been made in his presence.

That most of the kings failed to fulfil such promises can be seen from the historical books of Samuel and Kings, but that is no reason why the promises should not have been made.

So the psalm may become a vehicle for our own personal commitment to justice both in our own lives and in the society around us.

1   Devotion and justice shall be my song
        as I sing psalms to you, LORD.

2   I will behave wisely and well
        whatever happens to me;
   I will go about in my household
        with total integrity.

3   I will not set my sights on any worthless deed;
        I hate deviant behaviour, it shall have no hold on me.

4   I will harbour no crooked thoughts,
        I will have no truck with evil.

5   As for the man who whispers behind his neighbour's back,
        I will silence him for good.
   He who looks down on others and thinks himself above them,
        I cannot tolerate him.

6   I will look out for those in the land who are faithful
        to live with me;
   The one who behaves with integrity
        shall be my retainer.

7   There shall not live in my household
        anyone who practises deceit;
   no one who tells lies
        shall have any position where I can see him.

8   Each morning I will silence for good
        all in the land who are wicked,
   ridding the city of the LORD
        of all wrong-doers.

᎒᎒ Psalm 102

This psalm falls into three distinct parts. Verses 2-13 read like a prayer from an individual in trouble; vv.14-23 seem to mourn the affliction of Jerusalem and look forward to it being recognised by all as the place where the LORD meets his people; vv.24-29 resume the theme of personal sorrow but find confidence in God's eternity. There are two ways in which these three parts can be seen as making up one whole. First, an individual Israelite in trouble may be comparing his misfortunes with those of Jerusalem and finding some help from the comparison. Second, the singer may be the king who represents the nation and the apparent personal calamities of vv.2-13 may be metaphors for the people's distress connected with the debasement of Zion. However, it is not possible now to know for certain which was the original setting.

As usual the psalmist, whoever he is, does not hesitate to see the hardships as the result of God's anger (v.11) and as in Psalm 90, he compares human life with God's eternal nature (vv.12-13). Though Zion is to be consoled (see Isaiah 49.14-23) we are not told why this is necessary. Instead the emphasis is on the fact that Zion will again become famous as the centre for world-wide worship of the LORD. This feature occurs in some of those psalms which worship him as King (see Psalms 96-99). The final part of the psalm again makes the comparison which was made earlier in vv.12-13. The very world God made is destined to come to an end but God is eternal.

It is such a reflection on the nature of God himself which helps us still to cope with adversity and to retain our faith in the face of it.

2 LORD, hear my prayer,
     let my cry for help reach your ears.

3 Do not turn your back on me
     when I am in distress.
   Listen to what I have to say,
     answer me quickly when I call.

4 At the end of my days my life has gone up in smoke
     as though my body were burned on a bonfire.

5   Struck down, I have withered away like grass,
          for I have neglected to eat food.

6   My groaning is audible;
          I am all skin and bone.

7   I am just like a desert bird,
          like an owl living among ruins.

8   When I lie awake at night
          I feel like a lonely bird on a roof-top.

9   All day long my enemies taunt me,
          they make a fool of me, using my name in their oaths.

10   I have fed on ashes instead of food,
          I have diluted my drink with my tears

11   Because you have been so furious with me;
          you have picked me up and thrown me away.

12   The days of my life are like a lengthening shadow;
          though I am withering away like grass

13   You remain, LORD, for ever;
          succeeding generations will be reminded of you.

14   You will arise and console Zion,
          for the time to be gracious to her, the right moment, has
             arrived.

15   For we, your servants, take pleasure in her very stones
          and appreciate even the dust on her streets.

16   The nations will hold the name 'LORD' in reverence
          and all kings stand in awe of your glorious presence,

17   Because the LORD is the builder of Zion
          and he has revealed himself there in all his glory.

18   He has turned to the people who were made destitute,
          he has not treated their prayer with contempt.

19 This shall be written down for the rising generations,
        and people not yet born will praise the LORD.

20 For from his holy height he leaned over to see,
        the LORD looked down on the earth from heaven,

21 So as to hear the cries of the prisoner,
        to set free those under the sentence of death.

22 Therefore men will repeat the name of the LORD in Zion
        and rehearse his praise in Jerusalem

23 When nations are gathered together,
        when kingdoms assemble to worship the LORD.

24 On my way through life he has broken my pride and my
            strength,
        he has cut short my days.

25 'My God', I say, 'do not take me away half way through life,
        your life continues one generation after another.

26 Long ago you laid the foundations for the earth,
        you made the heavens with your own hands.

27 They will disappear but you will remain;
        they will wear out like clothes.
    You will cast them off like an old cloak
        and they will disintegrate.

28 But you remain God; your life will not end.

29 The children of us your servants will live in security;
        our descendants will stay safe in your presence.'

ৡ Psalm 103

Like the previous psalm this one also contrasts the frailty and finiteness of human life with the permanence of God, but the mood of the psalm is quite different. Perhaps they have been placed side by side to complement each other.

The psalmist begins by exhorting himself to praise God and reminding himself of God's forgiveness, devotion and care (vv.1-5). The 'you' in these verses is, of course, the psalmist himself. From verse 6 onwards, however, he begins to think of himself more as a part of God's people and the 'you' becomes 'us'. This is due, no doubt, to his recollection of the way God acted with Moses and his generation. Verse 8 recalls Exodus 34.6 and the psalmist recognises that it remains true for him and his contemporaries (vv.9-14). This expression of God's devotion towards his people and his forgiveness of their sins — without mention of sacrifice — is unequalled in the Old Testament and barely surpassed in the New. One generation passes away and another follows but God's devotion persists (vv.15-17).

In case people should be misled into thinking that obedience and disobedience are unimportant because 'God will forgive; that's his job' the psalmist goes on to remind himself and others of the need first for obedience (v.18) and then for a recognition of God's authority as divine King. Fatherhood (v.13) must never be understood sloppily. It always holds the notion of responsibility, of obedience and submission to the head of the family (see Deut. 21.18-21).

This thought of the Kingship of God brings the psalmist back to the attitude of praise in which he invites all in heaven and on earth to join before again exhorting himself to do the same.

The psalm has become so familiar and has meant so much to so many people that it would be superfluous to try to draw lessons from it or to show its relevance for today. It is timeless.

1   Kneel, my true self, and adore the LORD;
        all I am, kneel and adore the Holy One.

2   Kneel, my true self, and adore the LORD;
        do not forget all he has done for you.

3 He forgives all your wrong-doing;
    he cures all your diseases.

4 He saves you from death's door,
    his tender devotion is your crowning glory.

5 He gives you all you will ever need;
    you will be strong as an eagle, as in your youth.

6 The LORD puts things right,
    giving justice to the oppressed.

7 He used to tell Moses his way of behaving
    and the Israelites what he did.

8 The LORD is compassionate and gracious,
    slow to become angry and deeply devoted.

9 He does not prosecute his case against us for ever,
    nor does he remain angry for all time.

10 He does not deal with us as our sins deserve,
    nor repay us in proportion to our wrong-doing.

11 For as high as the sky above the earth,
    so deep is his devotion to his worshippers.

12 As far as East is from West
    so far has he set us apart from our acts of disloyalty.

13 Just as a father takes pity on his children
    so the LORD takes pity on his worshippers.

14 For he knows how we were shaped,
    he bears in mind that we are made of dust.

15 Man? He lives no longer than grass,
    he flourishes like the wild flower,

16 Then the wind blows on it and it is gone;
    no one can tell where it has been.

17   But the LORD's devotion to his worshippers lasts for ever,
          he does what is right for generation after generation.

18   For those who adhere to his covenant
          and remember and obey his rules.

19   The LORD has set up his throne in heaven;
          his royal authority extends over everything.

20   Kneel and adore the LORD, his heavenly messengers,
          strong warriors who do what he says,
          listening to the words he speaks.

21   Kneel and adore the LORD, all his heavenly court,
          his royal servants who do what pleases him.

22   Kneel and adore the LORD, everything he has made,
          in every place where his rule extends.

23   Kneel, my true self, and adore the LORD.

❧ Psalm 104

This psalm begins where the previous one left off, with an exhortation to the psalmist himself to praise God. It can be described as a 'nature' psalm, hence its frequent use at harvest festivals. The main theme is that every created thing depends on God for its continuance. The psalmist makes use of both Israelite tradition and ancient myths and poems from foreign lands, though, as usual, the myths become mere metaphors.

Verses 1-4 depict the LORD as King in heaven, riding on the clouds, a description also used of the Canaanite Baal. As King God is also creator (vv. 5-9). The waters of the great deep which, in ancient thought, surrounded the earth above and below and constantly threatened to engulf it (see Genesis 6-9) are held in check by him. Water, however, so necessary to all life, was provided by the LORD and not by Baal (see 1 Kings 18). The trees and hills provide homes for the birds and animals (vv. 16-18). The sun and moon, regarded by many nations as deities, follow the pattern laid down for them by God (vv.19-23). Wisdom (v.24) is not only an attribute of God, it is also the order which he imposes on the world. Leviathan, the sea-dragon of ancient myth, is reduced to one of God's sea-creatures (v.26). All creatures on earth or in the sea are provided for. As God breathed into the man-shaped dust and made it a living being (see Genesis 2.7) so he can withdraw his breath so that living things die. They are wholly dependent on him.

These reflections on the wonder of the created world lead the psalmist back to where he began, to praise and worship of God and a prayer that sinners who spoil God's creation may be removed from it so that it may not be further damaged. They have no place in a world so created by God. For all his convictions about God's goodness in creation and preservation the psalmist is not unaware of this other side of things, human wickedness.

It is possible for us to become so preoccupied with human sin and weakness that we forget all the good things with which God has surrounded us. This poem helps us to redress the balance.

1   Kneel, my true self, and adore the LORD.

     LORD, my God, you are very great,
         you dress in honour and majesty.

2   You wrap yourself in a robe of light,
         you stretch out the heavens like a tent.

3   He builds his house on the heavenly waters,
         he uses the clouds as his chariot
         and marches on the flying wind.

4   He employs the winds as his messengers,
         the fiery flames as servants in his court.

5   He set the earth on its firm foundations,
         it will remain for ever immovable.

6   The deep covered it like a cloak,
         the water level was above the mountains.

7   At your rebuke they took to flight,
         when you thundered at them they rushed away.

8 The mountains emerged, the valleys sank down
    where you had decided they should be.

9 You laid down the limits of the waters;
    they could not pass,
    nor could they return to cover the earth again.

10 You released the springs in the stream-beds,
    they flow between the hills.

11 They provide water for all wild animals,
    the wild asses quench their thirst there.

12 The birds in the sky nest nearby,
    from among the foliage they make their calls.

13 You water the hills from your home on high;
    as a result the earth receives enough moisture.

14 You make the grass grow for the cattle
    and vegetation for man to use,
    producing from the earth food

15 And wine which makes people happy,
    making their faces light up at the sight of oil
    and of food which sustains their lives.

16 The trees of the LORD have all they need,
    the cedars of Lebanon which he planted,

17 Where the birds build their nests,
    in whose tops the stork makes her home.

18 High hills are the haunts of the mountain goats,
    crags provide cover for the rock badgers.

19 The moon does what it has to do when it should,
    the sun knows when to set.

20 You make darkness and night falls
        in which every woodland creature creeps out.

21 The young lions roar for prey,
        seeking their food from God.

22 When the sun rises they gather
        to their dens and lie down there.

23 People go about their daily tasks
        and their work, until evening.

24 How many things you have made, LORD!
        You have made them all by wisdom;
        the earth is full of your creatures.

25 Here is the great sea, stretching away in all directions.
        In it countless creatures move silently about,
        creatures great and small.

26 There ships sail away;
        here too is Leviathan whom you made to play in it.

27 They all look expectantly to you
        to give them food when they need it.

28 When you provide it for them they gather it in,
        when you open your hand they are well satisfied;

29 When you turn your back on them they are dismayed,
        when you gather in their breath they die
        and return to the dust of which they are made.

30 When you exhale your breath things are created,
        you make the earth look new again.

31 May the glory of the LORD be seen for ever,
        may his creation make him happy,

32 He who looks on the earth and it trembles,
        who touches the mountains and they smoke.

33 I will sing to the LORD throughout my life,
       I will praise him with psalms while ever I live.

34 May my reflections please him;
       for my part, he makes me happy.

35 May sinners be removed finally from the earth,
       may wicked men live no longer.

       Kneel, my true self, and adore the LORD!
       Hallelujah!

🌿 Psalm 105

Psalms 105 and 106 belong together in the sense that both trace the history of God's chosen people using old traditions, one from the point of view of God's grace, the other from the point of view of Israel's disobedience. In the Rule of Discipline regulating life at Qumran in the 2nd century BC we read, 'the priests shall recite the favours of God manifested in his mighty deeds and shall declare all his merciful grace to Israel and the Levites shall recite the iniquities of the children of Israel, all their guilty rebellions and sins during the domination of Satan.' The fact that in 1 Chronicles 16 Psalm 105.1-15 is combined with Psalm 96 to be sung when the Ark was brought into Jerusalem by David probably indicates that in the great autumn Feast of Tabernacles when the LORD was acclaimed King there was an opportunity for people to renew their allegiance by recalling his grace and confessing their sin.

Psalm 105 recalls the story from the promise of Abraham to the settlement in Canaan. The theme seems to be summed up in v.8; it seeks to show how the promise to the patriarchs was fulfilled in spite of all obstacles. We have no means of dating the psalm because we do not know whether it makes use of the Pentateuch in its present form, which would place it after the exile in Babylon, or whether these traditions were already being recited in worship before the Pentateuch received its final shape.

The recital of God's acts in worship is not just a way of keeping their memory alive; it is meant to evoke a sense of wonder which breaks into praise — the final Hallelujah — and a sense of gratitude which gives birth to obedience.

1   Acknowledge the LORD; invoke him by name;
      tell out among all peoples what he has done.

2   Sing to him, sing psalms to him;
      reflect on his wonderful deeds.

3   Take pride in his sacred name;
      those who come seeking the LORD will be happy
         indeed.

4   Come, seek the LORD and his strength,
      come seeking his presence always.

5   Remember the wonders he has performed,
      the signs he has given and the verdicts he has
         pronounced,

6   You descendants of Abraham, his servant;
      you offspring of Jacob, his chosen one.

7   He is the LORD our God,
      his decisions affect the whole earth.

8   He has remembered the bond he forged for ever,
      the promise he made to a thousand generations,

9   The bond he forged with Abraham,
      the solemn promise he made to Isaac,

10   Which he confirmed to Jacob by decree,
      to Israel, as a bond to last for ever,

11   And which said 'I will give the land of Canaan to you,
      a territory which will be yours to possess.'

12   When they were few enough to be counted easily
      and lived as aliens in that land,

13 When they travelled to and fro among the nations
     from one kingdom to another,

14 He allowed no one to oppress them
     but reprimanded kings on their account,

15 Saying 'Do not touch those I have anointed,
     do no harm to my prophets.'

16 He summoned a famine on the earth,
     he denied them the food on which they relied.

17 He sent on ahead of them a man
     sold as a slave; Joseph it was.

18 They held his feet fast in fetters,
     his neck in an iron collar.

19 Until such a time as his predictions came true
     the LORD's promise put him to the test.

20 The king sent and released him,
     the one who ruled over nations set him free.

21 He made him master of his household,
     in charge of all he had,

22 To educate his princes as he wished
     and to teach his elder statesmen wisdom.

23 Then Israel came to Egypt,
     Jacob settled as an alien in the land of Ham.

24 God gave his people large families
     and made them too numerous for their enemies

25 Whose attitude he changed to one of hatred for his people,
     to crafty schemes against his servants.

26 He sent his servant Moses
     and Aaron whom he had chosen.

27   They threatened them with signs from the LORD,
        with wonders he would work in the land of Ham.

28   He sent darkness and it made everything dark,
        it did not disobey his commands.

29   He turned their water into blood
        and so killed off all their fish.

30   Their land was infested by frogs
        even in their royal apartments.

31   He said the word, and a swarm of flies arrived,
        and gnats all over the country.

32   He sent hail in place of their rains,
        flashes of lightning throughout the land.

33   He struck their vines and fig trees
        and split all the trees in their borders.

34   He said the word, and a swarm of locusts arrived,
        so thick they couldn't be counted.

35   They ate all the vegetation in the land,
        they ate everything the ground produced.

36   He struck down their every eldest son,
        those born first while they were at their most virile.

37   He led the Israelites out carrying gold and silver,
        no one among the tribes dropped out.

38   The Egyptians were glad to see them go
        for they had become terrified of them.

39   He spread out a cloud to screen them
        and a fire to provide light at night.

40   When they asked he brought them quails,
        he satisfied their hunger with food from heaven.

41 He broke open a rock and water gushed out;
　　　　it flowed in a river through the parched lands.

42 For he remembered his sacred promise,
　　　　made to his servant Abraham.

43 So he brought out his people rejoicing;
　　　　those he had chosen shouted for joy.

44 He gave them lands belonging to foreigners
　　　　and they entered into the fruits of other people's
　　　　　　labours.

45 The intention was that they should obey his decrees
　　　　and observe his laws.

　　　Hallelujah!

✄ Psalm 106

*If Psalm 105 ends with a call to obedience, Psalm 106 is a confession that
such obedience has not been forthcoming. It, too, begins by acknowledging
the LORD and recalling his mighty deeds (vv.1-2), but quickly moves on to a
confession of sin which the psalmist sees as continuing the tale of sin and
disobedience which began soon after the deliverance from Egypt. Such a
confession is necessary if the singer is to enjoy the benefits of belonging to
the chosen people.*

*There is the same uncertainty about the date as there is with Psalm
105, though vv.27 and 47, suggesting that the people are dispersed and
looking forward to restoration, may indicate the time of the exile in
Babylon. This, however, is by no means certain.*

*Verses 32-33 seem to be out of order since they refer to events in the
desert which, in the Book of Numbers, preceded the events at Peor in Moab
at the moment just prior to the entry into Canaan.*

*Recollection of the sins of ancestors is not meant in any way to transfer
to them the blame for the sins of contemporary society. It was not a case of
'The fathers have eaten sour grapes and the children's teeth are set on edge',*

a proverb the truth of which both Jeremiah and Ezekiel denied. The recital is rather an act of solidarity in sin with earlier generations, and divine compassion is still needed every bit as much as it was by those earlier generations if praise is to be sincerely offered and a place among God's people is to be enjoyed.

Verse 48 is a concluding doxology to Book 4 of the Psalms.

1 Hallelujah!
  Acknowledge the LORD for he is good,
    his devotion knows no end.

2 Who may speak of the mighty deeds of the LORD?
    Who tell aloud all the praise which is his due?

3 Happy are those who uphold justice,
    who do what is right on every occasion.

4 Remember me, LORD, when you are pleased with your people,
    take notice of me, too, when you help them,

5 That I may enjoy prosperity with those you have chosen,
    share the happiness of your nation
    and take pride along with those who belong to you.

6 Along with our ancestors we too have sinned,
    we have done wrong and wicked things.

7 Those ancestors, when they were in Egypt,
    did not consider your marvellous deeds
    nor reflect upon the depth of your devotion.

8 They rebelled against the LORD at the Sea of Reeds,
    but he rescued them to safeguard his honour,
    to reveal to men his power.

9 He spoke sternly to the Sea of Reeds and it dried up;
    he made them walk over the ground with water
      underneath
    as through a desert.

10 He rescued them from their foes,
          he reclaimed them from enemy hands,

11 But the water engulfed their enemies;
          there were no survivors.

12 So they came to believe what he said
          and they sang his praises.

13 But they quickly forgot what he had done
          and did not wait for his instructions.

14 In the desert they were overcome with desire,
          they tested God out in the wastelands.

15 He gave them what they asked for
          and stemmed their craving.

16 But in camp they became jealous of Moses
          and of Aaron who was consecrated to the LORD.

17 The ground opened and swallowed Dathan,
          it closed over Abiram and his followers.

18 Fire broke out among their supporters,
          flames set the wicked ablaze.

19 They made a calf at Horeb
          and bowed in worship before cast metal.

20 They exchanged their glorious God
          for a model of a grass-eating bull!

21 They forgot God who had saved them,
          who had done such great things in Egypt,

22 Working wonders in the Land of Ham,
          awesome deeds at the Sea of Reeds.

23 So he threatened to destroy them
          if Moses, his chosen servant,
      had not stepped into the breach before him
          to deflect his anger from doing so.

24 They dismissed the idea of a land to be desired,
        they did not believe God's promise.

25 They sat in their tents speaking in whispers,
        not listening to what the LORD was saying.

26 With raised hand he made a solemn threat
        to strike them down in the wilderness,

27 To scatter their descendants among foreign nations
        and disperse them in various countries.

28 They became adherents of Baal at Peor
        and ate sacrifices offered to gods who die.

29 They made God angry by behaving so,
        and a plague broke out among them.

30 But Phinehas took his stand as mediator
        and the plague was stemmed.

31 This act stood to his credit
        for one generation after another, for ever.

32 They made God angry near the spring of Meribah
        and through them Moses got into trouble;

33 For they put him in such a bad temper
        that he said things he had better not have said.

34 They did not wipe out the Canaanite peoples
        as the LORD had told them to do;

35 Rather they intermingled with those nations
        and learned from their example,

36 Worshipping and serving their idols
        which lured them into sin.

37 They sacrificed their sons and daughters,
        offering them to the demons.

38 They shed the blood of innocent people,
      their own sons and daughters
   whom they sacrificed to Canaanite idols;
      so the very land was made impure by their blood.

39 They behaved like harlots,
      defiling themselves by what they did.

40 The LORD was very angry with his people,
      those who belonged to him became abhorrent to him.

41 He placed them under the control of the nations
      and they were ruled by those who hated them.

42 Their enemies oppressed them
      and they were crushed by hostile powers.

43 Though God delivered them many times
      they, for their part, went on planning rebellion
      and so sank deeper into sin.

44 Yet he looked kindly on their distress
      whenever he heard them cry.

45 To help them he recalled his covenant with them,
      so deep was his devotion that he took pity on them.

46 He saw to it that they received compassion
      even from those who had taken them captive.

47 Save us, LORD, our God,
      gather us in from among the nations
   so that we may acknowledge you as the Holy One
      and take pride in praising you.

*   *   *

48 Blessed be the LORD, the God of Israel,
      from the beginning to the end of time.
   All the people shall respond 'Amen!'
      Hallelujah!

❦ Psalm 107

The central part of this psalm (vv.4-32) consists of four songs of thanksgiving for deliverance each with a refrain in vv.6-8, 13-15, 19-21 and 28-32. The conditions from which God has given deliverance are being lost and hungry in the desert, imprisonment, sickness and rough seas. In the Hebrew of v.17 'sickness' is not specifically mentioned: it reads 'Some are fools . . .'. The context, however, seems to require this slight change of the Hebrew. (This is made in the RSV translation but not in the NEB.)

In all probability we should see these four songs as meant to be sung in a corporate act of thanksgiving in which individuals can share by identifying themselves either literally or metaphorically with one or other of the rescued people. God changes fortunes, and all may rejoice in that.

Verses 2 and 3 cause a slight problem. In the first place they sound almost like a parenthesis and in the second they seem to refer to the return from exile in Babylon. If this is so then it is possible to see the four songs of thanksgiving as referring to the freedom of the Jews and their safe return. Perhaps the best interpretation is to say that the four songs are part of a pre-exilic psalm which was reinterpreted after the Exile and used as an act of corporate thanksgiving for the return.

The closing verses (32-43) may also have been added at this stage as a general statement that God can reverse fortunes in either direction, from good to bad for the wicked and from bad to good for the faithful. Such teaching is common enough among the Wisdom writings (see v.43). The reference to deserts and pools certainly reminds us of the promise of return in Isaiah 41.17-20.

The psalm shows, therefore, how earlier material could be re-interpreted and reused, sometimes in a new way, within scripture itself and it gives us some grounds for doing the same. In this particular instance the original significance is more meaningful to us than the reference to the return from exile, though this is another example of the way in which God, by his grace, can change fortunes.

1   Acknowledge the LORD, for he is good,
        his devotion knows no end.

2   Let those the LORD has rescued do this,
        those he has rescued from enemy hands,

3 Those he has gathered from various lands,
      from north, south, east and west.

4 Some wandered in the desert wastes,
      unable to find the way to a city they could live in.

5 They became hungry and thirsty too;
      their spirits began to droop.

6 In their distress they cried out to the LORD
      and he saved them from their troubles.

7 He led them by a direct route
      which brought them to a city they could live in.

8 Let them acknowledge the LORD's devotion,
      the marvellous things he has done for men and women.

9 He has met the needs of the thirsty
      and has filled the hungry with good food.

10 Some live in darkness black as pitch,
      prisoners suffering in iron bonds.

11 For they rebelled against God's commands
      and refused to do as the Most High said.

12 All heart was knocked out of them by hard labour,
      they stumbled but no one would help them.

13 In their distress they cried out to the LORD
      and he saved them from their troubles.

14 He brought them out of the darkness black as pitch
      and broke their chains.

15 Let them acknowledge the LORD's devotion,
      the marvellous things he has done for men and women.

16 For he has smashed open bronze doors
      and snapped in two their iron bars.

17 Some were sick because of their sinful behaviour,
   they brought suffering on themselves by their
   wrong-doing.

18 Everything they ate tasted vile;
   they knocked on death's door.

19 In their distress they cried out to the LORD
   and he saved them from their troubles.

20 He spoke, so that his word might heal them,
   he rescued them from the things which brought them low.

21 Let them acknowledge the LORD's devotion
   the marvellous things he has done for men and women.

22 Let them make their thank-offering
   and recite his deeds with joyful shouts.

23 Some went off to sea in ships,
   engaged in commerce over the wide sea.

24 These have seen what the LORD does,
   marvellous things on the ocean depths.

25 When he said so, the storm winds arose
   and tossed the waves high in the air.

26 Thrown up to the sky and then down to the depths,
   they surged to and fro in peril.

27 They reeled and staggered like drunken men
   and all their skill deserted them.

28 In their distress they cried out to the LORD
   and he brought them out of their troubles.

29 He quietened the storm to a whisper
   and the waves of the sea were stilled.

30 Then they were happy; for when it was calm
   he piloted them safely to their destination.

31 Let them acknowledge the LORD's devotion,
        the marvellous things he has done for men and women.

32 Let them sing high praise to him in the congregation,
        in the assembly of elders let them praise him.

33 He turns rivers into desert
        and springs into thirsty ground;

34 He makes fertile land salty
        because of the wickedness of those who live there.

35 He turns the desert into a pool
        and dry ground into springs of water.

36 He settled hungry people there
        and they built a town to live in.

37 They sowed seed and planted vineyards
        which produced a rich harvest.

38 He gave them blessing and their numbers grew,
        he did not allow their cattle to decrease.

39 When they did decrease and diminish
        through oppression, misfortune or suffering

40 God, who pours contempt on nobles
        and makes them wander in trackless wastes,

41 Raised up the needy out of their affliction
        and made their families as large as a flock of sheep.

42 The upright see it and are glad,
        but all wrong-doers hold their tongues.

43 Whoever would be wise, let him hold on to these things,
        let him pay close attention to the LORD's acts of devotion.

❧ Psalm 108

This psalm is made up of parts of two other psalms. Verses 2-6 are almost identical with Psalm 57.8-12, while verses 7-14 are the same as Psalm 60.7-14. The fact that the two passages could be combined like this to create a new psalm indicates again a certain freedom in the way the psalms were used.

Verses 2-6 show the same note of confidence as 57.8-12 but instead of being a response to the difficulties to be faced they function here as a confident introduction to troubles suggested by the use of 60.7-14. It is almost as though the prophetic oracle addressed to the king before battle in the earlier psalm is simply being quoted here as an encouragement on some other occasion. Beyond this we cannot go.

2   I have made up my mind, God,
        I will sing you songs of praise with my whole being.

3   Awake lute and lyre!
        I will awaken the new day.

4   I will acknowledge you among the people, LORD
        I will sing your praise among the nations.

5   For your devotion is greater than the height of heaven,
        your faithfulness reaches the skies.

6   Rise high, God, above the heavens,
        show your glory over all the earth.

7   Save us by your powerful right hand; answer our prayers
        so that those whom you love may be delivered.

8   God has promised — and he is holy —
        'I will triumph; I will share out Shechem,
        I will measure out territories in the valley of Succoth.

9   Gilead belongs to me; so does Manasseh.
        Ephraim is my helmet and Judah my sceptre.

10   Moab will be my wash bowl;
           over Edom I will fling my sandal,
           Philistia will be smashed to pieces against me.'

11   Who will lead me as far as Edom?
           Who will guide me to its fortified city?

12   Surely, God, you have deserted us,
           you no longer go out to battle with our armies.

13   Help us out of our distress
           for human help is useless.

14   With God's help we shall fight with courage,
           though it is he who will overrun our enemies.

❧ Psalm 109

This is a prayer of one falsely accused who pleads his case before the LORD in the Temple. It may be that the context is an appeal to the Temple court, similar to that in Psalm 7.

The first five verses express the psalmist's distress that although he has shown love towards them, his enemies are now attacking him. The main question concerns vv.6-19 and in particular whose words they are. Probably the majority of interpreters regard vv.7-19 as the psalmist's curses upon his accusers. The present translation takes the view that they are the words of his accusers as they attack him. The reason is not to soften in any way the extremely bitter curses which these verses contain by putting them on the lips of his enemies, for the psalmist himself reciprocates them in v.20. It is rather that vv.1-5 and 20-31 use the first person singular for the psalmist and the third person plural for his enemies, while vv.7-19 use the third person singular and it is more likely that this refers to the psalmist than to the plural enemies. These verses, then, demonstrate how false accusations and calls for judgement are made.

The situation seems to reflect accurately that envisaged in Deut. 19.16-21 and when the psalmist prays that the punishment his enemies have sought for him should be meted out to them he is simply asking that

*what is laid down in Deut. 19.19 should be carried out. In any case he makes.
little of this and moves on quickly to a prayer for acquittal and deliverance
from his enemies in court where he will praise God for his justice and affirm
his allegiance to him (vv.21-23).*

*So interpreted the psalm reminds us of the justice of God. Of course,
the innocent are not always acquitted and saved from trouble and it would
be wrong to imagine that this were so. But it was so for this psalmist and he
rightly rejoices in it.*

1   God whom I praise, do not remain silent,

2   For wicked, dishonest men oppose me;
    they have attacked me with lies.

3   They have expressed their hatred all round me,
    and campaigned against me for no reason at all.

4   In return for my love they have accused me,
    though I have prayed for them.

5   They have brought me evil in return for good,
    hatred in return for love.

6   'Appoint a wicked man to conduct his case,
    let an accuser take charge of his defence.

7   When he is tried may he emerge guilty,
    may his prayer be regarded as sin.

8   May his life be short,
    may someone else take charge of what he has.

9   May his children become orphans
    and his wife a widow.

10   May his children's homes become desolate,
    may they wander off to beg and seek help.

11   May creditors lay hands on all he has,
    may strangers rob him of what he has earned.

12 May there be no one to go on being kind to him,
      no one to be good to his children when he is dead.

13 May his line become extinct,
      his family name disappear in one generation.

14 May his father's wrongs remain in the LORD's mind,
      may his mother's sins never pass from his view.

15 May the LORD never lose sight of them,
      may he remove from the earth every memorial of them.

16 He was one who never thought of showing devotion,
      but instead hunted down to the death
      the weak, the poor, the dispirited.

17 He enjoyed a curse; it came easily to him;
      he found no joy in a blessing; it was far from his mind.

18 He cursed as easily as putting on his clothes,
      it came as naturally to him as the water he drank
      or the oil he put on his limbs.

19 It was like the clothes he put on,
      like the belt he always wore around him.'

20 May the LORD repay in the same coin those who accuse me,
      those whose false testimony threatens my life.

21 You are the LORD, my Lord,
      so deal with me that this becomes well-known,
      because your devotion is so strong rescue me,

22 For I am weak and in need,
      I am deeply wounded.

23 I am like a shadow which lengthens and is gone,
      like an insect shaken off the hand.

24 I have fasted so much I can hardly stand,
      my flesh has shrunk for lack of oil.

25   I have become an object of ridicule to them,
        when they see me they make faces at me.

26   Help me, LORD, my God;
        save me, devoted to me as you are.

27   Now may they recognise this as your doing;
        you, LORD, are the one who has done it.

28   They may curse, but you bless;
        they arose in court, but were disconcerted;
        now I am glad.

29   Those who accused me are covered with disgrace,
        they wear their shame like a cloak.

30   I fully and publicly acknowledge the LORD,
        standing in the middle of a crowd I will praise him.

31   For he conducts the defence of the poor,
        saving his life from those who carry out judgement.

❧ Psalm 110

This psalm raises innumerable problems of translation and interpretation which cannot be discussed here. A comparison with other translations will show where the difficulties lie. The interpretation is further complicated by its use in the Epistle to the Hebrews (chapter 1) as referring to Jesus, the exalted Messiah. We must initially try to dismiss this. If we do, and look at the psalm as here translated, then it seems almost certain that we are dealing with the coronation of a king. There are two divine oracles, vv.1 and 4, each followed by some comment. These seem to be spoken by a prophet fulfilling the role that Nathan played at the time of David (see 2 Samuel 7 and Psalm 89.19). The phrase 'A proclamation from . . .' (v.1) is exactly the same as that Amos frequently uses to round off his oracles. This oracle is addressed to the prophet's 'lord', that is, the king. He is to sit at the LORD'S

*right hand and therefore exercises his role as the representative of the LORD,
the divine King. This is the proper relationship between God and the king.
So installed, the LORD will extend his power (see Psalm 2.8-9).*

*The second oracle (v.4) establishes the king also as priest and sanctions
his priestly duties. Melchizedek was the priest-king of Jerusalem in pre-
Israelite days (see Genesis 14.18-20). There are good reasons for thinking
that David took over the role in Jerusalem when he captured it from a
successor of Melchizedek and so himself became priest-king. It is not clear
whether the word 'lord' in v.5 refers to the LORD or to the king as in v.1. In
any case the king is promised superiority over other nations. Verse 7 may
simply be a metaphor for the renewal of the king's strength, but it may
equally well have reference to some ritual drinking from the spring of Gihon
where Solomon was crowned (1 Kings 1.28).*

*It is not difficult to see how this psalm came first to anticipate the
coming of a future Messiah when kings were no longer crowned in Israel
and then, later, to refer to Jesus whom Christians saw as the fulfilment of
such Messianic hopes, especially after his resurrection and ascension.*

1   A proclamation from the LORD to my lord:
      'Sit at my right hand
  until I make your enemies
      a stool for your feet.'

2   The LORD will extend your authority and power;
      from Zion exercise your rule amid your enemies.

3   Your people will volunteer when you raise an army;
      in sacred dress young warriors will come to you,
      fresh as dew from the womb of the dawn.

4   The LORD has promised on oath, he will not go back on it:
      'You shall be a priest for ever
      in the tradition of Melchizedek.'

5   The Lord is your helper;
      when he gets angry he crushes kings.

6   Full of majesty, the king will execute judgement over the nations,
      as leader of a great land he will crush them.

7 He will drink from the stream along the way
        and so will hold his head high.

🐚 Psalm 111

*This is the first of four psalms often known as the Hallelujah Psalms
because they begin with this call to 'Praise the LORD'. Both 111 and 112 are
acrostic psalms, each line of the psalm beginning with a different letter of
the Hebrew alphabet in alphabetical order.*

*Because of this somewhat artificial arrangement it is not possible to
discern any logical development of thought, though the psalm is obviously
one which praises God for his great deeds. What these deeds are is not made
clear in vv.2-5 except that the provision of food may suggest the act of
creation. In v.9, however, the psalmist seems to have the Exodus from Egypt
in mind. The psalm is intended for corporate worship as can be seen by v.1,
but the final verse is typical of the Wisdom writings (see Proverbs 1.7,
Job 28.28).*

*Again we are reminded that one of the main elements in worship is the
recollection of what God has done and praise for his activities. This should
produce in the worshippers a proper response of humility and obedience.*

1 Hallelujah!
   I will acknowledge the LORD with my whole being,
        in the assembly, the gathering of honest men.

2 The things the LORD has done are great,
        they are studied by all who enjoy them.

3 His acts are splendid and glorious,
        he always does what is right.

4 He has given us something by which to remember his wonders;
        the LORD is gracious and compassionate.

5   He has provided food for his worshippers;
        he remembers his covenant for ever.

6   He shows his people how powerful he is
        by giving them land belonging to other nations.

7   All he does is reliable and just,
        all his precepts can be trusted.

8   They have a firm and lasting support,
        they are to be followed truly and fairly.

9   He sent and delivered his people;
        he set out his covenant laws for all time;
        holy and awesome is his name.

10 Reverence for the LORD is the first step to wisdom,
        good success comes to all who obey his laws.
        His people will never stop praising him.

🌿 Psalm 112

Whereas Psalm 111 concentrates on what God has done, Psalm 112, another acrostic, is concerned with the life of the man who makes the proper response of humility and obedience as set out in Psalm 111.10. On the one hand the psalm sets out the behaviour which should follow (vv.3-5, 9) and on the other it promises prosperity (vv.1-3, 7-8). In the final verse the psalmist notes the frustration of the wicked when he sees the success of the good man.

This teaching is again quite typical of the 'Wisdom' writings of the Old Testament, especially as found in Proverbs. However, we have already met many psalms in which good people suffer and complain about it and this point is most powerfully made in the Book of Job. We are not entitled, therefore, to deduce from this that the man who shows reverence and obedience to God will always prosper. Nevertheless the instinct which makes the psalmist extol this way of life is right. Obedience is not something we offer to ensure success; it is something we offer in response to God's gracious acts and if prosperity follows we should be thankful for it.

1 Hallelujah!
  Happy is the person who stands in awe of the LORD
    and is delighted to do as he commands.

2 His descendants will be powerful in the land;
    the family of those who live honest lives will be blessed.

3 There will be great wealth in his household;
    he will always do what he should.

4 He lights up the darkness of those who live honest lives;
    he does what is right with generosity and kindness.

5 It is a good thing to make generous loans,
    to fulfil promises to the letter.

6 Nothing can ever shake such a man;
    he will always be remembered for doing right.

7 He has no fear when he hears something bad about him,
    his courage is grounded on confidence in the LORD.

8 His courage never fails, he is not afraid
    as he looks forward to his opponents' downfall.

9 He gives liberally to the poor,
    always doing what he should.
  He can be proud of his wealth.

10 When the wicked sees him he will be furious,
    he will gnash his teeth in despair.
    Wicked people will have nothing to look forward to.

❧ Psalm 113

Psalms 113-118 became known in Jewish tradition as the Hallel psalms, to which Psalms 111 and 112 form a kind of introduction. 113 and 114 were sung before the Passover meal and 115-118 after it and they may have been used at the Last Supper (Mark 14.28) if this was a Passover meal.

This psalm is an act of praise to the LORD. The repetition of this personal name of God is important. The name which according to tradition was revealed to Moses at the burning bush on Sinai (Exodus 3.14) is probably connected with the verb 'to be' and it assured Moses that God was with him. Initially, therefore, it revealed little of the nature of its owner. Its full significance could be discerned only as his people followed him. It was proclaimed to the people when they came to Sinai (Exodus 34.6) but in time it became too holy for general use and could be spoken only by the priest in the Holy of Holies. The word 'lord' therefore came to be substituted for it and to distinguish it from the ordinary noun for 'lord' we print it in capital letters. The name stands for all that God is, as revealed in what he does.

The remarkable thing about this psalm is the way in which it dwells on the name LORD as belonging to the high and holy God (see Psalm 111.9) and then at once goes on to claim that this God, who lives above the heavens and the earth and looks down on both, is concerned for the poor and needy among his people, raising them to equal status with those who are rich and powerful (see Luke 1.46-55).

1   Hallelujah!
      Offer praise, you servants of the LORD,
            praise him who is the LORD.

2   Give thanks to him who is LORD
            both now and always.

3   From sunrise to sunset
            praise him who is LORD.

4   The LORD reigns on high above all nations,
            his glory shines above the skies.

5 Who is like the LORD our God?
       He makes his throne on high

6 But lowers his eyes to look down
       on heaven and earth.

7 He raises the poor from the dust,
       and lifts up the needy from the ashes,

8 Making them at home among nobles,
       among those of his people who are nobles.

9 The woman denied a family he makes at home,
       he makes her the happy mother of children.

❧ Psalm 114

It can easily be seen why this psalm was used at Passover. In a few short lines it recalls all the events from the Exodus to the settlement in Canaan. The fact that both Israel and Judah are mentioned in v. 2 may possibly indicate a time when the two separate kingdoms existed side by side, though together they made up the people of God. The events are not described in chronological order, especially if the shaking of the mountains in v. 4 is seen as referring to the events at Sinai as recorded in Exodus 19.

It is not so much the events themselves which evoke worship but the fact that behind them all stands God. Rather curiously, in view of Psalm 113, the personal name of God is not used in v. 7 of this psalm. The final verse is a highly poetic reference to the provision of water in the desert (see Exodus 17.5-6, Numbers 20.8-13).

Concentration in worship on the wonderful things that have happened to us can sometimes deflect our thoughts from the one who caused them to happen. The psalmist requires us to set our minds on the God who initiates them and to do so in wonder and awe.

1 Hallelujah!
   When Israel came out of Egypt,
       the family of Jacob from a foreign people,

2   Judah became sacred to the LORD,
        Israel displayed God's royal power.

3   The sea saw it and fled;
        the Jordan began to flow backwards.

4   The mountains shook like skipping rams,
        the hills quivered like young lambs.

5   What is it, sea, that makes you flee?
        What is it, Jordan, that makes you flow backwards?

6   What makes you shake, mountains, like skipping rams?
        What makes you quiver, hills, like young lambs?

7   Tremble, earth, before the Lord,
        before the God of Jacob,

8   Who turned the rock into a pool of water,
        the rocky outcrop into a fountain.

ꙮ Psalm 115

This psalm is best understood as a liturgy in which several people or groups of people share. Verses 1-8 may have been sung by the whole congregation or by a Temple prophet on their behalf. Verses 9-11 are prophetic calls to trust in God, to each of which a response is made. Verses 12-15 are a priestly blessing, following on the affirmation of trust, and the psalm concludes with a hymn of thanksgiving sung by the congregation.

The occasion on which the liturgy was first used cannot now be known for certain. It seems to presuppose some recent deliverance or victory which is attributed to God (vv. 1-3). As such it would, of course, be very appropriate after the return from exile in Babylon, but when the psalm came to be used at Passover the singers probably had the Exodus itself in mind.

Verses 1-8 thus contrast the God who rescued them from futile idols with a reminder in v. 8 that people tend to become like the God they worship. This was a theme common enough among the prophets and especially from

257

the prophet of the Exile (see Isaiah 40.18-20, 44.9-20, 46.1-7).

The following three verses (9-11) were spoken by a prophet, calling on the people to trust God, and not only on the people but the priesthood as well. The 'worshippers of the LORD' *in v.11 may refer to converts to Judaism so making a third group. This would explain the pronoun 'their' in the people's response in vv.10 and 11 which they also use of themselves in v.9.*

Verses 12-15 are the priest's blessing in response to the people's acknowledgement of God as their helper. Finally the people offer their praise to God, recalling that the dead cannot do so (vv.16-18). We have met this view of the state of the dead before. They go to an utterly empty and meaningless existence in Sheol (see Psalm 88.11-13).

While Christians may not share this pessimistic view of the future, the call to praise God and to acknowledge that all good comes from him and not from any other source remains as a constant challenge.

1   Not to us, LORD, not to us is any honour due.
     It is due to you for your devotion and faithfulness.

2   Why should the nations say,
     'Where, then, is their God?'

3   Our God is in heaven,
     he has done all he wished to do.

4   Their idols are made of silver and gold,
     they are the work of human hands.

5   They have mouths, but never speak,
     eyes, but they never see,

6   Ears, but they never hear,
     noses, but they never smell,

7   Hands, but they never feel,
     feet, but they never walk;
     no sound comes from their throat.

8   Just so may those become who made them,
     all who put their trust in them.

9   You, Israel, put your trust in the LORD!
        — He is their help and protector.

10 Priests of Aaron's line, put your trust in the LORD!
        — He is their helper and protector.

11 Worshippers of the LORD, put your trust in the LORD!
        — He is their helper and protector.

12 The LORD has remembered us; he will bless us.
        He will bless the people of Israel;
        he will bless the priests of Aaron's line;

13 He will bless the worshippers of the LORD,
        every single one of them.

14 May the LORD give you more and more,
        you and your children.

15 May you be blessed by the LORD
        who made heaven and earth.

16 The heavens above belong to the LORD,
        the earth he has given to mankind.

17 The dead do not praise the LORD,
        nor do those who go down to the silent grave.

18 As for us, we will thank the LORD
        from now on and forever.

Hallelujah!

᪥ Psalm 116

This is a personal song of thanksgiving for deliverance, though yet again the exact circumstances are hidden from us. The psalmist had probably been ill,

*for illness was seen as death extending its tentacles to draw a person down
from life to Sheol. In his distress the psalmist had almost given up hope
(vv.10-11) but had clung on to faith in God until God had rescued him. The
second half of the psalm (vv.12-19) expresses the psalmist's intention to
offer a thank-offering in fulfilment of a vow he had made during his illness.*

*Verse 16 ought perhaps to give us a clue to the author's identity. The
phrase 'slave-girl's son' is found otherwise only in Psalm 86.16. However,
the word 'slave-girl' is used of Hannah and her son was Samuel, a Levite
(1 Samuel 1.11). It is likely, therefore, that the psalmist was himself a Levite
and this is supported by the use of the phrase 'those devoted to him' in the
previous verse (15), a phrase which appears in other psalms to refer to
Temple officials (for instance, Psalm 4.4, 16.10, 89.20 etc.). That the
Levites or 'devoted ones' were subject to hardship and opposition may be
seen from Deuteronomy 33.8-11.*

*This psalm, like the others in the group, was used at the Passover
celebration and probably took on the meaning not only of individual
hardship, but of communal oppression and near-extinction as well.*

*As we use it now we are reminded again how relief from suffering
evokes both love for the God who gave relief and praise and confession of
God's goodness within the gathered congregation. Is this personal, audible
prayer within the context of corporate worship an aspect of worship which
we have tended to overlook?*

1   I love him! For the LORD hears
        my voice when I seek his favour.

2   Because he has listened to me
        I will call to him so long as I live.

3   Death has twined its ropes around me,
        Sheol has found and bound me;
        I meet with distress and sorrow.

4   I cry out, using the LORD's name,
        'Please, please, LORD, save me'.

5   The LORD is generous and does all he should,
        our God acts with compassion.

6 The LORD watches over those as yet without wisdom;
>   my affairs were at a low ebb
>   but he has brought me safely through.

7 I say to myself, 'Be at rest again
>   for the LORD has made up for all you suffered'.

8 For you have rescued me from death itself,
>   from weeping and from stumbling.

9 I can now walk freely in the LORD's presence
>   in the land of the living.

10 I stood firm in my faith, though I used to say,
>   'I am absolutely crushed'.

11 All too hastily I added,
>   'No one in the world can be trusted'.

12 How shall I repay the LORD
>   for all he has generously given me?

13 I will offer wine in gratitude for my deliverance
>   and will call to the LORD by name.

14 I will fulfil the vows I made to the LORD
>   in the presence of all his people.

15 Very rare, in the LORD's eyes.
>   is a sentence of death on those devoted to him.

16 I, LORD, even I, am your servant,
>   I am your servant, your slave-girl's son;
>   you have untied the ropes which bound me.

17 To you I will offer a thanksgiving sacrifice
>   and will call to you, the LORD, by name.

18 I will fulfil the vows I made to the LORD
>   in the presence of all his people,

19   In the courtyard of the LORD's Temple
         in the very centre of Jerusalem.

     Hallelujah!

🎝 Psalm 117

This, the shortest of the Psalms, is simply a call to praise and the grounds for that call are the familiar ones of God's devotion and faithfulness which are often thought of as being particularly evident in the great events of the Exodus from Egypt and settlement in Canaan. However they should no longer be limited to these events for these qualities may be seen by God's people in all our experiences.

1   Praise the LORD, all nations,
         praise him, all peoples.

2   For his devotion overwhelms us,
         and the LORD's faithfulness lasts for ever.

     Hallelujah!

🎝 Psalm 118

This is a song of thanksgiving by an individual for deliverance and victory. It is obviously composed for use in worship in the Temple as may be seen from vv.2-4 where the same three groups are called upon to make response as were exhorted to trust in God in Psalm 115. The repetition, especially in vv.5-14, also suggests a liturgical context, as does v.27. All this makes it likely that the individual who sang it was a representative Israelite,

262

probably the king. The occasion for which it was composed can no longer be known. It seems that Israel was surrounded by enemies but the king could nevertheless feel quite confident. Indeed from v. 15 onwards it would appear that the victory had already been achieved and therefore vv. 5-14 may be a recollection of distress from the perspective of victory. Verses 26-29 indicate that the victory was celebrated in a procession to the Temple. These verses remind us of Psalm 24 with their promise of blessing in vv. 26-27.

The striking thing about the psalm is the occurrence in almost every verse of the divine name, LORD, sometimes in the shorter form found in the word 'Hallelujah' (hallelu = praise; yah = the LORD). If, as is almost certain, this divine name conveys the reality of the presence of God (see Psalm 113) then its repeated use here makes it clear that the psalmist believes that God's presence makes possible things which without him would be impossible.

Whatever the psalm's original setting, it has remained ever since a source of confidence in the LORD and a reminder that it is important to rely on him rather than upon mere human endeavour.

1 Praise the LORD, for he is good,
    for his devotion knows no end.

2 Let Israel respond,
    'For his devotion knows no end'.

3 Let the priests of Aaron's line respond,
    'For his devotion knows no end'.

4 Let those who worship the LORD respond,
    'For his devotion knows no end'.

5 In dire straits I cried 'LORD!';
    the LORD replied by giving me room to be free.

6 I have the LORD beside me; I shall not be afraid
    whatever people do to me.

7 I have the LORD beside me to help me,
    I shall look in triumph on those who hate me.

8   It is better to seek security with the LORD
        than to rely on human help.

9   It is better to seek security with the LORD
        than to rely on human leaders.

10 Whole nations have surrounded me,
        by the LORD's authority I will cut them down.

11 They have surrounded me and are all round,
        by the LORD's authority I will cut them down.

12 They have surrounded me like bees,
    they come to meet me like a bush-fire;
        by the LORD's authority I will cut them down.

13 They pushed hard enough for me to fall over,
        but the LORD helped me.

14 I sing of the LORD and the strength he has given me;
        I owe my freedom to him.

15 Listen! Songs of freedom ring out
        in the camp of those who are victorious.

16 'By his power the LORD performs mighty deeds,
        by his power the LORD brings us out on top.'

17 By his power the LORD performs mighty deeds;
        I shall not die but live!
        I will recount what the LORD has done.

18 The LORD disciplined me severely,
        but he did not hand me over to death.

19 Open for me the victory gates!
        I will enter through them; I will praise the LORD.

20 This is the gate belonging to the LORD;
        victors may enter through it.

21 I will praise you because you have answered me,
    I owe my freedom to you.

22 I was a stone which the builders rejected
    but I have become the chief corner-stone.

23 The LORD was responsible for this;
    it is something for us to marvel at.

24 Today is the day! The LORD has done it!
    let us be happy and glad today.

25 Please, please, LORD, save me;
    please make me prosperous.

26 By the LORD's authority whoever enters receives blessing,
    from the LORD's Temple we bless you all.

27 The LORD is God; he has given us light,
    cordon off the pilgrimage as it approaches the altar.

28 You are my God, I will praise you;
    my God, I will praise you highly.

29 Praise the LORD, for he is good,
    for his devotion knows no end.

✎ Psalm 119

The main claim to fame of this psalm is its length. Because of its 176 verses it is rarely read in its entirety although one or two sections are well-known. It is another acrostic psalm but its complexity goes beyond that of any of the acrostics we have met so far. It is made up of 22 stanzas, one for each letter of the Hebrew alphabet in alphabetical order. Moreover all eight verses in each stanza begin with the same Hebrew letter.

    The main theme of the psalm is praise of and thanksgiving for the Law, for which eight synonyms are used, sometimes one in each verse of a stanza. For instance, in vv.73-80 we have commandments, word, decrees, promise, law, rules, instructions and precepts. This complexity shows that the psalm is anything but a spontaneous song; it is a carefully composed and constructed poem. This, along with its emphasis on the Law, suggests that the psalm was composed sometime after the Exile. Whether it was ever used in worship and if so in what way is difficult to say.

The chief importance of the psalm lies in its attitude to the Law. The contrast between Law and grace which is sometimes drawn in the New Testament has led some people to think that for the Old Testament too the Law was a heavy burden. Only by strict adherence to it could anyone be a member of the people of God. Deuteronomy 7 sets out the true order of things. God's love alone prompted him to deliver Israel from Egypt and then to provide them with the Law as a guide to their proper response to his grace. They were to love him in return and the Law was graciously given in order to help them to express that love in obedience to his will. This psalm reflects precisely this attitude to the Law. It is something good, something to be glad and happy about. It is this joy that the psalmist feels and expresses as he meditates on the Law.

| 1 | *Alep* | Happy are they who behave with integrity, |
| | | whose conduct conforms to the LORD's law. |

| 2 | | Happy are they who follow his instructions, |
| | | who seek him whole-heartedly, |

| 3 | | Who practise no injustice |
| | | but do as he directs. |

| 4 | | You set out your rules |
| | | for men to obey implicitly. |

| 5 | | If only my conduct is directed |
| | | to keeping your statutes |

| 6 | | Then I shall not be ashamed |
| | | when I have regard to your commandments. |

| 7 | | I will praise you in all sincerity |
| | | when I learn how right are your judgements. |

8   Your statutes I will keep;
                 do not ever forsake me.

9   *Bet*   How may a young man keep life's pathway clean?
                 By guarding it, as you have said.

10   I seek you with all my heart;
                 do not let me wander from your
                       commandments.

11   I have stored up your words in my mind
                 so as not to sin against you.

12   Thanks be to you, LORD;
                 teach me your statutes.

13   I use my voice to recite
                 all the decrees you have made.

14   I am happier following your instructions
                 than I am with any amount of wealth.

15   I meditate on the rules you have made
                 and have regard for your ways.

16   I am delighted to have your statutes;
                 I will never overlook your words.

17 *Gimel*   Be generous to me,
                 I will so live as to keep your word.

18   Uncover my eyes that I may see
                 wonderful things in your law.

19   I live as an outsider on earth;
                 do not conceal your commandments from me.

20   My desire to know your decrees
                 is completely overwhelming.

21   You rebuke the insolent;
            cursed are those who stray from your
                commandments.

22   Rid me of their taunts and insults,
            for I have followed your instructions.

23   Leaders may sit down to hatch plots against me ·
            but I will study your statutes.

24   Your instructions are a delight to me,
            they are my advisers.

25 *Dalet*   I lay prostrate in the dust;
            revive me as you have promised.

26   I told you all about myself and you answered me;
            teach me your statutes.

27   Show me how to live by your rules
            so that I may meditate on the wonderful
                things you have put there.

28   I shed tears of grief;
            settle me down as you have promised.

29 ·   Close off from me the path of falsehood,
            be gracious as you instruct me.

30   I have chosen the path of truth,
            I have accepted your decrees as my guide.

31   I have followed your instructions closely;
            LORD, do not make me feel ashamed.

32   I will rush along the paths you command,
            for you deepen my understanding.

33 *He*   Teach me to live by your statutes
            and I will do so from now on.

34   Help me to understand your law and keep it,
                and to do so whole-heartedly.

35   Lead me in the path marked out by your decrees,
                for I delight in it.

36   Bend my mind to your instructions
                and not to what I can get for myself.

37   Divert my attention from what is worthless,
                let me live by your word.

38   Confirm to me your promise
                made to those who stand in awe of you.

39   Prevent the insults I dread,
                for your instructions are good.

40   How much I want to keep your rules!
                Let me live by your rightful demands.

41   *Waw*   Approach me with devotion, LORD,
                save me, as you promised,

42   That I may have an answer for whoever taunts me,
                for I have trusted in your word.

43   Never stop me from speaking a true word
                for I have pinned my hopes on your decrees.

44   I will always keep your law
                for ever and ever.

45   I will walk about freely in the open
                for I have sought to keep your rules.

46   I will talk about your instructions before kings
                without feeling any embarrassment.

47   I shall find great delight in your commandments
                which I love so much.

48   I will raise my hands in prayer
         and meditate on your statutes.

49   *Zayin*   Remember what you said to me, your servant,
         on which my hope is founded.

50   This is a comfort to me in affliction,
         that your promise revives me.

51   Though insolent people have poured scorn on me
         I have not swerved from your law.

52   As I recall your decrees in the past,
         LORD, I find comfort in them.

53   I am furious with the wicked
         who ignore your law.

54   Your statutes have been music to my ears
         in the house where I live.

55   In the night I remember your name, LORD,
         and I keep your law.

56   This has been my concern,
         that I obey your rules.

57   *Het*   LORD, you are all I need;
         I have promised to do as you say.

58   I have tried hard to please you,
         be gracious to me, as you have promised.

59   I have weighed up my behaviour
         and returned to follow your instructions.

60   I have been quick, not slow,
         to keep your commandments.

61   I have been roped in by the wicked
         but have not overlooked your law.

62   I will get up at midnight to praise you
           for your just decrees.

63   I am at one with those who show you reverence
           and keep your rules.

64   Your devotion, LORD, fills the earth;
           teach me your statutes.

65   *Tet*   You have done well for me
           as you promised, LORD.

66   Teach me discernment and knowledge
           for I am faithful to your commandments.

67   Until I was humbled I used to stray
           but now I keep your word.

68   You are good; you are my benefactor;
           teach me your statutes.

69   Insolent people smear me with lies
           but I will keep your rules whole-heartedly.

70   They are as stupid as can be
           but I find great pleasure in your law.

71   It was good for me to be humbled
           so that I may learn your statutes.

72   The law you have proclaimed is better to me
           than any amount of gold and silver.

73   *Yod*   You made me and formed me with your own hands,
           give me the ability to learn your
              commandments.

74   May your worshippers be happy when they see me,
           for I have pinned my hopes on your word.

75   I know your decrees are right, LORD;
           you are faithful even when you afflict me.

76   Let your devotion be a comfort to me
                even as you promised me.

77   Treat me with compassion that I may live,
                for your law is my constant delight.

78   May the insolent be ashamed for discrediting me
                with lies;
                for my part, I will concentrate on your rules.

79   May those who show you reverence turn to me again,
                and those who are familiar with your
                      instructions.

80   I am determined to keep your statutes
                so that I shall not be ashamed.

81   *Kap*   I am exhausted waiting for your help;
                I have pinned my hopes on your word.

82   I am worn out watching for your promise;
                I say, 'How long before you comfort me?'

83   I am like a burnt out wineskin
                but I have never overlooked your rules.

84   How long must I wait?
                When will you exact justice on my persecutors?

85   Insolent people who ignore your law
                have dug pits for me to fall into.

86   Your commandments amount to fidelity;
                men hound me with lies; help me!

87   They have almost put an end to my life,
                whereas I have never disobeyed your rules.

88   Since you show devotion, spare my life
                and I will follow the instructions you give.

89	*Lamed*	Your word endures for ever, LORD; it stands firm in the heavens.
90		Your faithfulness lasts for all time; it stands firm in the earth you founded.
91		Your decrees stand firm even today; all these are your servants.
92		Unless your law had been a source of delight to me I should have perished amid my afflictions,
93		I will never neglect your rules for by them you have kept me alive.
94		I belong to you. Save me! For I have sought to keep your rules.
95		Wicked people are waiting to destroy me but I have looked closely into your instructions.
96		I have seen how everything comes to an end once it is finished but your commandment knows no bounds.
97	*Mem*	How I love your law! All day long I pore over it.
98		Your commandment makes me wiser than my enemies for it is available to me for ever.
99		I have more insight than all my teachers for I pore over your statutes.
100		I have more discernment than the elderly for I have obeyed your rules.
101		I have never set foot on any evil course and so have kept your word.

102 I have not deviated from your decrees
     for you yourself have shown me the way.

103 How welcome are your promises to me,
     more welcome than honey in my mouth.

104 From your rules I have gained insight,
     therefore I hate all deceitful behaviour.

105 *Nun* Your word is a lamp before my feet,
     shedding light on my path.

106 I have made and confirmed my solemn promise
     to obey your just decrees.

107 I am in deep, deep trouble, LORD,
     keep me alive as you promised.

108 Accept the prayers I freely offer, LORD,
     and teach me your decrees.

109 My life is continually at risk
     but I do not forget your law.

110 Wicked people have set traps for me
     but I have not overlooked your rules.

111 Your instructions are for ever my treasured
     possession,
     for they bring me great joy.

112 I am resolved to obey your statutes;
     the outcome will always be good.

113 *Samek* I hate two-faced people,
     but I love your law.

114 You are my shelter and my shield;
     I have pinned my hopes on your word.

115   You wicked, get away from me
           that I may keep the commandments of my
              God.

116   Support me, as you promised, that I may live,
           do not make me embarrassed by unfulfilled
              hopes.

117   Uphold me that I may stay safe,
           that I may always have regard for your
              statutes.

118   You cast aside all who stray from your statutes
           for they are deceitful liars.

119   You treat wicked people everywhere as trash,
           and so I love your instructions.

120   I feel such awe of you that my flesh creeps,
           I hold your decrees in reverence.

121   *Ayin*   I have done what is just and right;
           do not abandon me to my oppressors.

122   Guarantee my well-being,
           do not allow the insolent to oppress me.

123   I have become bleary-eyed with watching for your
              help,
           for you to do right, as you promised.

124   Deal with me as your devotion demands
           and teach me your statutes.

125   I am your servant; give me discernment
           that I may understand your instructions.

126   Now is the time for action, LORD;
           people have broken your law.

127   So I love your commandments
           more than gold even when it is refined.

128   Because of your rules I have lived an honest life;
     I hate all deceitful conduct.

129   *Pe*   Your instructions are marvellous
     and so I follow them.

130   When your words are opened up they give light
     and discernment to the inexperienced.

131   I could eat and breathe your commandments
     so much do I long for them.

132   Turn towards me and be gracious
     as is customary to those who love you.

133   Keep my feet firmly on the way you promised,
     let no wrong over-master me.

134   Free me from human oppression
     so that I may keep your rules.

135   Be radiant towards me
     and teach me your statutes.

136   My tears run down like rivers
     because people do not keep your law.

137   *Sade*   You do what is right, LORD,
     your decrees are just and true.

138   You have issued your instructions,
     they are right and wholly reliable.

139   My zeal was enough to destroy me
     because my opponents overlooked your
     words.

140   Your promise is tried and true
     and I, your servant, love it,

141   I am insignificant; people look down on me;
     but I do not overlook your rules.

142   You never cease to do what is right,
   your law is the truth.

143   I have found myself in dire straits,
   yet your commandments have been my
      constant delight.

144   Your instructions are always right;
   help me understand them that I may live.

145   *Qop*   I have called to you for all I am worth;
   answer me, LORD, I will keep your statutes.

146   I have called to you; save me
   that I may follow your instructions.

147   I rise before daybreak and cry for help;
   I pin my hopes on what you have said.

148   I lie awake through the night hours
   to meditate on your promise.

149   Hear my voice, as your devotion demands;
   LORD, let me live as your justice requires.

150   People carrying out a wicked plan draw near;
   they are far removed from your law.

151   You are near me, LORD,
   and all your commandments are true.

152   Long ago I got to know about your instructions
   that you meant them to last for ever.

153   *Res*   See the trouble I am in and rescue me
   for I have not overlooked your law.

154   As counsel for my defence, secure my release;
   let me live, as you promised.

155   Freedom is out of sight for the wicked
         for they have not sought to obey your statutes.

156   Your compassion knows no bounds, LORD,
         let me live, as your decree demands.

157   There are many who oppose and persecute me,
         but unswervingly I followed your instructions.

158   I have seen their treachery and been filled with
         loathing
         because they have not done as you said.

159   See how I love your rules, LORD,
         let me live as your devotion demands.

160   Your word is governed by truth
         and every one of your just decrees stands for
         ever.

161   *Sin*   Officials persecute me without cause,
         but I am overawed by your words.

162   I jump for joy because of your promise
         like one who finds great spoil.

163   I hate, I loathe falsehood,
         but I love your law.

164   Seven times a day I praise you
         for your just decrees.

165   Those who love your law prosper greatly,
         nothing can make them stumble.

166   I await your deliverance, LORD,
         and keep your commandments.

167   I follow your instructions
         and love them very much.

168   I keep your rules and instructions
            for I live out my life before you.

169   *Taw*   May my cry of joy reach you, LORD,
            give me understanding, as you said you
               would.

170   May my prayer catch your ear;
            rescue me as you have promised.

171   May praise come bubbling from my lips
            because you teach me your statutes.

172   May I sing aloud of your promise,
            for all your commandments are just.

173   May you reach out to help me,
            for I have chosen to obey your rules.

174   While I long for you to deliver me, LORD,
            your law is my constant delight.

175   May I stay alive and praise you;
            may your decrees help me.

176   I stray like a lost sheep; look for me!
            For I have not overlooked your
               commandments.

Psalm 120

In the Hebrew Bible Psalms 120-134 all bear the heading 'Song of Ascents', though it is no longer clear what this title means. It could suggest that at some stage, if not originally, they were used on pilgrimages to the Temple in Jerusalem. Certainly some of them would fit well in such a context.

This psalm, however, is a complaint from a person under attack by slanderers (vv. 2-3) and there is nothing to connect it with a pilgrimage. The psalmist is convinced that God hears him and will deal effectively with his attackers (v. 1). Although he lives among fellow-Jews he may just as well be living among foreigners, so strong are the attacks (v. 5).

So this psalm, like others, recognises that people who seek to live peaceful lives will often find themselves under verbal, if not physical attack. We may remind ourselves of Jesus who came on a mission of reconciliation and yet was slandered and rejected. Nevertheless the psalm reminds us that God is not deaf to the plight of such people.

1 When in distress it was to the LORD
        I cried, and he answered me.

2 'Save me, LORD, from those who lie about me,
        from those who slander me.'

3 What will he give you, you who slander me?
        What more will he place on your tongues?

4 A warrior's sharpened arrows!
        The red-hot ash of a broom bush too!

5 It has been hard for me,
        like going to live in Mesek
        or camping out in Kedar.

6 I have lived long enough
        among people opposed to peace.

7 I aim for peace when I speak,
        but they are all for conflict.

✿❧ Psalm 121

This psalmist certainly knew where to look for help when he needed it. He may have looked around the hill-top shrines where pagan gods were worshipped but he knew they were of no use to him: only the LORD could help him.

He may have been on his way to or from the Temple in Jerusalem as he sang this psalm, for v. 3, at least, looks like a priestly response. In the present translation the quotation marks are closed at the end of that verse though some take the whole of verses 3-8 to be priestly words of assurance. Here v. 3 is taken to be the psalmist's own recollection of words he had heard in the Temple which now reassure him, while verses 4-8 represent his own desire to convey to others the assurance he himself has gained.

Taken on its own the psalm could seem to express false confidence, for it is abundantly clear that the LORD does not always protect his own from danger or difficulty. It needs to be read, however, alongside psalms such as Psalm 120 which reveal the other side of the coin. Doubtless he was well aware of the misfortunes which can fall upon loyal servants of the LORD but he does not feel the need on every occasion to qualify his expressions of confidence by reference to them. Different circumstances call for different songs.

Consequently the psalm has been and will remain a source of inspiration and confidence for people confronted by uncertainty and wondering about alternative sources of help.

1   I will scan the hills with my eyes.
        From which direction will my help come?

2   My help comes from the LORD
        who made heaven and earth.

3   'May your guardian not let you fall!
        May he not become drowsy!'

4   See here! He never gets drowsy or falls asleep,
        the Guardian of Israel.

5   The LORD is your guardian,
        the LORD is your protector;
        he stands at your right hand.

6   In the day time the sun will not strike you down,
        nor will the moon at night.

7   The LORD will guard you from all harm,
        he will guard your very life.

8   The LORD will guard you at home or abroad
        from now on and for ever.

❧ Psalm 122

This is a psalm in praise of Jerusalem, seeking also the well-being of the city. Clearly the psalmist is either looking forward to or looking back on his pilgrimage there. It is not, however, a private visit; he summons others to go with him.

From the description of the city and the prayers related to it we may guess that the group was invited to Zion for the settlement of some dispute. Zion was the place from which the Law of the LORD went out (Isaiah 2.3, Micah 4.2) and where people went for judgement on difficult legal cases (Deut. 17.8-20, 1 Samuel 15.1-6). It may even be that there were inter-tribal disputes in the early days of Israel which needed to be settled in Jerusalem according to the Law which was upheld by the king and taught by the priests. The prayer for Jerusalem's peace may be either a prayer that there may be peace in Jerusalem or a prayer that the peace which Jerusalem has at its disposal may be experienced by those who go there. In the light of what has just been said it is here translated in the second sense.

In v.3 there is a serious problem for translators. The word in the second line really seems to mean 'joined together for itself' and it is hard to know just what this signifies. Since a similar word is used in Exodus 36.10-13 about the curtains surrounding the Tabernacle in the desert, it is here understood as referring to the encircling walls of Jerusalem.

Even if the psalm was originally used in this way there is no doubt that it also came to be used as an expression of longing to visit the holy city and it has retained this meaning. Christians have further interpreted it in terms of the joy in anticipation of finding peace and well-being in the presence of God wherever they worship him.

1 I was glad people were saying to me,
    'Let us go up to the LORD's house.'

2 We have been used to standing
    in your gateway, Jerusalem.

3 Jerusalem, built as a city
    enclosed within its walls,

4 Where tribes go up,
    the tribes of the LORD,
in accordance with Israelite law,
    to confess the name of the LORD.

5 For there judges sit in judgement,
    judges appointed by the Davidic house.

6 Pray for the peace which Jerusalem gives,
    'May those who love you be at ease,

7 May peace be found within your fortifications
    and rest within your fortresses.'

8 For the sake of my fellows and friends
    let me declare peace within you.

9 For the sake of the family of the LORD our God
    let me seek good for you.

ॐ Psalm 123

This short psalm was spoken or sung on behalf of the whole community during a time of oppression which we can no longer identify. It could have been during the exile in Babylon, but there were plenty of other occasions when the Israelites and Judaeans had to submit to their conquerors. The striking thing about the psalm is its recognition of the people's total dependence on the generosity of God as depicted by the metaphors in v.2.

They are 'fed up' with the oppression they experience (v.4) but can only wait for God to act. It is perhaps worth noticing that the prayers for retribution found in many other psalms (e.g. 5 and 139) are missing here.

The psalm serves as a reminder never to be so arrogant as to claim God's mercies as a right but always to recognise him as the King whom we serve and upon whose grace we must wait.

1   I will raise my eyes to you,
      my heavenly King.

2   As servants watch for their masters to be generous,
      as a maid watches for her mistress' gift,
so our eyes are fixed on the LORD our God
      until he is generous to us.

3   Be gracious, LORD, be gracious,
      for we have suffered too much contempt.

4   We choke on the mockery of those who live in luxury,
      on the contempt of those who look down on us.

❧ Psalm 124

If Psalm 123 is sung while waiting for deliverance from oppression, Psalm 124 is a song of thanksgiving for such deliverance. That the psalm was meant to be recited or sung by Israelites gathered for worship is indicated by the fact that the first verse looks like the priestly announcement of the first line of the song followed by a call to the worshippers to join in.

The theme is that God alone can set his people free from oppression — and he does so. The situation from which they have been rescued is, as usual, unclear since it is referred to only in a series of metaphors. As a result the psalm could be used on any number of different occasions when Israel had been set free from trouble.

Like Psalm 121 it is a reminder that we are dependent on God alone for help and that he alone sets us free, for as maker of heaven and earth all power belongs to him.

1 'Had it not been the LORD who was with us',
    let Israel please say it:

2 Had it not been the LORD who was with us
    when our fellow-men rose against us,

3 Then they would have swallowed us alive
    when their anger flared up against us.

4 Then the waters would have drowned us,
    the torrent would have swept over us.

5 Then it would have reached above our heads
    with raging waters.

6 The LORD be thanked, for he did not place us
    in their teeth to be torn like prey.

7 We were set free, like a bird
    which escapes from the trap which men set for it.
  The trap was broken!
    So we are free!

8 The LORD helps us when we call his name,
    he who made heaven and earth.

✌ Psalm 125

*This psalm opens with a confident expression of God's care and protection
of those who put their trust in him. They are enfolded in his care as Mount
Zion is enfolded by the surrounding hills (vv.1-2). Verse 3, however,
indicates some hardship which has overtaken Israel. Literally it reads 'The
sceptre of wickedness shall not be at rest in. . . .' This may refer to foreign
domination which often resulted in the Israelites having to comply with the
religious practices of their conquerors. Alternatively, but perhaps less
likely, it could refer to the seizure of power by wicked people who then seek*

to force their ways on the rest of the people. In either case such evil power will be short-lived.

Verse 4 stands out because it is addressed directly to God. It is a prayer for the good in the land. The following verse reverts to describing what the LORD will do to those who force others into wrong behaviour.

The final prayer for 'shalom' — peace and prosperity — may have been added as the psalm was used on subsequent occasions in worship.

It is not easy to hold on to confidence in God when wickedness seems to retain its hold on society for so long. This psalm helps us to do so.

1   Those who trust in the LORD
   are like Mount Zion
 which cannot be dislodged
   but lasts for ever.

2   Jerusalem — mountains enfold her;
   so too the LORD enfolds his people
   from this time and for ever.

3   For wickedness will not hold sway
   in the land assigned to the righteous,
 and so the righteous will not need
   to turn their hands to wrong-doing.

4   Do good, LORD, to those who are good,
   to those who mean to live good lives.

5   But those who influence others into their own crooked ways
   the LORD will lead away with the wrong-doers.

May Israel have peace and prosperity.

❦ Psalm 126

This well-known and beautiful psalm may have had either of two original settings. First the restoration of Zion may refer to the return from the

Babylonian Exile which is recalled with incredulity and great joy. If so, then verses 4-6 must be a prayer arising from the difficult times which followed this, to which the prophet Haggai bears witness. The task of re-establishing the returned exiles in the homeland was not easy and was made harder by famine (Haggai 1.7). Sowing, therefore, was done in a hopeless frame of mind, but the psalm reminds people that the God who brought them out of Babylon will also grant them good harvests. It may have been sung at the New Year festival in the autumn.

Alternatively, the psalm may have been used in the context of any such New Year festival. The restoration of Zion would then refer to the giving of rains after the summer drought, rains which ensured that the seeds sown in late autumn would spring to life. Such New Year celebrations were part of the Feast of Tabernacles which was full of joy and optimism. (See Zechariah 14.16-19 for the association of this feast with the Kingship of the LORD and the giving of rain.)

Whichever of these two original settings is correct, the psalm has provided later generations, including ourselves, with words to express unbounded joy when God changes the circumstances of life for the better.

1 When the LORD restored Zion
        it was as though we were dreaming.

2 We could not speak for laughing,
        we could only utter cries of joy.
    Then the saying arose among the nations,
        'The LORD has done something great with these people.'

3 The LORD has done something great with us:
        we were delighted.

4 Restore us again, LORD,
        as streams refresh the dry south.

5 Those who sow in tears
        will reap with shouts of joy.

6 Whoever weeps as he walks along his furrow
        carrying a handful of seed
    will surely come home in joy
        carrying his sheaves of corn.

287

❧ Psalm 127

This short psalm is a piece of instruction, perhaps given by some official in the course of public worship. It falls into two parts connected by the double meaning of the word 'house'. In verse 1 it means the actual building, but in verses 3-6 it refers to a person's household and especially to his children. Both parts speak of the folly and futility of human effort apart from God. The first part gives examples of human dependence on God in such things as house-building and civil defence. The second part, particularly v. 3, makes the same point with regard to children. Human participation there must be of course, but the gift is God's and therefore children rightly belong to him. This was recognised, for instance, by Hannah when she dedicated Samuel to the service of God (1 Samuel 1.27) and by Mary the mother of Jesus who similarly let go of her son.

In Israel children were a joy to their parents as well as protection for their future, for they were signs of the blessing of God. To have seven sons was to be blessed indeed (see Ruth 4.15, Job 1.1). Consequently, when parents became involved in disputes with others (v.6) they could feel secure because both they and their opponents knew that they had been blessed by God.

The psalm, then, does not advocate idleness any more than Jesus does in Matthew 6.24-33. It reminds those who read or recite it that every activity, if it is to be worth anything, must be related to the will and activity of God, for it is he who brings success to human enterprise. It makes the further point with regard to children that parents are not free to regard them as their own possessions to be disposed of at will. They belong to God first and to their parents only as a gift from God.

1   Unless the LORD builds a house
      those who do build it work to no purpose.
  Unless the LORD defends a city
      those who do defend it keep watch to no purpose.

2   It is no use your getting up early
      and going to bed late,
  or making a living by over-work;
      he gives his due to the one he loves.

3   Bear in mind, children belong to the LORD;
        he gives them to you as a reward.

4   Like arrows in a soldier's hand
        are children born to young people.

5   Happy is the soldier
        who fills his quiver with them!

6   Such people will never feel ashamed
        when they argue with opponents by the town gate.

❧ Psalm 128

*Like Psalm 127 this too is a psalm of instruction which enshrines much of
the teaching found in the so-called Wisdom literature, notably in the Book
of Proverbs. 'Reverence for the LORD' is the beginning and the foundation of
all wisdom (see Proverbs 1.7) and therefore leads to success and prosperity.
Success is here defined first in terms of food provided by a person's own crops
(v.2) and then in terms of family happiness (v.3). The vine is also used elsewhere as a symbol of a wife or lover (see Song of Solomon 7.8,12 and
possibly Isaiah 5.1-7).*

*The Wisdom literature usually speaks to the individual, but here
verses 5 and 6 make it clear that an individual's well-being is bound up
with that of his community, Jerusalem. This is, in fact, common to much
Old Testament thought. The individual is recognised and his individuality
is secure, yet he can hardly ever be thought of apart from his relationship
with others and especially with those who share the privilege and responsibility of being the people of God.*

*We cannot now say in what context a psalm such as this may have
been used in worship, but we do know that instruction in general was part
of the responsibility of the priest or Levite. We have seen already (Psalm 1)
that this kind of teaching must be understood as 'true' only in the most general sense and is offered more to encourage right attitudes to God than to
make theological statements about rewards for holding them. There are
other psalms which question the teaching's validity in particular cases (for
instance Psalm 73).*

We, too, have to see the psalm as a call for proper respect and reverence for God rather than as an infallible promise of prosperity as a reward for it.

1   Happy are those who revere the LORD,
        who do as he requires.

2   Your own produce will provide your food,
        you will be happy and prosperous.

3   Your wife inside your house
        will bear children as a vine bears grapes.
    Your children round your table
        will be like cuttings from an olive tree.

4   See, a man who reveres the LORD
        is blessed in this way.

5   May the LORD bless you from Zion!
    Watch Jerusalem prosper
        as long as you live,

6   Watch your children bear children
        as all goes well for Israel!

✱ Psalm 129

Like Psalm 124 this begins with the quotation of the first line of a song followed by a call to the people to join in. It is meant therefore as a corporate psalm and the use of the first person singular in verses 1-3 simply means that Israel is here personified. The psalm looks back throughout history to times of oppression ever since Israel was a 'boy', to the period of wandering in the wilderness after the people had been 'adopted' as God's son at the Exodus (Exodus 4.22, Hosea 11.1). Probably it was sung on many occasions when Israel suffered at the hands of foreign nations.

Nevertheless the psalm expresses the confidence that since God always does what is right the oppressor will be punished (vv.4-5). The prayer that this will happen again is couched in a metaphor of grass growing in the dust that accumulates on the flat roof of a house where there is insufficient soil or moisture for the seed to germinate with any success (v.6). The harvest would be no more than a handful of grass.

Verse 8 is sometimes thought to continue this figure by referring to passers-by who are unable to offer the usual greeting. The present translation sees the verse as referring back to the oppressors and understands the lack of a word of blessing on their part as the reason for their failure.

The enduring point about the psalm is the expression of confidence that God always does what is right even when the immediate circumstances make us doubtful of the fact.

1 'I have been under severe attack since boyhood';
    let Israel please say it.

2 I have been under severe attack since boyhood
    but have not been overcome.

3 Men have made long weals on my back
    like furrows cut by ploughmen.

4 The LORD does what is right;
    he has cut in pieces the flails of the wicked.

5 May all who hate Zion
    draw back from her in shame!

6 May they be like grass on a roof-top
    which withers before it can sprout.

7 No one can harvest a handful
    or bind an armful.

8 For those who passed by did not say,
    'The blessing of the LORD be upon you;
    in the LORD's name we bless you.'

✺ Psalm 130

The first six verses of this psalm are a personal cry for help from an Israelite who is in some unspecified trouble, but who sees it as due to his sinfulness. On the one hand he is clear that God has every right to punish sin and that he has no defence to offer. On the other hand he is equally sure of God's readiness to forgive (v.4). The recognition of this paradox serves only to increase his respect and reverence for God. Verses 5-6 then describe his eagerness as he waits for God's answer to his prayer.

Verses 7 and 8 are addressed to Israel and there is much uncertainty about the relationship between them and the earlier part of the psalm. It is probably best to understand them as spoken by the same psalmist as a call to each and every Israelite, rather than to Israel as a corporate entity, to follow his example and to 'wait' for God to answer prayer.

The importance of the psalm lies in the recognition that while God takes sin very seriously and no sinner can claim exemption from punishment, nevertheless, at the same time, he is ready to forgive those who seek his help. Christians believe that this finds its clearest expression in the Cross of Jesus which shows both the seriousness with which God views sin and the love which prompts him to offer forgiveness.

1   Out of my deep distress
      I call to you, LORD.

2   Lord, hear me calling,
      listen closely to my cry for help.

3   If you, LORD, should be on the watch for sins,
      LORD, who could withstand that?

4   But you are ready to forgive
      so that you may be revered.

5   I have waited for the LORD, I have waited.
      I have waited eagerly for his reply.

6   I have waited more eagerly
      than those who watch for morning watch for morning.

7   Wait, Israel, for the LORD,
      for he is always ready to show devotion
      and more than ready to set men free.

8   He alone will set Israel free
      from the effects of all their sins.

ꙮ Psalm 131

In this short psalm the psalmist lays claim to the qualities of humility and self-control (vv.1-2). Seen by themselves these verses appear self-righteous, but if we knew the context in which they were used we may well find that this was not their intention. They may, for instance, have been used alongside a psalm of lament over misfortune in which case we could see them as a confession of innocence (see Job 31). The previous psalm was just such a psalm and the two psalms were possibly meant to be used together. Both 130 and 131 have a similar pattern. Both are addressed directly to the LORD, but both include a call to Israel to wait on the LORD (130.7 and 131.3).

Pride and self-indulgence are basic sins from which all other sins stem. They are the sins for which the first man and woman were excluded from the Garden of Eden (Genesis 3) and they are regularly condemned by the prophets.

We should be careful, therefore, not to use the psalm to justify ourselves like the Pharisee in Jesus' parable in Luke 18.11-14. The psalm should rather remind us of the disposition we ought to show to God. At the same time it should warn us against that false humility which is ready to confess to sins which have not been committed in the belief that misfortune must always be due to our sin.

1   LORD, I do not harbour proud thoughts,
      I do not set my sights too high.
  I do not try to achieve goals
      too high or too difficult for me.

2   No indeed! I have calmed and quietened my desires.
        Like a child held tight against its mother
        so is my desire held on tight rein.

3   Wait, Israel, for the LORD
        from now on and for ever.

🐾 Psalm 132

The psalm falls naturally into two parts. Verses 1-9 are concerned with the Ark of the Covenant and recall the bringing of the Ark into Jerusalem as described in 2 Samuel 6, although in that account there is no mention of any promise made by David. Ephrathah in v.6 is associated with Bethlehem, David's birthplace, in Micah 5.2, while the neighbourhood of Jair refers to Kiriath Jearim where David found the Ark and from where he transferred it to Jerusalem. Verses 10-18 concern the Davidic line of kings who occupied the throne of Judah almost continuously up to the time of the exile in Babylon in 587 BC. The divine promise that this should be so is found in 2 Samuel 7. The two events are closely associated, then, both in 2 Samuel and here in this psalm. It is therefore likely that they were celebrated together in Israel's worship and that this psalm was part of the liturgy for that celebration.

As has already been mentioned elsewhere, there is no description in the Old Testament of the forms which Israel's worship took at the great festivals. We have to rely on hints that we find in the psalms and elsewhere. That there was a procession carrying the Ark into Jerusalem has already been suggested by Psalm 68.25-29. In his description of Solomon's dedication of the Temple the Chronicler uses vv.8-10 of this present psalm (2 Chronicles 6.41-42), thus we should probably see this psalm as one used in such a festival.

The two parts of the psalm are now nicely balanced by the fact that vv.1-9 are about David's promise to God, while vv.10-18 are about God's promise to David. There is no suggestion, however, that the fulfilment of God's promise is dependent on the fulfilment of David's.

The final two verses suggest that there was no longer a descendant of David on the throne and they express confidence that God will restore the royal line. They reflect a time when the first sixteen verses could no longer be used in their original sense since the Temple was in ruins and (presumably) the Ark destroyed and when the Davidic dynasty had been brought to an end. The original divine promise is therefore cast into the future, as in Psalm 2, as a hope of a coming Messianic (anointed) king, a hope which has persisted and which Christians see as fulfilled in Jesus.

1 Remember, LORD, all the suffering
    which David had to endure.

2 Remember the promise he made to the LORD,
    his vow to the Almighty God of Jacob.

3 'I will not enter my family tent,
    I will not climb into bed,

4 I will not close my eyes in sleep,
    nor my eyelids in slumber,

5 Until I find a place for the LORD,
    a home for the Mighty God of Jacob.'

6 Look, we heard about it in Ephrathah,
    we found it in the neighbourhood of Jair.

7 Let us enter God's home
    and make obeisance at his footstool.

8 Arise, LORD, and enter your resting place,
    you and your mighty Ark.

9 Your priests, let them show off your victories like new robes,
    those devoted to you, let them cry out in joy.

10 For your servant David's sake
    do not reject your anointed king.

11 The LORD promised on oath to David —
    he will never go back on his word —

'One of your own children
    I will place on your throne.

12   If your sons keep my covenant with them
    and the regulations I have taught them,
then their descendants always
    will sit on your throne after you.'

13   For the LORD has chosen Zion,
    he wanted it as a place to live in.

14   'This is where I shall rest for ever,
    here I will live, for so I want to do.

15   I will amply provide for her destitute,
    I will satisfy her needy with food.'

16   Your priests, let them show off your salvation like new robes,
    those devoted to you, let them cry out in joy.

17   'There I will raise up a king to continue David's line.
    I have a shining successor ready for my anointed.
18   His enemies I will cover with shame,
    but his crown shall sparkle on his head.'

❧ Psalm 133

It is difficult to decide whether the 'brothers' in this psalm refers to actual brothers who live together in the family circle, in which case the psalm extols domestic harmony, or to brothers in the extended sense of fellow-Israelites, in which case the psalm extols corporate worship at the great festivals in Jerusalem. References to the anointing of priests in v.2 may, but does not necessarily, suggest the latter.

The anointing oil and the precious dew are fitting similes for the blessing of the LORD. Such blessing includes material things such as crops, wealth and children and can be summed up in the word 'life' (see Psalm 16).

The last line did not suggest eternal life as we understand it. It is a promise that God gives fullness of life for as long as people are physically alive. There is also perhaps a hint of the belief that in some way a person lives on in his children.

Whichever of the above interpretations we may regard as original, the psalm is now capable of being used, quite appropriately, in either sense. Further, for Christians who believe in eternal life through Jesus who rose from the dead and still lives, the final sentence may be read as a promise of this for those who live in harmony.

1   How precious, how lovely it is
       when brothers live in complete harmony;

2   As precious as the oil poured over the head
       and running down over the beard,
   over the beard of the priest descended from Aaron,
       and continuing to run over the collar of his robes;

3   As precious as the dew on Hermon,
       the kind which falls on the hills of Zion.
   For on such the LORD sends his blessing,
       life which lasts for ever.

✍ Psalm 134

Like Psalm 133, this psalm too is concerned with blessing. The Hebrew literally speaks of God's servants 'blessing' the LORD in verses 1 and 2 and of the LORD blessing his servants in v.3. It was tempting to follow most translations and to use the word 'bless' throughout in order to bring out the pattern of the psalm. However, the word must have a different meaning since man cannot bless God in the same way as God blesses man (see Psalm 133). In any case the phrase 'bless the LORD' has become a religious cliché which has little meaningful content. When the Hebrew word is used with God as subject and man as object then it has the meaning indicated in Psalm 133; but when it is used with man as subject and God as object it means some-

thing like 'thank' or possibly 'adore'. Here it is the response to God's blessing.

The servants of the LORD (v.1) are either Temple officials or Israelite worshippers in general sharing in a night vigil.

The psalm still calls on those who use it to respond to the LORD's blessing not in any perfunctory way but with a real spirit of gratitude and adoration.

1 Say thank you to the LORD
    all you servants of his,
who spend your nights
    standing in his Temple.

2 Raise your hands to the holy place
    and say thank you to the LORD.

3 From Zion may the LORD bless you,
    he who made heaven and earth.

❧ Psalm 135

This is a hymn in praise of the LORD for all that his name conjures up in the thoughts of his worshippers. It reminds them, as they hear it in worship, of his creative power (vv.6-7), his redemptive power (vv.8-12) and of his superiority over other gods (vv.15-18). The response is therefore to thank or 'bless' God (see Psalm 134).

The psalm uses language and incidents which may be found elsewhere in the Psalms (see Psalms 115 and 136) but this is probably due to their currency as the vocabulary and themes of worship rather than to any direct borrowing. It is often noticed that the wanderings in the wilderness and the events at Sinai are not mentioned; but then neither is the oppression of the Israelites in Egypt or the first nine plagues. Indeed the crossing of the Red Sea is alluded to only in general terms (v.9) whereas the events leading up to the settlement in Canaan are mentioned more fully (vv.10-12). It is not meant to be a comprehensive history but is rather a poetic reminder of the whole story of Israel's early life.

The ridiculing of idols is reminiscent of the prophets, especially Isaiah 40-55 (see also Psalm 115). The various groups who are called to thank the LORD also remind us of Psalm 115. This makes it very likely that the psalm was used in celebration at one or more of Israel's great festivals.

To look back to the beginnings of one's religious inheritance is a valuable exercise. It is a reminder of God's continuous activity on behalf of his people and his ability to exercise that power still. For similar reasons Christians look back to the events of Jesus' life, sometimes singling out one, for instance at Christmas and Easter, but always remembering them all.

1 Hallelujah!
   Praise him who is the LORD,
       praise him, you servants of the LORD,

2 Who stand in the LORD's house
       in the temple courts of our God.

3 Hallelujah! For the LORD is good,
       sing praises to him for he is our delight.

4 For the LORD chose Jacob for himself,
       Israel as his special people.

5 I know that the LORD is great,
       our Lord is greater than any other gods.

6 The LORD made whatever he pleased
       in heaven and earth, in seas and deeps,

7 Bringing up mists from the ends of the earth.
   He made lightning flashes to accompany the rain,
       fetching the wind out of his stores.

8 He struck down the eldest sons in Egypt,
       both human and animal.

9 He gave evidence of his wonderful power
       by his deeds against Pharaoh and his servants.

10 He defeated many nations
       and killed powerful kings;

11 Sihon, the Amorite king,
      Og, the king of Bashan
      and all the Canaanite city states.

12 He gave their lands for Israel to inherit,
      Israel his own people.

13 LORD, you will be well-known for ever,
      you will be remembered by successive generations.

14 For the LORD will take his people's side,
      he will have pity on his servants.

15 Other nations worship idols of silver and gold
      made by human hands.

16 They have mouths but cannot speak
      and eyes but they cannot see;

17 They have ears but cannot hear,
      nor can they even breathe.

18 May those who make them and trust in them
      become as useless as the idols themselves.

19 Thank the LORD, people of Israel,
      thank the LORD, Aaronite priests,

20 Thank the LORD, Levitical priests,
      thank the LORD, you his worshippers.

21 Blessed be the LORD from Zion,
      he who lives in Jerusalem.
   Hallelujah!

❧ Psalm 136

Here is another psalm which recalls God's past dealings with his people. It does so more fully than Psalm 135, beginning with the creation (vv. 5-9) and going on to the deliverance from Egypt (vv. 10-15), the wanderings in the desert (v. 16) — without any specific mention of the events at Mount Sinai — the settlement in the promised land (vv. 17-22) and God's subsequent care (vv. 23-25). The absence of any mention of the covenant at Sinai is somewhat surprising. Perhaps at the time the psalm was composed this had not achieved the position of importance in Israel that it later came to have.

The second line of each verse is clearly a response to be offered by the congregation and this sets the psalm firmly in the context of public worship. It would be particularly suitable for the spring festival of Passover and Unleavened Bread, but it would not be out of place either in the autumn Feast of Tabernacles.

Once more the recollection of God's gracious use of his power on his people's behalf and of his constancy is the ground for his people's praise.

1 Acknowledge the LORD for he is good,
    his devotion knows no bounds.

2 Acknowledge the God of gods,
    his devotion knows no bounds.

3 Acknowledge the Lord of lords,
    his devotion knows no bounds.

4 Who alone has done the impossible,
    his devotion knows no bounds.

5 He made the heavens, such was his ability,
    his devotion knows no bounds.

6 He laid down the earth upon the seas,
    his devotion knows no bounds.

7 He made the great lights in the sky,
    his devotion knows no bounds.

8   The sun to dominate the day,
         his devotion knows no bounds.

9   The moon and stars to rule the night,
         his devotion knows no bounds.

10   He killed the Egyptians' eldest sons,
         his devotion knows no bounds.

11   And led Israel out from among them,
         his devotion knows no bounds.

12   Reaching out to them with his strong hands,
         his devotion knows no bounds.

13   He split the Red Sea in two,
         his devotion knows no bounds.

14   He led the Israelites through it,
         his devotion knows no bounds.

15   But drowned Pharaoh and his army in it,
         his devotion knows no bounds.

16   He guided his people through the desert,
         his devotion knows no bounds.

17   He defeated great kings,
         his devotion knows no bounds.

18. And killed them, majestic as they were,
         his devotion knows no bounds.

19   Sihon, the Amorite king,
         his devotion knows no bounds.

20   And Og, king of Bashan,
         his devotion knows no bounds.

21   And gave their land for Israel to inherit,
         his devotion knows no bounds.

22 Israel his own people,
      his devotion knows no bounds.

23 He remembered us when we were down,
      his devotion knows no bounds.

24 And wrenched us free from our oppressors,
      his devotion knows no bounds.

25 He provides food for man and beast,
      his devotion knows no bounds.

26 Acknowledge the God of heaven,
      his devotion knows no bounds.

❧ Psalm 137

The psalm begins by looking back to a time during the exile in Babylon when the captive Jews had to endure the mockery of the Babylonians. It may be that it was written soon after the return to Judah in 538 BC. Verses 8 and 9 do not necessarily contradict this because the city of Babylon was not destroyed when Cyrus captured it that year. Alternatively it is possible to see it as written in Babylon looking back to an occasion earlier in the Exile. The present translation rather assumes this latter situation.

It offers us no information about conditions in the Exile other than the understandable gloating of the Babylonians. The songs of Zion, such as Psalms 46 and 48, had spoken of Jerusalem as God's dwelling place and therefore eternally safe and secure. The fact that Jerusalem was now in ruins cast serious doubts either upon God's power or upon his devotion or upon both. The Babylonians were not slow to make fun of the sorrowing, bewildered Jews.

The Edomites (v.7) who lived to the South of Judah were delighted at Judah's defeat for it gave them a chance to occupy and make use of Judaean territory (see Lamentations 4.21, Ezekiel 25.12-14, 35.1-9, Obadiah).

The last two verses are an embarrassment to us because of their ferocity, especially against the children. They can be understood only against the background of the desperation felt by the Jews and their strong belief in the

justice of God which required the annihilation of the Babylonian people.
They make it hard for many today to use the psalm in its entirety, beautiful
as the first six verses may be. Christians in particular are aware of another
way of dealing with evil by overcoming it with suffering love as seen in the
Cross of Jesus.

1 There we sat beside Babylon's streams
      and we wept when we remembered Zion.

2 Upon the willows which grew there
      we hung up our harps,

3 Though there our captors demanded songs.
      They made fun of us telling us to be happy,
      'Sing us one of the songs of Zion'.

4 How could we sing the LORD's song
      on foreign soil?

5 If I should forget you, Jerusalem,
      may my hand forget how to play.

6 May my song stick in my throat
      if I do not remember you,
   if I do not think more highly of Jerusalem
      than of my own greatest happiness.

7 Remember, LORD, the day Jerusalem fell;
      hold it against the Edomites
   that they said, 'Strip it, strip it
      down to its very foundations'.

8 Babylon, a woman doomed to destruction,
      happy the man who repays you
      in kind for what you have done to us.

9 Happy the man who seizes your children
      and smashes them against the rock.

✃ Psalm 138

Since it uses the first person singular this psalm may be regarded as a personal thanksgiving for deliverance from trouble in the past which gives the singer confidence to face trouble in the present. A closer reading, however, suggests the strong possibility that the psalmist is representing the whole community. The occasion cannot now be determined but the period of the Exile and the impending return to Judah would be appropriate. There is some support for this view in the fact that the psalm is placed after Psalm 137 which comes from that period. Also verse 5 is reminiscent of Isaiah 40.5, while making obeisance towards the Temple reminds us of the Book of Daniel which is set in the exilic period, though the practice may have begun earlier than this.

Whatever its date the psalm is about the devotion and fidelity of God which are demonstrated in his actions on behalf of his people (vv.1-3) and which can be seen by people everywhere (vv.4-5).

Verses 6-8 hold together two aspects of God which are found throughout the Old Testament — the greatness of God as far superior to men and the nearness of God and his concern for all people high and low (see, for example, Isaiah 66.1-2).

These two truths about God which are found in the Old and the New Testaments alike must be held as complementary if our understanding of God is to be based on what we find in the Bible. God who is supreme over all things and whose fullness is beyond our human grasp is nevertheless present with us and near to us individually however great or humble we may be.

1   I acknowledge you whole-heartedly,
        in your divine presence I sing psalms to you.

2   I make obeisance towards your holy Temple,
        I acknowledge that you are the LORD
   because of your devotion and fidelity;
        for you greatly enhanced your reputation by fulfilling
          your promise.

3   One day I called, and you answered me,
        you give me inner strength and make me proud.

4   All the kings in the world will acknowledge you
        when they hear the promises you have made.

5   They will watch closely how the LORD acts,
        for the glory of the LORD is great.

6   For, high as the LORD is, he still sees ordinary folk
        and recognises the high and mighty at a distance.

7   Though my way is surrounded by trouble
        you ensure I stay alive.
    Because my enemies are angry you stretch out your hand,
        your strong right hand saves me.

8   The LORD accomplishes it for me,
        LORD, your devotion knows no bounds;
        do not refrain from your activities.

✺ Psalm 139

The proximity of God as described in Psalm 138 is not always a pleasant experience. It means, as this psalmist recognises, that people can hide nothing from him, not even their most inward thoughts (vv.1-4). Escape from this all-seeing eye of God is impossible (vv.5-12). At the same time this omnipresence of God is a source of confidence since it means that he is there with his people to guide them (v.10). The intimate knowledge which God has of each person is because he made them (vv.13-16). As he contemplates all this the psalmist is filled with a sense of awe (vv.17-18).

Verses 19-22 stand out awkwardly and are often omitted when the psalm is now recited. They strike a discordant note similar to the final verses of Psalm 137. Yet there are no good grounds for thinking that they are not the psalmist's own words. His view of God as all-seeing means that God can see the wickedness in other people, especially those who set themselves up in opposition to him. That being so, divine justice demands that God's enemies be destroyed and so he prays that this may happen.

Finally, the psalmist invites God to inspect his own life and thoughts so that he may be guided on a course which is not wicked (vv.23-24).

We may wish to pray for God to deal with the wickedness in the world in a different way from that sought by the psalmist, but the destruction of wickedness is something we all long for. The reminder that God knows us as intimately as this will save us from pride and self-righteousness as we pray.

1   LORD, you have examined me and you know.

2   You know me through and through, sleeping or waking;
       you discern from a distance what I have in mind.

3   You sift through all I do, on the move or at rest;
       you get used to the way I behave.

4   For though I do not utter a word,
       you know, LORD, what I intend to say.

5   Whether I go forward or backward you hem me in,
       you keep me under your control.

6   Such knowledge is too wonderful for me,
       it is high and beyond my reach.

7   Where can I go to escape from you?
       Where can I run from your presence?

8   If I ascend to the heavens, you are there;
       if I prepare a bed in Sheol, you are there too.

9   If I take wing to the Eastern sunrise
       or make my home beyond the Western sea,

10 There, too, you will lead me by the hand,
       you will hold me firmly in your grasp.

11 If I say, 'Surely the darkness will hide me
       and night shut out the light behind me'

12 Even then the darkness will not make it too dark for you,
       but night will light up like the day.
       Darkness and light will become the same.

13 For you it was who made me an intelligent being,
        who put me together inside my mother.

14 I can acknowledge you for this reason —
        I am set apart in a way which fills me with awe.
    The things you have made are wonderful,
        of that I am well aware.

15 You could see my human frame,
        what I was made, in secret,
        with great complexity in the places below the earth.

16 You saw the various parts of me,
        they are all recorded in your book.
    Over a period of time they took shape
        and not one of them was lacking.

17 How important to me are the things you have in mind!
        How many they add up to, God!

18 Should I count them they outnumber the sand.
        I awoke to life and still I was with you.

19 If only you would kill the wicked, God,
        these men of violence who rebel against you,

20 Who speak to you with malicious intent
        and complain to you for no reason.

21 I certainly do hate those who hate you, LORD,
        and detest those who stand in opposition to you.

22 I hate them with implacable hatred
        and regard them as my enemies.

23 Examine me, God, and discover what I think,
        inspect my thoughts and see how disturbed they are.

24 See whether my behaviour causes any hurt,
        and guide me along the way that stretches ahead.

🎕 Psalm 140

Like verses 19-22 of the previous psalm this too attacks the wicked and prays for their defeat and demise. It is probably best to regard it as a prayer from an individual rather than as one spoken by the king representing his nation. This means understanding 'strife' in v.2 and the 'arms' of v.8 as figures of speech and not literally.

The reason for the attack on the wicked is different from that in Psalm 139. Here it is because the psalmist himself is being attacked by them. It is therefore a prayer for deliverance which will of necessity involve the defeat of his enemies. The prayer is offered in confidence because of his belief in God as powerful and because of past experience of God's help (vv.7-8). Behind this, however, there is again, as in Psalms 137 and 139, a basic belief in the justice of God exercised especially on behalf of those who cannot look after themselves (v.13). This will mean that honest and good people will confess their allegiance to the LORD and will live in his presence.

Once more we may feel uncomfortable about the prayer that wicked people should be paid back in their own coin (vv.10-12) but the insistence on the justice of God is valuable even if we need to complement it with a fuller recognition of his mercy and with a different way of overcoming evil — with good.

2   Rescue me from the wicked, LORD,
       protect me from men of violence,

3   Who think up evil schemes
       and are always stirring up strife.

4   Their words are sharp like a snake's tongue,
       they speak with the venom of an asp.

5   Keep me out of the hands of the wicked, LORD,
       protect me from men of violence
       who plan to cut my feet from under me.

6   In the hollows they set hidden traps for me,
       using ropes they spread out their nets,
       along the path they lay snares for me.

7   I said to the LORD, 'You are my God,
        listen to my cry for help',

8   LORD, my Lord, you have the strength to save me,
        you have shielded me when men have taken up arms
            against me.

9   LORD, do not give the wicked what they want,
        do not promote their evil schemes.

10 When they stand proudly around me
        let the trouble they threaten overwhelm them.

11 May coals of fire be dislodged and fall on them,
        may they tumble into a deep pool and never come up.

12 As for the man who speaks hostile words,
        may he never be at home in the land;
    and as for the man who acts violently,
        may disaster hunt him down rapidly.

13 I know that the LORD takes up the cause of the poor
        and ensures justice for the needy.

14 Surely those who do right will confess you as LORD,
        those who are honest will live in your presence.

৩৪ Psalm 141

*Like so many others this psalmist finds himself in trouble and under attack
from his enemies, though who they are is, as usual, by no means clear. His
only means of defence is to appeal to God and this is what he does. The
request that his prayer may be regarded as equivalent to an offering in the
Temple suggests that he was unable to get to Jerusalem. This may have been
because he was in exile, but it may equally well have been because he lived at
a distance from the capital.*

*   In offering his prayer he recognises that his thoughts, words and deeds*

ought to be free from evil, but he also knows that only God can keep them so (vv.3-4). Consequently he considers any rebuke from a good man to be valuable (v.5).

From this standpoint he can go on to pray that his enemies may be punished by God as they deserve to be (vv.6-7). At the same time he is, of course, concerned for his own safety (vv.8-10).

Again and again we have found in the psalms that pleas for help are coupled with prayers for the destruction of enemies, whether personal or national, because the wicked are seen as enemies of God himself who cannot tolerate such an affront and must act in judgement. It calls us to take sin seriously even if our attitude towards enemies has changed.

1 LORD, I have summoned you; come to me quickly.
       Listen to what I say when I call to you.

2 Let my prayer be an offering of incense to you,
       my uplifted hands an evening sacrifice.

3 LORD, keep my speech under control,
       post a sentry on my lips.

4 Keep my thoughts off anything bad,
       prevent me from occupying myself with evil deeds.
   You pronounce wrong-doers guilty
       so I will not share their fancy foods.

5 If a man who does right strikes me that is a kindness,
       if he chastises me it is like oil on the head;
       let not my head refuse it.

   But I will still pray about the wicked things men do.

6 May their judges fall into the hands of the Rock.
       (Men will hear what I say and find it pleasing.)

7 As when a man opens up the ground and digs a grave
       may their bones be scattered at the entrance to Sheol.

8 For my part, I look towards you, LORD my God;
       I seek safety with you; do not expose me to danger.

9   Protect me from the traps they set for me,
         from the snares of wrong-doers.

10 Let wicked men fall into their own nets
         while I pass by in safety.

✁ Psalm 142

This psalm is a simple plea for rescue from people who are intent on attacking the psalmist either verbally or physically. In this case, however, there is no prayer for retribution upon them.

The psalm makes two main points. First, although the psalmist feels completely alone, humanly speaking, he is convinced that God will hear his prayer and that God is all he needs. Second, he sees his release from trouble as a demonstration to other people that God acts justly. Whether he was actually in prison (v.8) or simply felt imprisoned by his opponents we are not in a position to say.

The points he makes are still valid. He surely does not intend to denigrate human help but rather to say that when all human help fails we can still rely on God to help us. Further, when God helps us that will not only bring congratulations from others but will also bear witness to him.

2   I cry out aloud to the LORD,
         aloud I seek his favour.

3   I pour out my complaints before him,
         I tell him all about my distress.

4   My spirits are drooping badly
         but you know the path I must tread;
    along the road I must travel
         men have set hidden traps for me.

5   Look to the right and see!
         There is no one there to take notice of me.

I have no way of escape;
there is no one to bother about me.

6 I cry to you, LORD.
I say, 'In you I find shelter,
you are all I need in life.'

7 Pay attention to my cry,
for I am very low indeed.
Rescue me from those who dog my steps,
for they are too strong for me.

8 Release me from my prison
so that I may confess you are the LORD.
Those who do right will crowd around me
for you will have dealt with me as I deserve.

🍃 Psalm 143

This is another passionate plea for help from a person who is at the end of his tether because of attacks made upon him (vv. 3 and 7). He makes no claim to absolute innocence; rather he recognises that no one can do that (compare Job 4.17 for a similar view expressed by one of Job's friends and Job 9.2-3 for Job's own view). He can only trust in God's mercy and he feels sufficiently confident of this to pray for help. Such confidence is derived from his knowledge of what God has done for his people in the past (v. 5).

The psalmist assures us that since God is gracious and dependable we too may rely upon him in times of need.

1 LORD, hear my prayer.
Keep faith with me and listen to my cry for help,
do what is right and give me an answer.

2 Do not put me on trial,
for no living thing can be innocent before you.

3   An enemy has dogged my steps;
         he has crushed out my life on the ground.
     He has made me live where all is dark
         like those who died long ago.

4   My spirits have drooped badly,
         my heart is desolate in my breast.

5   I remember the olden days.
         I mull over all you did,
         I think long about the deeds you performed.

6   I spread out my hands in prayer towards you,
         I thirst for you like a drought-stricken land.

7   Quick, LORD, answer me!
         I am at my last breath.
     Do not turn your back on me
         or I shall be like the dying on the way to the Pit.

8   Tell me each morning of your devotion
         for you are the one I trust.
     Show me which way I should go
         for from you I seek what I need.

9   Rescue me from my enemies, LORD,
         for to you I run for shelter.

10   Teach me to do what pleases you,
         for you are my God.
     Be well-disposed towards me
         and lead me over level terrain.

11   Revive me, LORD, and keep your reputation.
         Do what is right and release me from my distress.

12   Show me devotion and wipe out all my enemies;
         destroy all those who oppress me;
         for I am your servant.

꩜ Psalm 144

That this psalm was spoken by the king as the representative of his people is fairly clear. What is less clear is the occasion for which it was composed and on which it was used. It may be seen as a royal prayer before battle in which the king acknowledges that his martial skills have been given to him by God who has made his kingdom secure (vv.1-3). Almost quoting Psalm 8 he confesses human inadequacy and dependence on God even by a king (vv.4-5). Drawing on traditional language he prays for God to appear (compare Psalm 18 and Exodus 19) and keep him safe as he has done previous kings (vv.6-12). The passage in brackets seems out of place here and has probably been copied in error from v.12. Finally the king prays for material prosperity for his people (vv.13-16).

There is, however, another way of understanding the psalm. It may have been sung by the king in the annual ritual of re-enthronement at the Feast of Tabernacles. This possible ritual was described in the introduction to Psalm 18. It involved a dramatic representation of the death of the king as the focus of his people and his restoration to life by God who appeared to him, followed by his exaltation over other kings and the promise of rain and therefore prosperity for his people. Even if this second interpretation is correct it still remains true that it may have been used later as a victory psalm (see Psalm 18).

Now the psalm can no longer be used in either of these two ways. It can be a reminder, however, that even people in power are dependent upon God and that any success they may achieve is due to him.

1   Thanks be to the LORD, my Rock!
        He trains me to use my hands for fighting,
          my fingers for making war.

2   He is my shelter and my stronghold,
        my place of security and safety.

3   He is my shield and I find shelter with him,
        he keeps nations in subjection to me.

4   LORD, what is man and why are you familiar with him?
        What is a mere human and you consider him?

5   Man is like a breath of wind,
        his days are a passing shadow.

6   LORD, draw your heavens aside and come down,
        touch the mountains and they will smoke.

7   Send flashes of lightning scattering in all directions,
        shoot your arrows and make the thunder rumble.

8   Reach down from on high,
        catch hold of me and rescue me from deep waters.
        (From the hands of foreigners

9   Who tell lies under oath
        and raise their right hand dishonestly.)

10 God, I will sing a new song to you,
        I will sing you praises to the ten-stringed lute,

11 Who gave victory to the kings
        and snatched your servant David to safety.

12 Snatch me away from the cruel sword,
        rescue me from the hands of foreigners
    who tell lies under oath
        and raise their right hands dishonestly.

13 Make our sons happy like plants
        which grow tall while still young;
    our daughters like stone columns
        cut for the building of the Temple.

14 May our barns be full,
        providing all kinds of produce,
    may our flocks increase by thousands,
        by tens of thousands in the fields.

15 May our cattle be heavy with young,
        going full term without miscarriage
        and causing no anguished cry in the open squares.

16 Happy are the people to whom this shall happen!
      Happy are the people who have the LORD as their god!

🎕 Psalm 145

*This is an acrostic psalm (see Psalms 9 and 10, 25, 119). The verse beginning
with the fourteenth letter of the alphabet is missing from the Hebrew text. It
is found, however, in one Hebrew manuscript from Qumran and in the
Greek translation called the Septuagint. Here it is translated from these
sources as the first half of v.14.*

*Although the acrostic form tends to inhibit a well-developed argu-
ment the psalm has a clear overall theme. It is concerned with the greatness
of God and the responsibility of his people to make this known. While most
of the psalm speaks of the LORD in the third person, vv.4-7 are addressed
directly to him. There is probably little significance in this change. It is one
which occurs not infrequently in prayer.*

*The fact that the psalm celebrated the kingship of the LORD probably
means that it was used originally in the great autumn festival (see Psalms
47, 93, 95-99).*

*The function of the worshipping community is to repeat, for the
benefit of each new generation, the account of what God has done. This
applies as much to the Christian Church at worship as to the Israelites
in ancient Israel or to Jews in the present day. For Christians, of course,
the 'mighty deeds' will above all include those events recorded in the
New Testament.*

1 *Alep*   I will sing high praise to you, my God and King,
                I will never cease to give you thanks.

2 *Bet*   Every day I will thank you,
                I will never cease praising you.

3 *Gimel*   The LORD is great and worthy of high praise,
                his greatness is beyond comprehension.

4	*Dalet*	Each generation will commend your work to the next, they will tell again of your mighty deeds,
5	*He*	Of your splendid, glorious majesty. I will meditate on the story of your marvellous doings.
6	*Waw*	It tells how fierce and awesome were your deeds; now I will recount your prodigious exploits.
7	*Zayin*	They will freely recite the commemoration of your goodness; they will shout about the help you have given.
8	*Het*	The LORD is generous and compassionate, full of patience and deep devotion.
9	*Tet*	The LORD is good to everyone, his compassion extends to all he has made.
10	*Yod*	All you have made will confess you, LORD, those devoted to you will give you thanks.
11	*Kap*	They will speak of your royal glory and tell of your mighty deeds,
12	*Lamed*	Making known to all mankind your mighty deeds, your majestic royal glory.
13	*Mem*	Your reign will continue for ever, your rule will last through every generation.
14	*Nun*	The LORD's faithfulness is reflected in all he says, his devotion in all he does.
	Samek	The LORD supports all who are stumbling, he lifts up all who are down.
15	*Ayin*	Everything looks up expectantly to you, you give them their food when they need it.

| 16 | *Pe* | You supply every creature generously, |
| | | giving them all they could wish for. |

| 17 | *Sade* | The LORD's righteousness is reflected in all he says, |
| | | his devotion in all he does. |

| 18 | *Qop* | The LORD draws near to all who summon him, |
| | | to all who summon him in sincerity. |

| 19 | *Res* | For his worshippers he does all they could wish for, |
| | | he hears their cry for help and saves them. |

| 20 | *Sin* | The LORD keeps guard over all who love him, |
| | | but he will destroy all the wicked. |

21	*Taw*	I will put my praise of the LORD into words,
		and men everywhere will thank him by name,
		continually, for ever.

❧ Psalm 146

The last five psalms in the Psalter all begin and end with 'Hallelujah', 'Praise the LORD'. Psalm 146 contrasts the rule of human leaders with that of the divine king. It is not that human rulers are wrong, but they are liable to failure simply because they are human. Therefore it is wiser always to trust in God the all-powerful creator who acts according to his true nature.

The list of the activities of God which reveal this true nature is an impressive one, dealing as it does with his activities on behalf of those who are in various ways deprived. Similar statements may be found in Isaiah 29.18-19, 42.7 and especially in Isaiah 61.1-4. This is how the LORD's justice or righteousness finds expression and human rulers ought really to reflect this in their own government.

The psalmist knew that this was not so in practice. Kings and nobles did not reflect God's justice. Isaiah 11.1-7 therefore looked forward to an ideal king who would do so and this became part of the Messianic hope. This hope, however, does not find expression in this psalm; rather people are called to trust in the LORD.

The New Testament, however, depicts Jesus as fulfilling such Messianic hopes and as behaving in this way throughout his life. The psalm itself calls us to put our trust, then, in this God. Seen in the wider context outlined above it also reminds us of what is required of us as those who seek to live in accordance with God's will.

1   Hallelujah!
  Praise the LORD, my true self.

2   I will praise the LORD as long as I live,
  I will sing praises to God all my life.

3   Do not put your trust in nobles,
  in human leaders who are incapable of saving you.

4   They will expire and return to the soil,
  on that day their thoughts will die with them.

5   Happy the man who has the God of Jacob to help him,
  who pins his hopes on the LORD, his God.

6   He is the Maker of heaven and earth,
  the sea and every creature in it,
  he remains true to himself for ever.

7   He ensures justice for the oppressed,
  he gives food to the hungry,
  the LORD sets prisoners free.

8   The LORD gives sight to the blind,
  the LORD raises up those who are down,
  the LORD loves those who do right.

9   The LORD protects the aliens,
  he gives relief to the orphans and widows,
  he makes the wicked take the wrong road.

10   The LORD will be king for ever,
  your God, Zion, for generation after generation.

Hallelujah!

꧁ Psalm 147

This hymn of praise to God falls into three parts (vv.1-6, 7-11 and 12-20) each beginning with a call to praise. The first part (vv.1-6) suggests an exilic or early post-exilic date since Jerusalem appears to be in ruins and some of its people in exile. The verses alternate between expressions of God's greatness (vv.4 and 5) and his will to help the needy (vv.3 and 6).

The second part (vv.7-11) also speaks of God's power and the way that power is used for the benefit of all created beings. Yet what gives him pleasure is not the physical characteristics of these beings, but supremely the humble respect, obedience and worship which men offer to him.

Part three is concerned with the word of God. It was by this that the world was created (Genesis 1 and Psalm 33.6). Here his word can both make and melt the ice and snow. In this sense his word has a universal range. His word, in the sense of commandments, however, has been given especially to Israel so that his chosen people may be obedient.

The fact that God's word is made known to Israel is not a cause for pride alone. It also involves the responsibility of making it known to others. It is from Jerusalem that the word goes forth (see Isaiah 2.3, Micah 4.2).

Worship, then, requires people to praise God for those universal gifts which he makes available to all, but the psalm calls us also to obedience. At the same time it calls for praise for those gifts which he gives to his own people, but we should never forget the responsibility this lays upon us not only to praise him but also to make known his will.

1   Praise the LORD, for that is good,
       make music to our God for it is pleasing.
       Praise is a lovely thing.

2   The LORD is rebuilding Jerusalem,
       he gathers in the banished Israelites.

3   He heals those whose spirit is crushed
       and binds up their wounds.

4   He decides how many stars there shall be
       and gives names to every one of them.

5　Our LORD is great and very strong,
　　　　his understanding is indescribable.

6　The LORD raises up those brought low,
　　　　he crushes the wicked to the ground.

7　Respond to the LORD with thanks,
　　　　play music to our God on the harp,

8　Who hides the sky behind the clouds
　　　　and gets the rain ready for the earth,
　　　　and makes the hills sprout with grass.

9　He provides food for the animals,
　　　　for the young ravens when they call for it.

10　It is not the strength of the horse he admires,
　　　　it is not the mobility of man which gives him pleasure;

11　He does take pleasure in people who show him reverence,
　　　　in those who wait in expectation of his devotion.

12　Praise the LORD, Jerusalem!
　　　　Praise your God, Zion!

13　For he has strengthened the bolts on your gates,
　　　　he has blessed your people inside them.

14　He gives prosperity within your borders,
　　　　and satisfies your needs with best quality wheat.

15　He sends his message to the earth,
　　　　his word travels at full speed.

16　He makes the snow lay like wool,
　　　　he scatters the hoar-frost like ashes.

17　He sprinkles his frost around like crumbs,
　　　　no one can withstand the cold he sends.

18 He sends word, and his word melts them,
            he makes the wind blow and the waters begin to trickle.

19 He makes public his word to Jacob,
            his statutes and rules to Israel.

20 He has not done this for any other nation;
            they do not know his rules.

    Hallelujah!

ꝏ Psalm 148

*This is another call to praise, addressed this time to everything which God
has made. As in Psalm 147.15-18 creation was effected simply by God's
command. Since all things owe their existence to him, all things owe him
also their praise.*

*As it stands verse 14 brings the psalm to an end with a call to God's
special people to join in the praise offered by all other things on account
of the special position which God has given them. In this sense it provides
a fitting climax for a hymn meant to be used in Israel's worship. Some
people regard the last two lines as the title of the next psalm, but this
seems to rob the present psalm of its proper climax.*

*The psalm reminds us of St Francis' 'Canticle to the Sun', upon which
the hymn 'All creatures of our God and King' is based. In our modern, down-
to-earth attitude the highly poetic call to inanimate objects to join in praise
of God may seem out of place. It gives expression, however, to the belief that
all things owe their existence to God and are dependent on him. Praise is the
proper response to such a belief and if it is due from inanimate objects how
much more is it due from those who feel themselves close to God.*

1   Hallelujah!
            Praise the LORD from the heavens,
            praise him in the heights.

2 Praise him, all his angels,
     praise him, all his heavenly host.

3 Praise him, sun and moon,
     praise him, all the shining stars.

4 Praise him, all the heavens
     and the waters above the heavens.

5 Let them praise the LORD by name,
     for when he issued a command they were created.

6 He gave them all a permanent place,
     he made a decree which always remains in force.

7 Praise the LORD, from the earth,
     sea monsters and all deep waters,

8 Fire and smoke, hail and snow,
     stormy wind which does as he says,

9 Mountains and hills,
     fruit trees and cedars,

10 All animals wild and tame,
      things which crawl and birds that fly,

11 Kings and people on earth,
      princes and rulers everywhere,

12 Young men and girls,
      old men and boys.

13 Let them praise the LORD by name,
      for he is supreme above all others,
      his splendour is above heaven and earth.

14 He has made his people powerful;
      those devoted to him will praise him,
      the Israelites, the people closest to him.

Hallelujah!

✢ Psalm 149

The theme of this psalm is again the praise of God by his chosen ones. However, as it progresses it turns into a cry for vengeance upon other nations who do not worship the LORD and who are therefore regarded as his enemies. It is not clear whether they are so regarded because they had attacked and humiliated God's people (v.4), but even if this was the case, we still cannot with certainty assign the psalm to any particular occasion for this happened more than once in Israel's history. Verse 6 could suggest the time of Nehemiah when those rebuilding Jerusalem were told to work with one hand and hold their sword in the other (Nehemiah 4.17).

Alternatively, it has been suggested that the psalm was written as part of the dramatic representation in worship of the defeat of evil and the victory of Israel's God in the festival of his enthronement (see Psalms 93, 95-99).

We cannot explain away the idea of vengeance which we have come across frequently in other psalms. If, as suggested in Psalms 4, 12, 16 etc, the term 'devoted servant' refers to the Levites then we have to bear in mind the fact that according to Exodus 32.25-29 they were chosen and set aside for the purpose of killing the wicked who had defected from God.

We may therefore wish to express things differently but the fight against evil continues and to engage in it is an honour.

1   Hallelujah!
       Sing to the LORD a new song,
        sing his praise in the gathering of his devoted servants.

2   Let Israel be happy with God who made them his people,
        let Zion's children rejoice in their King.

3   Let them praise him as LORD in the dance,
        let them play for him on tambourine and harp.

4   For the LORD accepts his people,
        he gives a garland of victory to the humiliated.

5   Let his devoted servants rejoice in their abundance,
        let them shout for joy as they recline at table.

6   Let the highest praise of God be on their lips
        and a double-edged sword in their hand,

7   To wreak vengeance on the nations
        and to punish the people,

8   To bind their kings with fetters
        and their nobles in iron chains,

9   To carry out the sentence which is laid down.
        This is the honour granted to all his devoted servants.

Hallelujah!

❧ Psalm 150

*The final psalm in the Book of Psalms is fittingly a call to praise God with
enthusiasm and with every possible accompaniment. His holiness, the fact
that he is God, and his supreme power and greatness demand it and evoke it.*

*The highest and most glorious activity of man is to come before God in
prayer and praise. The Psalms indicate that we may approach him with
frankness and honesty in anxiety and complaint, but above all with a
consciousness of who he is, the God of power and the God of grace to whom
the praise and adoration of our whole being is due.*

1   Hallelujah!
        Praise God as the One who is holy,
        praise him as supremely strong,

2   Praise him as being all-powerful,
        praise him as immeasurably great.

3   Praise him with a trumpet sound,
        praise him with lute and harp.

4 Praise him with tambourine and dance,
      praise him with strings and flute.

5 Praise him with a crashing cymbal,
      praise him with jubilant cymbals.

6 Every breathing thing, praise the LORD.

  Hallelujah!